B. J. Summers' Guide to Coca-Cola

SECOND EDITION

Identifications
Current Values
Circa Dates

COLLECTOR BOOKS
A Division of Schroeder Publishing Co., Inc.

The current values in this book should be used only as a guide. They are not intended to set prices, which vary from one section of the country to another. Auction prices as well as dealer prices vary greatly and are affected by condition as well as demand. Neither the Author nor the Publisher assumes responsibility for any losses that might be incurred as a result of consulting this guide.

Searching For A Publisher?

We are always looking for knowledgeable people considered to be experts within their fields. If you feel that there is a real need for a book on your collectible subject and have a large comprehensive collection, contact Collector Books.

Front Cover:

Clockwise from top:
Gold dipped special occasions bottle, $35.00.
Sprite Boy cardboard fan, $75.00.
Royal Palm seltzer bottle, $125.00.
"Soda Jerk" metal serving tray, $650.00.
Cardboard poster, "Hospitality," $900.00.
Cardboard carton stuffer sign, $45.00.
Cardboard die cut clown, $800.00.

Back Cover:

Clockwise from top:
Center piece of cardboard festoon, $1,200.00.
Cardboard sports favorites, $100.00 – 200.00 each.
Metal picnic cooler, $130.00.

Cover design by Beth Summers
Book design by Karen Smith

Collector Books
P.O. Box 3009
Paducah, Kentucky 42002-3009

Copyright © 1999 by B.J. Summers

Contents

Dedication & Acknowledgments

I would like to dedicate this book to a great lady and an invaluable help with this value guide — Gail Ashburn.

I would like to extend my sincere thanks to the following people and businesses without whose help this book would have been impossible.

Affordable Antiques Inc.
933 S. 3rd St.
Paducah, KY 42001
Ph. 502-442-1225

Easy to find on Paducah's I–24 loop, Oliver Johnson usually has some Coke collectibles worth the visit. If you don't find what you need, he can usually locate it for you.

Alfred and Earlene Mitchell
c/o Collector Books
P.O. Box 3009
Paducah, KY 42002-3009

One of the nicest couples you could ever know, who have been collecting since the sixties. They were kind enough to allow us to photograph much of their collection and answer a constant stream of questions. Al and Earlene are very active collectors. They buy, sell, trade, and are very active in collectors' clubs.

Gary Metz's Muddy River
    Trading Co.
263 Lakewood Dr.
Moneta, VA 24121
Ph. 540-721-2091
Fax 540-721-1782

Gary Metz probably produces one of the best advertising auctions in this country. While his emphasis is primarily on Coca-Cola and other soda products, he certainly isn't limited to those fields. Gary is probably one of the nicest people you'll ever meet. Give him a call and send for his next catalog to open up a whole new level of collecting.

Antiques, Cards, and Collectibles
203 Broadway
Paducah, KY 42001
Ph. 502-443-9797

Three floors of antiques and collectibles housed in an old historic hardware store in downtown Paducah. Owner Ray Pelley offers a good general array of collectibles along with some great Coca-Cola ones.

Charlie's Antique Mall
303 Main St., P.O. Box 196
Hazel, KY 42049
Ph. 502-492-8175

Located in the historic antique community of Hazel, Ky., on Main Street, this place has it all. The manager, Ray Gough, has some great dealers with a wide variety of antiques and collectibles and some of the friendliest help you'll find. This border town mall can keep even the pickiest collector busy for the better part of a day.

Farmer's Daughter Antiques
6330 Cairo Rd
Paducah, KY 42001
Ph. 502-444-7619

Bill and Jane Miller have one of the neatest shops you'll ever find. The mix of advertising (Bill's specialty), and primitives (Jane's specialty) is a winning combination in everyone's book. Their shop is easily located, just a mile off 1-24 at exit 3. You can't miss the big barn — stop by and talk to one of the friendliest couples in the antique world.

Chief Paduke Antiques Mall
300 S. 3rd St.
Paducah, KY 42003
Ph. 502-442-6799

This full-to-overflowing mall is located in an old railroad depot in downtown Paducah with plenty of general line advertising, including good Coke pieces, plus a good selection of furniture. Stop by and see Charley or Carolyn if you're in this area.

Collectors Auction Service
Rt. 2 Box 431, Oakwood Dr.
Oil City, PA 16301
Ph. 814-677-6070

Mark Anderton and Sherry Mullen offer a couple of great mail and phone advertising auctions each year. While their main focus is on oil and gas collectibles, there have been a good many Coca-Cola collectibles offered. It is worthwhile to check them out.

Gene Harris Antique Auction
    Center, Inc.
203 South 18th Avenue, P.O. Box 476
Marshalltown, IA 50158
Ph. 515-752-0600

If you have been collecting for any time at all, you probably know about this auction house. Seems like there is always an ad in the antique papers for one of their sales. Not only will you find advertising offered but watches and clocks, china, dolls, and almost anything else you can imagine.

Eric Reinfeld
87 Seventh Avenue
Brooklyn, NY 11217
Ph. 718-783-2313

An avid Whistle and Coca-Cola collector all wrapped into one. Give Eric a call if you're interested in selling or buying advertising relating to these two catagories.

Michael and Debbie Summers
3258 Harrison St.
Paducah, KY 42001

My brother and sister-in-law are avid collectors and have been invaluable help in compiling information for this book. Mike and I have spent many days chasing down treasures at auctions.

Patrick's Collectibles
612 Roxanne Dr.
Antioch, TN 37013
Ph. 615-833-4621

If you happen to be around Nashville, Tenn., during the monthly flea market at the state fairgrounds, be certain to look for Mike and Julie Patrick. They have some of the sharpest advertising pieces you'll ever hope to find. And if Coca-Cola is your field, you won't be able to walk away from the great restored drink machines. Make sure to look them up — you certainly won't be sorry.

Pleasant Hill Antique Mall
& Tea Room
315 South Pleasant Hill Rd.
East Peoria, IL 61611
Ph. 309-694-4040

Bob Johnson and the friendly staff at this mall welcome you for a day of shopping. And it'll take that long to work your way through all the quality antiques and collectibles here. When you get tired, stop and enjoy a rest at the tea room where you can get some of the best home cooked food found anywhere. All in all, a great place to shop for your favorite antiques.

Creatures of Habit
406 Broadway
Paducah, KY 42001
Ph. 502-442-2923

This business will take you back in time with its wonderful array of vintage clothing and advertising. If you are ever in western Kentucky, stop and see Natalya and Jack.

The Illinois Antique Center
308 S.W. Commercial
Peoria, IL 61602
Ph. 309-673-3354

Overlooking the river in downtown Peoria, Ill., this huge warehouse has been remodeled by Dan and Kim and now has a wonderful selection of antiques and collectibles. Always a great source of advertising signs, statues, and memorabilia. You'll find an ample supple of smiling faces and help here. Plan on spending the better part of a day.

Rare Bird Antique Mall
212 South Main St.
Goodlettsville, TN 37072
615-851-2635

If you find yourself in the greater Nashville, Tenn., area stop by this collector's paradise. Jon and Joan Wright have assembled a great cast of dealers who run the gamut of collectible merchandise. So step back to a time when the general store was the place to be, and be prepared to spend some time.

Riverside Antique Mall
P.O. Box 4425
Sevierville, TN 37864
Ph. 423-429-0100

Located in a new building overlooking the river, this is a collector's heaven. It's full of advertising, with lighted showcases and plenty of friendly help. You need to allow at least half a day for a quick look through this place that sits in the shadows of the Smokey Mountains.

Bill and Helen Mitchell
226 Arendall St.
Henderson, TN 38340
Ph. 901-989-9302

Bill and Helen have assembled a great variety of advertising with special emphasis on Coca-Cola, and they are always searching for new finds. So if you have anything that fits the bill, give them a call or drop them a letter.

Richard Opfer Auctioneering, Inc
1919 Greenspring Drive
Timonium, MD 21093
Ph. 410-252-5035

Richard Opfer Auctioneering, Inc provides a great variey of antique and collectibles auctions. Give his friendly staff a call for his next auction catalog.

Wildflower Antique Mall
Exit 220-Interstate 57 & Rt. 45
Pesotum, IL 61863
Ph. 217-867-2704

Serving central Illinois along I-57, this exceptionally clean mall is conveniently located just off exit 220. It is full of advertising and collectibles and has a better-than-average supply of Coca-Cola items.

Wm. Morford
RD #2
Cazenovia, NY 13035
Ph. 315-662-7625

Wm. Morford has been operating one of the country's better cataloged phone auction businesses for several years. He doesn't list reproductions or repairs that are deceptive in nature. Each catalog usually has a section with items that are for immediate sale. Try out this site and tell him where you got his name and address.

If I have omitted anyone who should be here, please be assured it is an oversight on my part and was not intentional.

Pricing & Introduction

Pricing is always a difficult part of any value guide. My purpose in this book is not to set a value, nor do I wish to move the market in any one particular direction. It is my desire to help the collector by giving information about actual values. To achieve this end, each listing is coded to show how the price was obtained. If the price is followed by "C," then the price was given to me by a collector. A "B" indicates an auction price, while "D" represents a dealer price. This should help the reader/collector in determining a selling or buying value.

There are several factors that will determine the value of almost any item. Condition is to a collector as location is to a realtor. Condition should always be a prime factor in determining price. Give a mint price only when the item is in mint condition. Unfortunately, we all can see mint prices being charged for items that should bring only good condition price. I have attempted to place a condition on each listing which should also help the reader with values.

Rarity also plays a role in value. If the item is one-of-a-kind or you know of only a couple more in existence, the value could be higher for a piece less than mint. Ask yourself, how often will I find this item ? How badly do I want this piece? How long until I see it again? These questions play a part in determining the value of a piece.

Location is also a factor to address in a value. I live in the heartland of the country. Values here, generally speaking, will be less than on either coast, but as always, there are exceptions.

A wise collector is an informed collector. There are several other guides on the market that will help you learn. *Schroeder's Antiques Price Guide, Goldstein's Coca-Cola Collectibles, B.J. Summers' Guide To Advertising Memorabilia Volume 1 & 2,* and *Huxford's Collectible Advertising* are all excellent sources.

How do you introduce a product that needs no introduction? A product that had its beginnings in a backyard kettle, yet has captured the heart and spirit of the American public. Generations have grown up with this magic elixir playing a major part in both business and social functions. Our whole concept of Santa Claus as the jolly gift giver evokes the image of none other than Haddon Sundblom's Coca-Cola Santa. Most of us have great memories of Coke and fries at the local Dairy Queen. Some of us that are slightly older have other memories. Like enjoying peanuts in our Coke.

In compiling this value guide, I attempted to help not only the beginner, but also the advanced collector. The American collector will pay almost any price to relive a comfortable time with pleasant memories. The Coca-Cola Company with its fantastic product and proliferation of Americana advertising allows us to relive those special times.

I hope this book will help the reader broaden his or her collecting experience.

See page 12 for listing.

Aluminum die cut "Drink Coca-Cola In Bottles" in script, truck radiator sign, 1920s, 17½"x7½", EX, $335.00 B.

Muddy River Trading Co./Gary Metz.

Autumn Leaves, five piece festoon, designed for use on a soda fountain back bar, 1927, G, $900.00 C.

Muddy River Trading Co./Gary Metz.

Bottle hanger, Santa Claus in refrigerator full of bottles being surprised by small child, 1950s, F, $8.00 C. Mitchell Collection.

Bottle hanger with artwork of 6-pack in food basket, 1950s, 8"x7", EX, $500.00 C. Bill Mitchell.

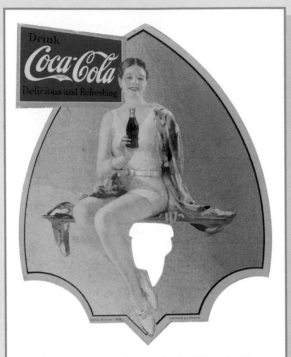

Bottle topper, Bathing Girl, "Drink Coca-Cola Delicious and Refreshing," rare, 1929, VG, $1,800.00 B. Muddy River Trading Co./Gary Metz.

Bottle topper, Canadian, great graphics by Fred Mizen, "Refresh Yourself," 1926, 13"x13", EX, $3,600.00 C. Muddy River Trading Co./Gary Metz.

Bottle topper, plastic, "We let you see the bottle," 1950s, EX, $400.00 C. Mitchell Collection.

Bottle topper, woman with yellow scarf and parasol, 1927, 8"x10", VG, $2,000.00 B.

Muddy River Trading Co./Gary Metz.

Cardboard, bather in diamond blue background pictured with a Coke button and a bottle, framed and under glass, 1940, 23"x22", NM, $1,475.00 C. Mitchell Collection.

Cardboard, bather in round blue background, framed and under glass, by Snyder & Black, rare, 1938, 22", NM, $2,500.00 C. Mitchell Collection.

Cardboard Christmas tree string sign with dynamic wave "Drink…," 1970s, 14"x24", G, $32.00 D. Wildflower Antique Mall.

Cardboard clown balancing on a bottle, 1950, EX, $800.00 B.

Muddy River Trading Co./Gary Metz.

Cardboard, cut-out, Coca-Cola policeman, waist up view with "Stop for pause, Go refreshed" ribbon in front, great graphics, hard to find, 1937, 45"x32", G, $1,050.00 B. Muddy River Trading Co./Gary Metz.

Cardboard cut-out, "Drink Coca-Cola, The Pause that Refreshes," used as a window display by Niagara Litho Co., N.Y, 1940s, 32½"x42½", VG, $975.00 C. Mitchell Collection.

Cardboard cut-out, model with a bottle and a colorful parasol, easel back, 1930s, 10"x18½", EX, $1,600.00 C. Mitchell Collection.

Cardboard, cut-out, woman with glass of Coke, similar to 1930 serving tray, 1930, 21"x38", F, $525.00 B. Muddy River Trading Co./Gary Metz.

Cardboard, die cut, embossed, WWII battleship, framed under glass, 26"x14", NM, $1,300.00 B. Muddy River Trading Co./Gary Metz.

Cardboard, die cut, "Drink Coca-Cola, Delicious and Refreshing, Ours is Ice Cold," 1900s, 9"x19", F, $425.00 C. Bill Mitchell.

Cardboard, die cut, "Every Bottle Sterilized," framed and matted, 1930s, 14"x12", EX, $1000.00 C. Bill Mitchell.

Cardboard, die cut, fishing boy and dog with original pond, unusual find, 1935, 36" tall, G, $2,500.00 B. Muddy River Trading Co./Gary Metz.

Cardboard, die cut, sailor girl with "Take Home" flags, matted and framed, 1952, 11"x7", NM, $375.00 B.

Muddy River Trading Co./Gary Metz

Cardboard, die cut, "Serve Coca-Cola" button with candles, EX, $115.00 C.

Al & Earlene Mitchell.

Cardboard, die cut, service girl in uniform with bottle of Coke, 1944, 25"x64", EX, $600.00 B.

Gene Harris Antique Auction Center, Inc.

Cardboard, die cut with attached hangers for wall or window display, Bathing Girl, 1910, F, $1,450.00 B.

Muddy River Trading Co./Gary Metz.

Cardboard, die cut, woman sitting on bench with bottle, "Delicious and Refreshing, Coca-Cola in bottles," 1900s, 18"x28½", G, $5,500.00 C. Bill Mitchell.

Cardboard, dimensional arrow sign, heavy brown cardboard, hard to find, 1944, 20"x12", G, $150.00 B. Muddy River Trading Co./Gary Metz.

Cardboard, embossed die cut, easel back sign featuring girl in woods illustrated in a beveled mirror with advertising at bottom marked "Kaufmann and Strauss Company, New York," 1903, 4½"x10½", EX, $15,500.00 B.

Muddy River Trading Co./Gary Metz.

Cardboard, "Drink Coca-Cola," couple on a beach with a large towel, 1932, 29"x50", Hayden-Hayden, F, $600.00. Mitchell Collection.

Cardboard, girl with a bottle, 1940s, EX, $600.00 B. Muddy River Trading Co./Gary Metz.

Cardboard, "Have a Coke," sign featuring Sprite Boy advertising King Size, has a hanger and easel back attachment, 1957, 18" sq., EX, $170.00 B.

Muddy River Trading Co./Gary Metz.

Cardboard, horizontal, "Drink Royal Palm Beverages Made from Pure Cane Sugar by the Coca-Cola Bottling Company," 1930s, 17"x11¼", F, $60.00 B. Muddy River Trading Co./Gary Metz.

Cardboard, horizontal, featuring silhouette girl running, "Let's watch for 'em," 1950s, 66"x32", NM, $800.00 B.
Muddy River Trading Co./Gary Metz.

Cardboard, horizontal poster, "Coke… For Hospitality" featuring artwork of people at cookout, framed under glass, 1948, 36"x24", NM, $425.00 B.
Muddy River Trading Co./Gary Metz.

Cardboard, horizontal poster, featuring Sprite Boy advertising family size too, in original wooden frame, 1955, 36"x20", EX, $500.00 B. Muddy River Trading Co./Gary Metz.

Cardboard, horizontal poster, featuring Sprite Boy with six-pack of Coke, 1946, 41½"x27½", F, $525.00 B.
Muddy River Trading Co./Gary Metz.

Cardboard, horizontal poster, "Planning hospitality," with artwork of hand taking bottle from 6-pack, 27"x16", EX, $325.00 C. Al & Earlene Mitchell.

Cardboard, horizontal poster, "You taste its quality" featuring artwork of woman with flowers and a bottle of Coke, framed under glass, 1942, 36"x20", NM, $1,150.00 B.
Muddy River Trading Co./Gary Metz.

Cardboard, "I'm heading for Coca-Cola," woman in uniform getting off airplane, in original wooden frame, 1942, 16"x27", VG, $600.00 B. Mitchell Collection.

Cardboard in wooden frame, "Betty," 1914, 30"x38", VG, $2,750.00 D. Mitchell Collection.

Cardboard, large horizontal "Mind Reader," woman on chaise being offered a bottle of Coke, EX, $625.00 B.
Muddy River Trading Co./Gary Metz.

Cardboard, large horizontal poster, featuring party scene with Coke iced down in a tub, hard to find item, 1952, F, $300.00 B.
Muddy River Trading Co./Gary Metz.

 Cardboard, large vertical poster, "Mom knows her groceries," featuring woman at refrigerator, 1946, G, $400.00 C.

Muddy River Trading Co./Gary Metz.

 Cardboard, lobby poster featuring Clark Gable and Joan Crawford, "Dancing Lady," 1930s, EX, $1,900.00 B.

Muddy River Trading Co./Gary Metz.

Cardboard, "Pause," clown and an ice skater, in original wooden frame, 1930s, EX, $800.00 B.

Muddy River Trading Co./Gary Metz.

Cardboard, "Play Refreshed," woman on a carousel horse, in original wooden frame, 1940s, EX, $1,200.00 B.

Muddy River Trading Co./Gary Metz.

Cardboard poster, "Come over for Coke," with hostess at serving table with food and bottles of Coke, 1947, 36"x20", fair, $235.00 B. Collector's Auction Services.

Cardboard poster, cameo, Lillian Nordica, 1905, F, $9,000.00 C.

Cardboard poster, featuring Sprite Boy displaying two bottle sizes, 1955, 16"x27", NM, $225.00 C. Muddy River Trading Co./Gary Metz.

Cardboard poster, "Coke has the taste you never get tired of," with artwork of young girl with 45rpm record and bottle of Coke, 1960s, 36"x20", EX, $125.00 C. Al & Earlene Mitchell.

Cardboard poster, featuring three women, "Friendly Pause," 1948, 16"x27", NM, $1,500.00 B.

Muddy River Trading Co./Gary Metz.

Cardboard poster, "for good eating" with staggered bottles, 1950s, 36"x20", G, $225.00 C.

Al & Earlene Mitchell.

Cardboard poster, "Good taste for all," 1955, 16"x27", NM, $225.00 B.

Muddy River Trading Co./Gary Metz.

Cardboard poster, girl on lifeguard stand, 1929, 17"x29¾", VG, $1,000.00 B. Muddy River Trading Co/Gary Metz.

Cardboard poster, horizontal, "All set at our house," with boy holding cardboard six-pack carrier, 1943, EX, $650.00 B.

Muddy River Trading Co./Gary Metz.

Cardboard poster, horizontal, "Be really refreshed… Enjoy Coke"/"Take Home Plenty of Coke," with scene at swimming pool, 1959, 21½"x37½", G, $250.00 D.

Cardboard poster, horizontal, "Coke belongs," young couple with a bottle, 1944, EX, $700.00 B.
Muddy River Trading Co./Gary Metz.

Cardboard poster, horizontal, "Coke Time join the friendly circle," people in pool around cooler on float, 1955, 36"x20", EX, $375.00 B.
Muddy River Trading Co./Gary Metz.

Cardboard poster, horizontal, "Face your job refreshed," woman wearing visor beside a drill press, 59"x30", VG, $750.00 C.

Cardboard poster, horizontal, "Hospitality Coca-Cola," girl lighting a candle with a bottle in foreground, 1950, 59"x30", EX, $900.00 D.

Cardboard poster, horizontal, "Lunch Refreshed," 1943, EX, $1,000.00 B.
Muddy River Trading Co./Gary Metz.

Cardboard poster, horizontal, "Me too," young boy looking up at large bottle, two sided, 62"x33", G, $450.00 C.

Cardboard poster, horizontal, "Play refreshed," woman in cap with fishing rig and a bottle, 1950s, 36"x20", VG, $350.00 C. Mitchell Collection

Cardboard poster, horizontal, "The drink they all expect," couple getting ready to entertain with finger sandwiches and iced bottles, 1942, NM, $600.00 B. Muddy River Trading Co./Gary Metz.

Cardboard poster, horizontal, "The pause that refreshes," girl in yellow dress propped against table holding a bottle, in a reproduction frame, 36"x20", EX, $900.00 B.

Muddy River Trading Co./Gary Metz.

Cardboard poster, horizontal, "The rest-pause that refreshes," three women in uniform, 1943, 36"x20", EX, $425.00 B.

Muddy River Trading Co./Gary Metz.

Cardboard poster, horizontal, "They all want Coca-Cola," girl delivering a tray with four hamburgers, framed under glass, 36"x20", EX, $375.00 B.

Muddy River Trading Co./Gary Metz.

Cardboard poster, horizontal, "Thirst knows no season," woman drinking from a bottle in front of skis, framed, 1940, 56"x27", EX, $450.00 B.

Muddy River Trading Co./Gary Metz.

Cardboard poster, horizontal, "To be refreshed," girl holding a bottle in each hand, in reproduction frame, 1948, EX, $325.00 B.

Muddy River Trading Co./Gary Metz.

Cardboard poster, horizontal, "Welcome Home," 1944, 36"x20", VG, $300.00 B.

Muddy River Trading Co./Gary Metz.

Cardboard poster, horizontal, "What I want is a Coke," girl on sandy beach in swim suit reaching for a bottle, in original wooden frame, hard to find, 1952, VG, $1,100.00 D.

Cardboard poster, "Hospitality," artwork of woman and girl, both in sun bonnet, add $250.00 if in original wooden frame, 1950s, 36"x20", EX, $275.00 C. Al & Earlene Mitchell.

Cardboard poster, in frame, featuring girl in swim suit with a bottle of Coke, "Yes," 1947, 15"x25", F, $375.00 B.

Muddy River Trading Co./Gary Metz.

Cardboard poster, large horizontal, "America's Favorite Moment," a couple in a diner booth, each with a bottle, 1940s, 36"x20", EX, $250.00 B. Muddy River Trading Co./Gary Metz.

Cardboard poster, large horizontal, "Good Pause Drink Coca-Cola in Bottles," 1954, 36"x20", G, $500.00 C.

Mitchell Collection.

Cardboard poster, large vertical, "Drink Coca-Cola 50th anniversary," two women in period dress of 1886 and 1936 sitting together, 1936, 27"x47", VG, $1,250.00 B. Muddy River Trading Co./Gary Metz.

Cardboard poster, Lillian Nordica, "Coca-Cola Delicious and Refreshing 5¢," standing beside Coca-Cola table with her hand resting on screen at rear of room, rare, 1904, 26"x40", EX, $9,000.00 C.

Cardboard poster, "Now! King Size too!" Sprite Boy with a six-pack of king size Coca-Cola and a six-pack of regular Coca-Cola, 1955, 16"x27", G, $95.00 C. Mitchell Collection.

Cardboard poster, "The best is always the better buy," girl with grocery sack and six-pack, framed under glass, 1943, EX, $975.00 B. Muddy River Trading Co./Gary Metz.

Cardboard poster, "The pause that refreshes" with girl on beach in swim suit, add $250.00 if in original aluminum frame, 1950s, 36"x20", F, $250.00 C.

Al & Earlene Mitchell.

Cardboard poster, vertical, "Coke Time," head shot of woman, bottle in hand, and various sports activities, 1950s, F, $200.00 D. Mitchell Collection.

Cardboard poster, vertical, "Coke Time," in original wooden frame, 1943, EX, $950.00 B. Muddy River Trading Co./Gary Metz.

Cardboard poster, vertical, double sided, Old Man North on one side and bottles on the other, French Canadian, 16"x27", $150.00 B. Muddy River Trading Co./Gary Metz.

Cardboard poster, vertical, "Drink Coca-Cola Delicious and Refreshing," cowboy holding a bottle, 1941, 16"x27", G, $525.00 C. Mitchell Collection.

Cardboard poster, vertical, "Drink Coca-Cola," Hostess Girl, 1935, 30"x50", G, $350.00 B. Muddy River Trading Co./Gary Metz.

Cardboard poster, vertical, "Drink Coca-Cola" on button, girl at stadium in the fall holding a program and a bottle, framed under glass, 1940, 30"x50", EX, $1,400.00 B. Muddy River Trading Co./Gary Metz.

Cardboard poster, vertical, "Drink Coca-Cola" upper left hand corner, girl on towel at beach, bottle, framed under glass, rare, hard to find, 1930s, 30"x50", EX, $1,700.00 B. Muddy River Trading Co./Gary Metz.

Cardboard poster, vertical, "Entertain your thirst," two ballerinas at a green bench, framed under glass, 1942, 16"x27", VG, $600.00 B. Muddy River Trading Co./Gary Metz.

Cardboard poster, vertical, "Extra-Bright Refreshment," couple at party holding bottles, 33"x53", G, $200.00 C.

Cardboard poster, vertical, "Face the sun refreshed," pretty girl in white dress shielding her eyes from the sun with one hand while holding a bottle with the other, 1941, 30"x53½", VG $625.00 C.

Cardboard poster, vertical, "For the party," soldier and woman on bicycle for two, 29"x50½", EX, $425.00 B. Muddy River Trading Co./Gary Metz.

Cardboard poster, vertical framed, "Home Refreshment on the way," 24½"x50", VG, $425.00 B.
Muddy River Trading Co./Gary Metz.

Cardboard poster, vertical, "Have a Coke," girl with bottle in each hand in front of drink machine, 1940s, 16"x27", EX, $325.00 B.
Muddy River Trading Co./Gary Metz.

Cardboard poster, vertical, "Home refreshment," woman holding a bottle with the refrigerator door ajar, 1950s, 16"x27", NM, $550.00 B.
Muddy River Trading Co./Gary Metz.

Cardboard poster, vertical, "Join me," fencer resting against a chest cooler with a bottle, in reproduction frame, 1947, 16"x27", EX, $775.00 B.
Muddy River Trading Co./Gary Metz.

29

Cardboard poster, vertical, "Nothing refreshes like a Coke," couple on bicycles, 1943, EX, $1,700.00 B.
Muddy River Trading Co./Gary Metz.

Cardboard poster, vertical, "On the refreshing side," couple with bottles, 1941, 30"x50", VG, $575.00-B.
Muddy River Trading Co./Gary Metz.

Cardboard poster, vertical, "Refreshment," pretty girl in fancy dress at a pool setting with bottles on table, 1949, 33½"x54", VG, $475.00 C.

Cardboard poster, vertical, "Refreshment right out of the bottle," girl with skates drinking from a bottle, 1941, EX, $750.00 B. Muddy River Trading Co./Gary Metz.

Cardboard poster, vertical, "Right off the ice," girl at ice skating rink, 1946, 16"x27", EX, $375.00 B.
Muddy River Trading Co./Gary Metz.

Cardboard poster, vertical, "So Easy," woman illuminated by candle getting ready for small gathering, 1950s, VG, $400.00 C. Mitchell Collection.

Cardboard poster, vertical, "Start Refreshed," couple at roller skating rink, 1943, 16"x27", EX, $350.00 B.

Muddy River Trading Co./Gary Metz.

Cardboard poster, vertical, "The drink they all expect," similar to horizontal poster of this year but showing full length artwork of couple preparing for entertaining, 1942, EX, $700.00 B.

Muddy River Trading Co./Gary Metz.

Cardboard poster, vertical, "Thirst knows no season," couple building a snowman, graphics are great, 1942, 30"x50", NM, $700.00 C.

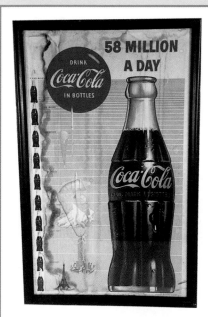

Cardboard poster, vertical, "Welcome Pause," girl in yellow with tennis racquet at chest vending machine, 1940s, 16"x27", $275.00 B. Muddy River Trading Co./Gary Metz.

Cardboard, poster, vertical, with large bottle in foreground and places and events in background, "58 Million a Day," 1957, 17½"x28½", F, $95.00 D.

Cardboard poster, vertical, woman sitting on a dock with a parasol behind her, holding a glass, "7 million drinks a day," 1926, 18"x31", VG, $1,500.00 B. Muddy River Trading Co./ Gary Metz.

Cardboard poster, "Wherever thirst goes," great graphics of girl in row boat with a bucket of iced Coca-Cola, 1942, EX, $500.00 B. Muddy River Trading Co./Gary Metz.

Cardboard poster with entertainer singing in front of microphone with bottle, "Entertain your thirst," 1940s, 36"x20", EX, $600.00 B. Gene Harris Antique Auction Center, Inc.

Cardboard poster with Johnny Weissmuller and Maureen O'Sullivan sitting on springboard, "Drink Coca-Cola, Come up smiling," 1934, 13½"x29½", EX, $2,800.00 C. Mitchell Collection.

Cardboard poster, woman sitting wearing a broad brimmed hat with flowers, holding a Coca-Cola 5¢ bamboo fan and glass, framed, 1912, EX, $4,750.00 D.

Cardboard poster, "Wherever you go," travel scenes in background, 1950s, EX, $195.00 C. Mitchell Collection.

Cardboard poster, "Yes," girl on beach with bottle, if found in original frame add $400.00 to this price, 1946, 56"x27", EX, $450.00 C. Mitchell Collection.

Cardboard, rack sign featuring Eddie Fisher on radio, 1954, 12"x20", EX, $130.00 B. Muddy River Trading Co./Gary Metz.

Cardboard, promotional sign for cups featuring Sprite Boy, 1940s, 15"x12", F, $350.00 B.

Muddy River Trading Co./Gary Metz.

Cardboard poster, "Zing-For your supper with ice cold Coke," young cartoon man in early version space suit with food and a bottle, 1960s, $115.00 C. Mitchell Collection.

Cardboard, sign featuring straight sided bottle "Demand the Genuine by Full Name, Nicknames Encourage Substitution," 1914, 30"x18", F, $500.00 B.

Muddy River Trading Co./Gary Metz.

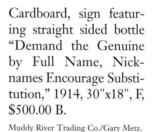

Cardboard, rack sign for 12 oz. cans with large diamond cans, 1960s, NM, $75.00 D.

Farmers Daughter.

Cardboard, St. Louis Fair, woman sitting at table with a flare glass that has a syrup line, 1909, F, $6,000.00. D

Cardboard, stand up, "For the emergency shelf," folds in middle, EX, $285.00 B. Muddy River Trading Co./Gary Metz.

Cardboard, string hung die cut "Float with Coke," 1960s, 10" dia., EX, $75.00 C. Al & Earlene Mitchell.

Cardboard, "The pause that refreshes at home," large horizontal poster, featuring woman with bottle, and 6 for 25¢ carrier, add $375 for original frame, 1940s, 56"x27", EX, $450.00 C. Al & Earlene Mitchell.

Cardboard, 3-D, "Boy oh Boy," pictures boy in front of cooler with a bottle in hand, 1937, 36"x34", VG, $825.00 C. Mitchell Collection.

Cardboard, trolley car sign, matted and framed, "Around the corner from anywhere," 1927, EX, $2,600.00 B.
Muddy River Trading Co./Gary Metz.

Cardboard, trolley car sign, "Relieves fatigue, Sold everywhere" good graphics, 1907, 20"x10¼", F, $3,400.00 B.
Muddy River Trading Co./Gary Metz.

Cardboard, trolley car sign, "Tired?, Coca-Cola relieves fatigue," 1907, 20½"x10¼", F, $2,300.00 B.
Muddy River Trading Co./Gary Metz.

Cardboard, trolley sign, "Drink Coca-Cola Delicious and Refreshing," if mint the value would increase to the $3,500.00 range, 1914, F, $800.00 C. Mitchell Collection.

Cardboard, sports favorite, hanging, complete set consists of 10 signs; individual signs go in the $100.00–$200.00 range, 1947, EX, complete set, $2,000.00 – 2,400.00 C. Mitchell Collection.

Cardboard, two piece set, display sign and a paper window banner, "We sell Coca-Cola part of every day - Served ice cold," printed by Snyder & Black, 1942, EX, $500.00 C. Mitchell Collection.

Cardboard, two sided die cut foldout sign featuring girl with glass "Be Really Refreshed," 1960s, 13"x17", EX, $425.00 B.

Muddy River Trading Co./Gary Metz.

Cardboard, vertical poster featuring girl at water, 1938, 30"x50", EX, $4,000.00 B.

Muddy River Trading Co./Gary Metz.

Cardboard, vertical sign featuring a burger plate and a bottle of Coke, "A good combination," EX, $85.00 C. Al & Earlene Mitchell.

Cardboard, "Welcome friend," red and white lettering on simulated oak background, 1957, 14"x12", EX, $195.00 C. Mitchell Collection.

Celluloid bottle, "Drink Coca-Cola Delicious and Refreshing," 1900, 6"x13¼", VG, $2,300.00 C.

Cardboard, window display, cameo fold-out, 1913, VG, $5,200.00 B. Muddy River Trading Co./Gary Metz.

Celluloid disc, foreign, Spanish, rare, yellow and white on red, 1940s, 9", NM, $325.00 C.

Celluloid hanging "Highballs" sign, with original hanging chain, gold lettering on black background, 1921, 11¼"x6", EX, $6,200.00 D.

Chalkboard, painted metal, made in U.S.A, American Art Works Inc. Coshoctin, Ohio, 1940, 19¼"x27", F, $200.00 C.

Celluloid, round, "Coca-Cola," white lettering on top of a bottle in center with red background, 1950s, 9" dia., EX, $175.00 D.

Coca-Cola fashion girl, one of four fashion girls, framed and under glass, 1932, EX, $5,800.00 C.

Mitchell Collection

Countertop light-up sign, "Drink Coca-Cola" with glass in spotlight at bottom center, back lit with red and white bulbs, manufactured by Brunhoff Mfg. Co., red and white, 1930s, 12"x14", EX, $6,200.00 B.

Muddy River Trading Co./Gary Metz.

Decal, paper, unused, "Drink Coca-Cola Ice Cold," bottle in shield, 1934, 18"x15", EX, $130.00 B. Muddy River Trading Co./Gary Metz.

Decal, "Drink Coca-Cola in Bottles," framed, 1950s, 15"x9", NM, $45.00 B. Muddy River Trading Co./Gary Metz.

Die cut Coca-Cola bottle sign, 1951, 6' tall, G, $525.00 B. Muddy River Trading Co./Gary Metz.

"Drink Coca-Cola, Cures Headache...Relieves Exhaustion at Soda Fountains 5¢," framed under glass, 1890–1900s, VG, $1,500.00 B. Muddy River Trading Co./Gary Metz.

Festoon, five piece Square Dance back bar display with the original envelope, 1957, 18"x11', G, $1,400.00 B.

Muddy River Trading Co./Gary Metz.

Festoon, nine piece back bar display, hard to find, complete with original envelope and instruction card, 1958, 12' long, NM, $1,600.00 B.

Muddy River Trading Co./Gary Metz.

Festoon, people in period dress from 1886 to 1951, pictured is the center piece only, 1951, NM, $1,200.00 B.

Muddy River Trading Co./Gary Metz.

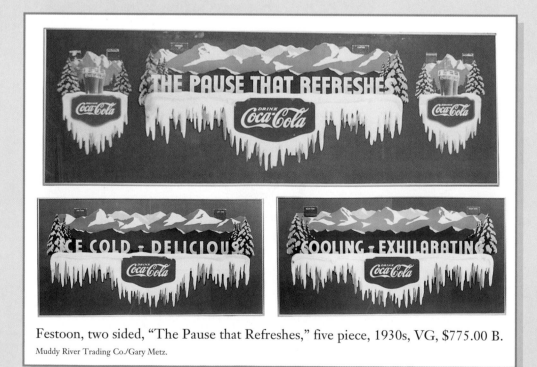

Festoon, two sided, "The Pause that Refreshes," five piece, 1930s, VG, $775.00 B.

Muddy River Trading Co./Gary Metz.

Festoon, state tree complete with original display envelope, 1950s, EX, $550.00 C. Mitchell Collection.

Festoon, verbena, center piece only shown, price is for complete 5-piece set with ribbons, $1,500.00 B.

Muddy River Trading Co./Gary Metz.

Fiberboard, round, pressed and raised, by Kay Displays, scarce, 13" dia., G, $600.00 B. Muddy River Trading Co./Gary Metz

Glass and metal light-up, "Work safely work refreshed," cardboard insert, with original packing box, 1950s, 16"x16", EX, $675.00 B. Muddy River Trading Co./Gary Metz.

Glass front light-up sign that has an illusion of movement, featuring "Have a Coke " arrow and a cup of Coke, hard-to-find item, 1950s, 17"x10"x3", NM, $1,400.00 B.

Muddy River Trading Co./Gary Metz

Glass, oval, "Drink Coca-Cola 5¢," silver lettering on maroon colored background, 1906, 9"x6¾", VG, $2,300.00 C.

Glass, round, "Drink Coca-Cola 5¢," gold trademark with blue background, 1900s, 8" dia., F, $2,200.00 D.

Glass, round mirror, "Drink Carbonated Coca-Cola 5¢ in Bottles," G, $475.00 C. Mitchell Collection.

Illusion light-up sign, plastic front, 1960s, 11", NM, $775.00 B.
Muddy River Trading Co./Gary Metz.

Light-up counter sign, "Serve Yourself" base with "Drink..." and clock on sign body, 1950s, 9"x20", EX, $850.00 D.
Pleasant Hill Antique Mall & Tea Room/Bob Johnson.

Light-up, plastic and glass, "Pause and Refresh," "Quality carries on" on right side with bottle in hand, same artwork as appears on fans of this vintage, 1940s, 19"x15½", EX, $675.00 B.

Muddy River Trading Co./Gary Metz.

Light-up counter top "Pause" motion sign, with original box, 1950s, EX, $875.00 C.

Light-up, plastic and metal, round, double sided, "Drink Coca-Cola Sign of Good Taste," 1950, 16" dia., EX, $550.00 B.

Muddy River Trading Co./Gary Metz.

Light-up, plastic, rotating, "Shop Refreshed Drink Coca-Cola," 1950s, 21" tall, G, $525.00 B.

Muddy River Trading Co./Gary Metz.

Light-up, plastic with metal base, "Drink Coca-Cola, Sign of Good Taste," 1950s, VG, $500.00 C. Mitchell Collection.

Light-up "Work Safely" plastic with cardboard insert and Coca-Cola paper cup on left of lower panel, 1950s, 15½" sq., G, $725.00 B. Muddy River Trading Co./Gary Metz.

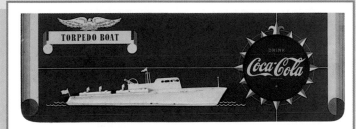

Masonite and wood destroyer ship sign, 1940s, EX, $300.00 C. Mitchell Collection.

Masonite and aluminum cooler sign with arrow through outside circle, 1940s, M, $525.00 C. Mitchell Collection.

Masonite, die cut, pretty blond girl holding a glass and a bouquet of flowers, 1940s, 42"x40", VG, $550.00 B. Muddy River Trading Co./Gary Metz.

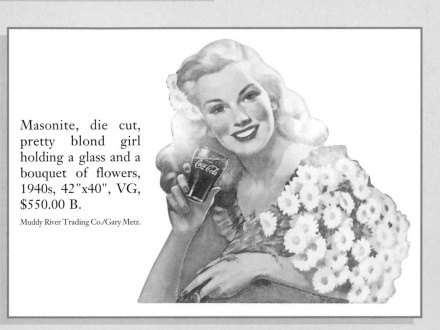

Masonite, die cut sign with teenagers on records, hard to find, 1950s, 12", EX, $2,200.00 B. Muddy River Trading Co./Gary Metz.

Masonite, horizontal, "Drink Coca-Cola Fountain Service," fountain heads on outside of lettering, 1930–40s, 27"x14", EX, $1,200.00 B. Muddy River Trading Co./Gary Metz.

Masonite, Kay Displays sign featuring a metal button in center of wings that have a Sprite Boy decal on each end, 1940s, 78"x12", EX, $850.00 B. Muddy River Trading Co./Gary Metz.

Metal and glass light-up sign with clock, "Please Pay When Served," 1950s, 20"x9", EX, $650.00 C. Eric Reinfeld.

Masonite, Sprite Boy in arrow through cooler, 1940s, EX, $850.00 C. Mitchell Collection.

Metal and plastic light-up counter sign, waterfall motion, "Pause and Refresh," 1950s, EX, $1,150.00 B. Muddy River Trading Co./Gary Metz.

Metal, cooler panel insert, "Serve yourself, Please Pay the Clerk," yellow & white on red, 1931, 31"x11", G, $140.00 B. Muddy River Trading Co./Gary Metz.

Metal bag holder, painted, "For Home Refreshment Coca-Cola," Sprite Boy, 36"x17", VG, $500.00 D.

Metal, double sided fountain service sign, 1934, 23"x26", NM, $1,600.00 D.

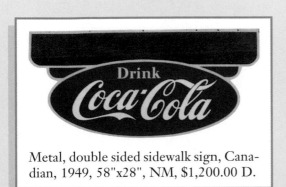

Metal, double sided sidewalk sign, Canadian, 1949, 58"x28", NM, $1,200.00 D.

Metal, "Drink Coca-Cola, Delicious and Refreshing," bottle on left side, "The Icy-O Company Inc., Charlotte, N.C.," EX, $850.00 B. Muddy River Trading Co./Gary Metz.

Metal, double sided, "In any weather Drink Coca-Cola," thermometer on one side fits on outside of screen door, while the "Thanks, Call Again" fits on the inside of the door, rare, 1930s, EX, $2,100.00 **B.** Muddy River Trading Co./Gary Metz.

Metal, "Drink Coca-Cola," with bottle at right of message, 1950s, 54"x18", EX, $275.00 C. Eric Reinfeld.

Metal, fishtail, painted, "Coca-Cola Sign of Good Taste," bottle on right side of sign, 31¾"x11¾", G, $200.00 C.

Metal, fishtail, painted horizontal, "Coca-Cola, Sign of Good Taste," white lettering on red background on white frame with green stripes, 1960s, 46"x16", EX, $225.00 D.

Metal, flange, Italian, American made sign, white & yellow on red, 1920s, 16"x12", NM, $1,500.00 **B.** Muddy River Trading Co./Gary Metz.

Metal, horizontal, "Drink Coca-Cola," Sprite Boy in spotlight, red background outlined in yellow with white lettering, 57"x18", VG, $475.00 C.

Metal "Have a Coke" with spotlight bottle in a metal frame, 1940s, 18"x54", EX, $325.00 D.

Patrick's Collectibles.

Metal, horizontal, painted, "Enjoy Coca-Cola," red background with white lettering, white background block on right side with bottle centered in box, 1960, 32"x11¾", $150.00 C.

Metal, "Ice cold" with cup in center, 1960s, 20"x28", NM, $300.00 B. Muddy River Trading Co./Gary Metz.

Metal lollipop, "Drink Coca-Cola Refresh!," not on proper base, 1950s, $495.00 D. Riverview Antique Mall.

Metal, painted "Drink…" sign with bottle in spotlight, 1948, 54"x18", G, $325.00 D.

Patrick's Collectibles.

Metal, "Pause Refresh yourself," various scenes in yellow border, lettering, 1950s, 28"x10", VG, $225.00 C. Mitchell Collection.

Metal, rolled frame edge, "Coke adds life to everything nice" with dynamic wave, 1960s, EX, $275.00 D.

Rare Bird Antique Mall/Jon & Joan Wright.

Metal policeman crossing guard with original base. This is a very volatile piece. I've seen them sell for as little as $600.00 or as high as $3,500.00, 1950s, G, $1,300.00 D.

Metal rolled frame edge with "Pick up 12… Refreshment for all," with artwork of 12-pack carton, 1960s, 50"x16", EX, $550.00 D.

Rare Bird Antique Mall/Jon & Joan Wright.

Metal, "Serve Coke at Home," 16" button at top, 1948, EX, $675.00 D.

Affordable Antiques.

Metal, sidewalk, "For Headache and Exhaustion Drink Coca-Cola," with 4" legs, manufactured by Ronemers & Co, Baltimore, M.D, 1895–90, G, $7,500.00 B.

Muddy River Trading Co./Gary Metz.

Metal sign with rolled framing edge, "things go better with Coke" with bottle at right of message, 35¼"x35¼", G, $275.00 D, Patrick's Collectibles.

Metal two sided rack sign, "Serve Coca-Cola Sign of Good Taste," 1960s, 17"x10", G, $95.00 B.

Muddy River Trading Co./Gary Metz.

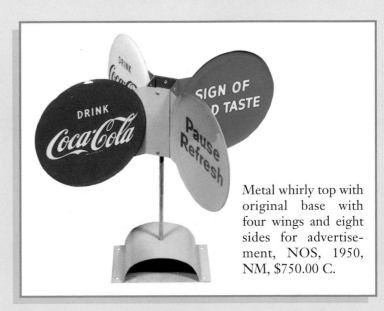

Metal string holder with double sided panels, "Take Home Coca-Cola in Cartons," featured with six pack for 25¢, 1930s, EX, $1,100.00 B. Muddy River Trading Co./Gary Metz.

Metal whirly top with original base with four wings and eight sides for advertisement, NOS, 1950, NM, $750.00 C.

Mileage and driving time chart from Rand McNally with Coke message information around map, 1950s, 24"x18", EX, $275.00 C. Al & Earlene Mitchell.

Neon sign with original wrinkle paint, 1939, 17"x13½", G, $1,700.00 B. Muddy River Trading Co./Gary Metz.

Neon, "Coca-Cola in bottles," great colors with metal base, 1950s, EX, $3,000.00 D. Muddy River Trading Co./Gary Metz.

Oil cloth, Lillian Nordica, "Coca-Cola at Soda Fountain 5¢ Delicious Refreshing," rare, 1904, 25"x47", EX, $12,000.00 C.

Oil on canvas that has been dry mounted on board featuring soda jerk with glasses of Coke, back is marked Forbes litho, 1940s, 22"x17", F, $2,300.00 B. Muddy River Trading Co./Gary Metz

Original artwork of outdoor retail location, 1970s, 30"x20", EX, $50.00 B.

Muddy River Trading Co./Gary Metz.

Paper, bottler's calendar advance print, Garden Girl on a golf course, framed under glass, rare, 1919, NM, $8,000.00 C.

Mitchell Collection.

Paper, calendar print sent to bottlers in advance of calendar, two models on a beach outing, framed under glass, rare, 1917, NM, $8,000.00 C. Mitchell Collection.

Paper calendar print sent to Coca-Cola bottlers a year in advance of the calendar, Autumn Girl, rare, framed under glass, 1921, NM, $8,000.00 C.

Mitchell Collection.

Paper, calendar top, girl sitting on slat back bench wearing a large white hat with a red ribbon and drinking from a bottle with a straw, framed, 1913, 16"x24", G, $4,500.00 C.

Paper, "Come in… we have Coca-Cola 5¢," Sprite Boy with glasses, 1944, 25"x8", VG, $350.00 B. Muddy River Trading Co./Gary Metz.

Paper, Edgar Bergen and Charlie McCarthy, CBS Sunday Evenings, 1949, 22"x11", EX, $195.00 C. Mitchell Collection.

Paper, Gibson Girl, matted and framed, if in mint condition price would go to about $5,000.00, 1910, 20"x30", F, $3,000.00 C. Mitchell Collection.

Paper, girl in white dress with large red bow in back with a bottle and a straw, matted and framed under glass. There are two versions of this, the other one is identical except the waist bow is pink, 1910s, F, $3,800.00 C. Mitchell Collection.

Paper poster featuring a bottle of Coke on snow, printed on heavy outdoor paper, 1942, 57"x18", EX, $130.00 B. Muddy River Trading Co./Gary Metz.

Paper, Hilda Clark, oval "Drink Coca-Cola 5¢" sign on table, framed under glass, 1901, EX, $7,500.00 C.

Paper poster featuring man and woman with flared glasses and the globe motif, 1912, 38"x49", F, $16,500.00 B. Muddy River Trading Co./Gary Metz.

Paper poster, horizontal, "Let's have a Coke," couple in uniform, 1930s, 57"x20", G, $850.00 B.

Muddy River Trading Co./Gary Metz.

Paper poster, horizontal, "Such a friendly custom," two women in uniform at soda fountain, 1930s, G, $350.00 B.

Muddy River Trading Co./Gary Metz.

Paper poster "Refresh," on heavy outdoor paper, 1940s, 57"x18", EX, $275.00 B.

Muddy River Trading Co./Gary Metz.

Paper poster, "Ritz Boy," first time Ritz Boy was used, framed under glass, 1920s, F, $700.00 C. *Mitchell Collection.*

Paper poster, "Sold Everywhere 5¢," has been trimmed, but is a rare piece, 1908, 14"x22", M, $10,000.00 – 11,000.00; F, $1,050.00 B.

Muddy River Trading Co./Gary Metz.

Paper poster "Treat yourself right" featuring man with a sandwich opening a bottle of Coke, 1920s, 12"x20", F, $550.00 B

Muddy River Trading Co./Gary Metz.

Paper poster, vertical, "Drink Coca-Cola Delicious and Refreshing," matted, framed under glass, 1927–28, 12"x20", VG, $675.00 B.

Muddy River Trading Co./Gary Metz.

Paper poster, vertical, "Pause a minute Refresh yourself," roll down with top and bottom metal strips, 1927–28, 12"x20", EX, $1,800.00 B. Muddy River Trading Co./Gary Metz.

Paper, "That taste-good feeling," boy with Coca-Cola and hot dog, 1920s, EX, $650.00 B.

Muddy River Trading Co./Gary Metz.

Paper, two women drinking from bottles sitting in front of an ocean scene with clouds in the sky, 1912, 16"x22", VG, $4,500.00 C.

Paper, "which" Coca-Cola or Goldelle Ginger Ale, this one has been trimmed with lettering eliminated, framed and under glass, if mint value would increase to $8,500.00, 1905, G, $4,500.00 C. Mitchell Collection.

Paper, window display, die cut, glass shaped, "Drink Coca-Cola," rare, 12"x20", EX, $1,800.00 B.

Muddy River Trading Co./Gary Metz.

Plywood and metal arrow and bottle sign "Drink Coca-Cola Ice Cold," 1939, 17" dia., G, $400.00 C.

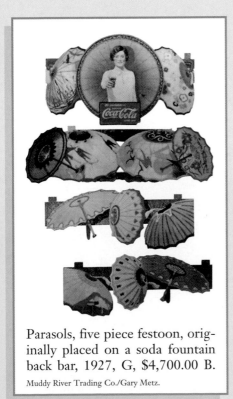

Parasols, five piece festoon, originally placed on a soda fountain back bar, 1927, G, $4,700.00 B.

Muddy River Trading Co./Gary Metz.

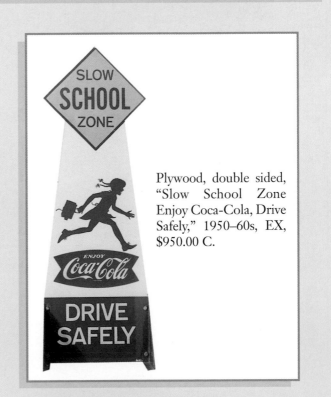

Plywood, double sided, "Slow School Zone Enjoy Coca-Cola, Drive Safely," 1950–60s, EX, $950.00 C.

  Plywood, triangle die cut sign with down arrow, "Ice Cold Drink Coca-Cola," Kay Displays, 1930s, EX, $575.00 B.

Muddy River Trading Co./Gary Metz.

 Porcelain, Canadian fountain service sign, 1935, 27"x14", NM, $1,200.00 B.

Muddy River Trading Co./Gary Metz.

Porcelain, "Buvez Coca-Cola," with Sprite Boy in spotlight, French, 1940s, 58"x18", EX, $750.00 B. Muddy River Trading Co./Gary Metz.

Porcelain, "Delicious, Refreshing" with bottle in center, 1950s, 24" sq., EX, $225.00 B.

Muddy River Trading Co./Gary Metz.

 Porcelain double sided "Drink.." sign, Made in Canada P & M 49, 1940s, 58"x27.5", G, $450.00 B,

Collectors Auction Services.

 Porcelain double sided dispenser sign with metal frame, 28"x27", G, $850.00 B.

Collectors Auction Services.

 Porcelain flange, die cut, "Rafraichissez vous Coca-Cola," foreign, VG, $400.00.

Porcelain, double sided flange sign, "Drink Coca-Cola Here," 1940s, NM, $850.00 B.

Muddy River Trading Co./Gary Metz.

Porcelain, double sided flange, "Iced Coca-Cola Here," red, white and yellow, 18"x20", EX, $700.00 B.

Collectors Auction Services.

Porcelain double sided lunch sign, 1950s, 28"x25", NM, $1,500.00 B.

Muddy River Trading Co./Gary Metz.

Porcelain, "Drink Coke," "Ask for it either way," 1940s, 9" dia., EX, $375.00 C. Mitchell Collection.

Porcelain, "Drink Coca-Cola" shield sign, white & yellow on red, 1942, 3' x 2', F, $225.00 B.

Muddy River Trading Co./Gary Metz.

Porcelain, flange, "Have a Coca-Cola," 1951, 17"x19", EX, $400.00 B.

Muddy River Trading Co./Gary Metz.

Porcelain, fishtail sign with turned ends, "Drink Coca-Cola," white on red, 1950s, 44"x16", M, $325.00 B. Muddy River Trading Co./Gary Metz.

Porcelain, flange, "Refresh Yourself, Coca-Cola Sold Here Ice Cold" on shield shaped sign, 1930s, 17"x20", G, $525.00 B.
Muddy River Trading Co./Gary Metz.

Porcelain, French Canadian flange sign, "Buvez Coca-Cola Glace," 1950s, 18"x19", NM, $200.00 B.
Muddy River Trading Co./Gary Metz.

Porcelain, horizontal, "Coca-Cola Sold Here Ice Cold," red background trimmed in yellow with white lettering, 1940s, 29"x12", G, $275.00 D.

Porcelain, horizontal, "Drink Coca-Cola Fountain Service," yellow background, 1950s, 28"x12", $700.00 B.
Muddy River Trading Co./Gary Metz.

Porcelain, outdoor advertising sign, "Drug Store, Drink Coca-Cola, Delicious and Refreshing," red, white, and green, 1933, 5' x 3½', EX, $1,100.00 B.
Muddy River Trading Co./Gary Metz.

Porcelain one sided neon, "Drug Store… Fountain Service",, 86"x58"x8", G, $3,500.00 B. Collectors Auction Services.

Porcelain, sidewalk sign and legs, double sided, "Stop Here Drink Coca-Cola," 1941, 27"x46", VG, $875.00 B.

Muddy River Trading Co./Gary Metz.

Porcelain outdoor bottle, tall vertical, "Drink Coca-Cola," believed to be a foreign sign where English was the dominant language, 1950–60s, 16"x4', NM, $550.00 B.

Muddy River Trading Co./Gary Metz.

Reverse glass, "Drink Coca-Cola," 1920s, 10"x6", EX, $1,200.00 B.

Reverse glass, "Drink Coca-Cola," metal frame that could be illuminated from the back, 1930s, 13"x9", F, $700.00 C. Mitchell Collection.

Reverse glass with original chain and frame, "Drink Coca-Cola," rare version in red, white lettering on red background, 1932, 20"x12", EX, $3,500.00 B.

Muddy River Trading Co./Gary Metz.

Reverse glass, "Drink Coca-Cola," for back bar mirror, 1930s, 11" dia., G, $550.00 C. Mitchell Collection.

Santa cardboard poster, "Coke adds life to Holiday Fun" with artwork of Santa holding list and bottle, 1960s, 36"x20", EX, $85.00 C. Al & Earlene Mitchell.

Starburst light-up with Coca-Cola bottle in center, "Drink Coca-Cola," fishtail at bottom, 1960s, 14"x16", EX, $550.00 B. Muddy River Trading Co./Gary Metz.

Tin, bottle, Christmas, 1933, 3' tall, EX, $1,000.00 C.

Tin, bottle, die cut embossed, 3' tall, VG, $350.00 B. Muddy River Trading Co./Gary Metz.

Tin bottle, embossed, 1931, 4½"x12½", VG, $375.00 B. Muddy River Trading Co./Gary Metz.

Tin, bottle, oval, "Drink A Bottle of Car-bonated Coca-Cola," rare, 1900s, 8½"x10½", EX, $7,500.00 C.

Tin, button, white painted with bottle in center, 1940s, 24" dia., NM, $400.00 B. Muddy River Trading Co./Gary Metz.

Tin, button, with mechanic on duty under the button, 1950–60s, VG, $465.00 D. Riverview Antique Mall.

Tin, button with Sprite Boy decal, white, 1950s, 16", NM, $775.00 B. Muddy River Trading Co./Gary Metz.

Tin, Canadian sign featuring 6 oz. bottle on right, 1930s, 28"x20", G, $325.00 B. Muddy River Trading Co./Gary Metz.

Tin, Canadian six-pack in spotlight "Take home a carton," 1940, 36"x60", G, $200.00 B.
Muddy River Trading Co./Gary Metz.

Tin, carton rack with great rare sign at top, hard to find this one, 1930s, 5' tall, NM, $825.00 B.
Muddy River Trading Co./Gary Metz.

Tin, die cut bottle sign, 1932, 12"x39", VG, $575.00 C.

Tin, die cut six-pack sign, featuring carrier with handle, advertising 6 for 25¢, 1950, 11"x13", EX, $775.00 B.
Muddy River Trading Co./Gary Metz.

Tin distributors, oval, from McRae Coca-Cola Bottling Co. in Helena, GA, featuring pretty long-haired girl, 1910, EX, $3,500.00 D.

Tin, double sided die cut arrow flange, "Drink Coca-Cola Ice Cold," with button at top and bottle in lower arrow point, EX, $475.00 C.

Tin, double sided flange fishtail sign, red on white and green, 1960s, 18"x15", G, $300.00 C.

Tin, "Drink Coca-Cola" button with silver metal arrow, 1950–60s, 18" dia., VG, $725.00 C. Mitchell Collection.

Tin, "Drink Coca-Cola Enjoy that Refreshing New Feeling," painted fishtail with Coca-Cola bottle on right side, 1960s, 32"x12", VG, $195.00 C.

Tin, "Drink Coca-Cola Ice Cold," 1923 with embossed bottle at left, note shadow on bottle, 1937, 28"x20", G, $525.00, B.
Muddy River Trading Co./Gary Metz.

Tin, "Drink Coca-Cola Ice Cold" in red arrow pointing right at bottle in white background, red & white, 1952, 27"x19", NM, $250.00 B. Muddy River Trading Co./Gary Metz.

Tin, "Drink Coca-Cola" sign with marching bottles, note shadow on bottles, 1937, 54"x18", NM, $800.00 B. Muddy River Trading Co./Gary Metz .

Tin, "Drink Delicious Refreshing Coca-Cola," Hilda Clark, very rare, 1900, 20"x28", EX, $15,000.00 C.

Tin, "Drink Coca-Cola," 24" iron frame, one side has a 16" button while the opposite side as a 10" plastic button with a small light which creates a back light, VG, $975.00 C.

Tin, "Drink Coca-Cola," with couple at right of message holding bottle, 1940s, 35"x11", EX, $575.00 D. Patrick's Collectibles.

Tin, embossed "Drink Coca-Cola Delicious and Refreshing" with bottle at left of message, with trademark in tail, 1930s, 36"x12", EX, $550.00 C. Al & Earlene Mitchell.

Tin, embossed "Gas Today" with spotlight blackboard in center, 1936, 18"x54", G, $700.00 B. Muddy River Trading Co./Gary Metz

Tin, embossed over cardboard with string holder, "Drink Coca-Cola," 1922, 8"x4", EX, $900.00 B. Muddy River Trading Co./Gary Metz.

Tin, embossed, Buvez Coca-Cola, painted, foreign, 17¼"x53", G, $125.00 C.

Tin, featuring Elaine holding a glass, 1916, 20"x30", VG, $5,500.00 C.

Tin, flange bottle logo, rare and somewhat difficult to find, "Enjoy Coca-Cola In Bottles," 1950s, 18", G, $475.00 B. Muddy River Trading Co./Gary Metz.

Tin, flange, "Drink Coca-Cola" with bottle in spotlight at lower corner, 1947, 24"x20", G, $575.00 D. Rare Bird Antique Mall.

Tin, flange with filigree at top of piece, 1936, 20"x13", EX, $700.00 B. Muddy River Trading Co./Gary Metz.

Tin, flat "Refresh yourself," sign "Drink Coca-Cola Sold Here Ice Cold," yellow & white on red, 1927, 28"x29", VG, $425.00 B. Muddy River Trading Co./Gary Metz.

Tin, Hilda Clark, considered rare due to the fact this artwork is rarely found in the tin version, 1903, 16¼"x19½", EX, $3,700.00 B. Muddy River Trading Co./Gary Metz.

Tin, Hilda Clark, round, "Coca-Cola Drink Delicious and Refreshing," very rare and hard to find piece, 1903, 6" dia., EX, $5,500.00 C.

Tin, horizontal embossed, "Drink Coca-Cola," 1923 bottle on left side, 35"x12", EX, $350.00 B.

Muddy River Trading Co./Gary Metz.

Tin, Hilda Clark, showing her drinking from a glass while seated at a table with roses and stationery, very rare, 1899, VG, $15,500.00 C.

Tin, horizontal, "Drink Coca-Cola," red background, silver border on self frame with bottle in spotlight in lower right-hand corner, 1946, 28"x20", EX, $340.00 B.

Muddy River Trading Co./Gary Metz.

Tin, horizontal, "Drink Coca-Cola," self-framing, white, VG, 32"x10½", 1927, VG, $725.00 B. Muddy River Trading Co./Gary Metz.

Tin, horizontal embossed, "Drink Coca-Cola Ice Cold," matted and framed, white and yellow lettering on red and black background, bottle in left part of sign, 1936, 28"x20", EX, $800.00 B.

Muddy River Trading Co./Gary Metz.

Tin, "Ice Cold Coca-Cola Sold Here," yellow & white on red, 1933, 20" dia., G, $225.00 B.

Muddy River Trading Co./Gary Metz.

Tin, Lillian Nordica, oval framed, "Coca-Cola Delicious and Refreshing," featuring Coca-Cola table and oval "Drink Coca-Cola 5¢," rare, 1904, 8½"x10¼", EX, $8,000.00 D.

Tin, Lillian Nordica, oval framed with framed back drop showing "Delicious and Refreshing 5¢," 1905, 8¼"x10¼", EX, $7,500.00 C.

Tin, Lillian Nordica, self framed, embossed, promoting both fountain and bottle sales, 1904–05, EX, $8,500.00 C.

Tin "Now Enjoy Coca-Cola at home," featuring hand carrying cardboard six-pack, rare and hard to find, Canadian sign, 1930s, 18"x54", F, $1,050.00 B.

Muddy River Trading Co./Gary Metz.

Tin over cardboard with beveled edge, for China use, rare, 11"x8", EX, $675.00 C. Bill Mitchell.

Tin, painted, "Coca-Cola," made in U.S.A/AAW 10-37, red background with white lettering and bottle in center outlined in green, 1934, 45" dia., EX, $425.00 D.

Tin, painted, "Drink Coca-Cola in Bottles 5¢," horizontally lettered, if this sign were EX to M price would increase to the $1,100.00 – $1,400.00 range, 1900s, 34½"x11¾", F, $400.00 C.

Tin, painted, "Drink Coca-Cola," shoulders and head of girl drinking from a bottle, yellow and white lettering on red background, self framing, 1940, 34"x12", EX, $425.00 B. Muddy River Trading Co./Gary Metz.

Tin, painted litho, "Drink Coca-Cola In Bottles 5¢," bottle on each side, framed, 1907, 34½"x12", EX, $625.00 D.

Tin, painted vertical, "Serve Coca-Cola at home," yellow and white lettering on red background with a six-pack spotlighted in the center, 1951, 18"x54", EX, $300.00 B.

Muddy River Trading Co./Gary Metz.

Tin "Pause… Drink Coca-Cola," considered to be rare due to the 1939 – 40 cooler in the left-hand spotlight, all on red background horizontal lettering, self framing, 1940, 42'x18', EX, $2,400.00 B. Muddy River Trading Co./Gary Metz.

Tin, "Pause" sign with bottle in spotlight, 1940, 18"x54", NM, $1,200.00 B.

Muddy River Trading Co./Gary Metz.

Tin, pilaster sign, featuring bottle with 16" button at top of unit, 1948, 16"x54", NM, $675.00 D.

Affordable Antiques.

Tin, round Sprite Boy with bottle and button, embossed edge, string hung, 1940s, 12¾" dia., EX, $775.00 C.

Tin, self framing, horizontal oval, "Coca-Cola," girl in foreground offering a bottle, 1926, 11"x8", EX, $375.00 C.

Tin, self-framing new Betty, "Drink Coca-Cola" sign, yellow & white on red, 1940, 28"x20", F, $225.00 B.
Muddy River Trading Co./Gary Metz.

Tin, self framing rectangle, "Coca-Cola," oval inside rectangle framing girl presenting a bottle, 1926, 11"x8½", EX, $2,000.00 C.

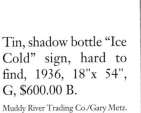

Tin, shadow bottle "Ice Cold" sign, hard to find, 1936, 18"x 54", G, $600.00 B.
Muddy River Trading Co./Gary Metz.

Tin, sidewalk sign featuring 24 bottle case "Take a case home today," 1957, EX, $200.00 B.
Muddy River Trading Co./Gary Metz.

Tin sidewalk, embossed, "French Wine Coca," with 9" legs, close-up of center inset (right), 1885–88, 27¾"x19¾", VG, $7,500.00 B.
Muddy River Trading Gary Metz.

Tin, sign with rolled edge,"Enjoy Big King Size... Ice Cold Here" fishtail design, 1960s, 28"x20", G, $225.00 D. Patrick's Collectibles.

Tin, six-pack die cut sign with spotlight on carton, hard to find, 1958, 11"x12", NM, $1,500.00 B.

Muddy River Trading Co./Gary Metz.

Tin, six-pack, embossed die cut, 1963, 3'x2½', EX, $725.00 B. Muddy River Trading Co./Gary Metz.

Tin, six-pack, embossed die cut, featuring a King Size six-pack, 1963, 3'x2½', EX, $700.00 B. Muddy River Trading Co./Gary Metz.

Tin, "Take Home a carton," self framing border, Canadian, 1950, 35x53, $625.00 B.

Muddy River Trading Co./Gary Metz.

Tin, "things go better" sign featuring "Drink" paper cup, hard to find, red, green, and white, 1960s, 28"x20", NM, $600.00 B.

Muddy River Trading Co./Gary Metz.

Tin, two sided die cut arrow sign "Ice Cold Coca-Cola Sold Here," 1927, 30"x8", VG, $400.00 C.

Tin, vertical, "Drink Delicious Refreshing Coca-Cola," Hilda Clark, one of the oldest signs known to exist, and the first celebrity to endorse the product, lettering under pen reads "Coca-Cola makes flow of thought more easy and reasoning power more vigorous," 1899, 20"x28", VG, $10,500.00 B.

Muddy River Trading Co./Gary Metz.

Tin, vertical painted, "Drink Coca-Cola Ice-Cold Delicious and Refreshing," green background with button at top and yellow lettering beneath button, 1941, G, $250.00 D.

Trolley car sign, matted and framed, "Four Seasons," 1923, 20¼"x10¼", NM, $4,000.00 B. Muddy River Trading Co./Gary Metz.

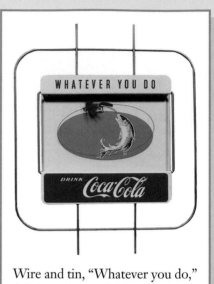

Wire and tin, "Whatever you do," fish jumping or fishing fly, 1960, 14"x18", EX, $195.00 C.

Wire and tin, "Whatever you do," saddle on fence, 1960s, 14"x18", EX, $195.00 C.

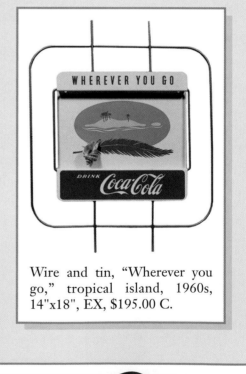

Wire and tin, "Wherever you go," tropical island, 1960s, 14"x18", EX, $195.00 C.

Wire and tin, "Wherever you go," skier coming down a snow slope, 1960s, 14"x18", EX, $195.00 C.

Wood and masonite, Kay Displays, sign advertising Sundaes and Malts with 12" button in center and Sprite Boy on each end, 1950s, 6'6"x1', EX, $1,050.00 B. Muddy River Trading Co./Gary Metz.

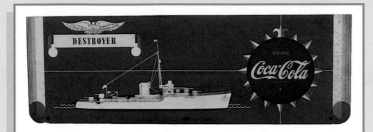

Wood and masonite, wartime torpedo boat, 1940, EX, $275.00 C. Mitchell Collection.

Wood and wire, Kay Displays sign with bowling scene, 1940s, 16" dia, EX, $425.00 B.
Muddy River Trading Co./Gary Metz.

Wood finish with chrome accents "Thirst asks nothing more," difficult to locate this piece, 38"x10", G, $775.00 B.
Muddy River Trading Co./Gary Metz.

Wood and plastic, "Drink Coca-Cola" in fishtail sign, 15½"x12", VG, $75.00 D.

Wood, "Here's Refreshment," bottle and horseshoe on plank, 1940s, EX, $325.00 C. Mitchell Collection.

Wood, Silhouette Girl, metal hanger, 1940, EX, $475.00 C.
Mitchell Collection.

Wood, Sprite Boy Welcome Friend, 1940, 32"x14", EX, $550.00 C. Mitchell Collection.

EVERY BOTTLE *Coca-Cola* STERILIZED

Wooden, hand painted, truck sign double sided with the maker's name on one side, with original metal brackets, "Every Bottle Sterilized," white lettering on red background, 1920s, 10' x 1', F, $425.00 B.
Muddy River Trading Co./Gary Metz.

Wooden medallion, Kay Displays, "Drink Coca-Cola," bottle with leaves at bottom, 1930s, EX, $1,300.00 D.

Wooden, three piece set manufactured by Kay Displays, 1930s, 37"x10" center, 9"x11½" end pieces, NM, $2,800.00 B.
Muddy River Trading Co./Gary Metz.

Wooden, three piece Kay Displays made of plywood and metal, featuring embossed icicles, displayed at Weidelich Pharmacies until it closed in the early 1960s, 1936, 36"x20" center, 36"x18" end pieces, G, $4,000.00 B. Muddy River Trading Co./Gary Metz.

America's Fighting Planes, set of 20 scenes of planes in action, price at $50.00 each if set is incomplete, 1940s, EX . . . . $1,200.00 C

Banner, "Be Really Refreshed... Around The Clock," 1950s, EX . . . . $40.00 C

Banner, canvas, featuring a 24 bottle case with area at bottom for the price, 9' tall, EX . . . . $145.00 C

Banner, paper, "Home Refreshment," carton at left, 1941, 51"x13", NM. . . . . $75.00 C

Banner, paper, "King Size," 1958, 36"x20", NM . . . . $110.00 C

Banner, "Take Coke Home," 108", EX . . . $150.00 C

Banner, "Welcome to Super Bowl XXVIII," 102"x34", EX. . . . . $65.00 D

Bottle hanger, "Ice Cold Coca-Cola King Size," red, white, and green, M . . . . $5.00 C

Bottle hanger, Santa Claus holding a bottle with information card about "Twas the Night Before Christmas," fold out story inside, 1950s, M . . . . $15.00 C

Bottle hanger, Santa Claus in refrigerator full of bottles, being surprised by small child, 1950s, F . . . . $3.00 D

Bottle topper, plastic, "We let you see the bottle," 1950s, G . . . . $300.00 D

Canvas awning, Refreshment Center, red & white stripe, 1950s, 5' x 2', EX . . . . $575.00 C

Canvas banner, "Take Coke Home," pricing information at bottom, 24 bottle case in center, 9' tall, EX . . . $425.00 D

Cardboard advertisement for a deck of playing cards that can be purchased with six coupons taken from six-pack cartons, Piqua Coca-Cola Bottling Company, 1938, 12"x18" . . . . $45.00 C

Cardboard advertisement, horizontal, "Have a Coke," woman holding a bottle, 36"x20", EX . . . . $250.00 B

Cardboard airplane hangers, complete set of 20 in original envelope, if sold separately price at $35.00 to $50.00 each, 1943, EX . . . . $1,000.00 C

Cardboard, an African-American family enjoying Coca-Cola, 1958, EX . . . . $75.00 C

Cardboard and wood price board for 6½ oz. and 12 oz. sizes with original tin frame, 1950, 25"x15", VG. . . . $145.00 D

Cardboard and wood right angle display featuring three 6-packs and carriers, "Easy to Carry," carriers have wooden handles, 1947, 42"x33", EX . . . . . $275.00 D

Cardboard, bather in diamond blue background pictured with a Coke button and a bottle, framed and under glass, 1940, 23"x22", EX . . . . $1,250.00 C

Cardboard, bather in round blue background, framed and under glass, by Snyder & Black, rare, 1938, 22", EX . . . . $1,800.00 C

Cardboard bottle display, cut out, featuring a girl in a swimsuit, "So Refreshing," 1930, 9"x17½", VG. . . . $475.00 D

Cardboard bottle display of girl holding tray, 1926, 11½"x14", NM . . . . $3,500.00 B

Cardboard bottle rack, "Enjoy Coca-Cola," 1970–80s, 18", red and white, EX . . . . $12.00 D

Cardboard, boy and girl with bottles, "Coke for me too," 1946, 36"x20", EX . . . . $725.00 C

Cardboard, Canadian poster featuring artwork of girl on ping pong table with a bottle of Coke, framed under glass, 14"x28", G. . . . . $600.00 D

Cardboard, Canadian trolley card, "Drink Coca-Cola, Made In Canada," 1920s, 21"x11", F. . . . . $170.00 C

Cardboard, carton insert, a lady's hand shown carrying a six-pack, "Take Home This Handy 6 Bottle Carton," by Niagara Litho, 1936, G . . . . $85.00 D

Cardboard, carton insert, "Good With Food," 1930s, NM. . . . . $150.00 D

Cardboard, carton insert, "Good With Food," 1930s, F . . . . $75.00 C

Cardboard, carton insert, "Refresh Your Guests," 1930, VG. . . . . $175.00 C

Cardboard, carton insert, "Six for 25¢ Plus Deposit," 1930s, NM . . . . $400.00 C

Cardboard, carton insert, slanted red billboard logo "Easy to Serve," 1930, EX. . . . . \$125.00 D

Cardboard, clown balancing on a bottle, 1950, G. . . . . \$500.00 C

Cardboard, Coca-Cola polar bear stand up , 6' tall, EX . . . . \$65.00 D

Cardboard, cup sign with Sprite Boy, 1950s, 15"x12", EX. . . . . \$75.00 B

Cardboard, cut out, Athletic Games, 1932, EX. . . . . \$55.00 C

Cardboard, cut out, "Buy Coca-Cola Have for Picnic Fun," shows two couples having a picnic, 1950s, EX. . . . . \$95.00 C

Cardboard, cut out, "Buy Coca-Cola, Have for Picnic Fun," shows two couples having a picnic, 1950s, G. . . . . \$75.00 D

Cardboard, cut out, cherub holding a tray with a glass in a glass holder, 14½", EX. . . . . \$3,800.00 B

Cardboard, cut out, couple at sundial, "It's Time to Drink Coca-Cola" on edge of dial, 1911, 29"x36", G . . . . \$3,500.00 B

Cardboard, cut out, "Drink Coca-Cola, The Pause that Refreshes," used as a window display by Niagara Litho Co. N.Y, 1940s, 32½"x42½", G . . . \$800.00 D

Cardboard, cut out, featuring glass in hand, has a 3-D effect, 1958, 19"x21", G . . . . \$300.00 D

Cardboard, cut out, man and woman at sundial, both are holding flare glasses, 1913–1916, 30"x36½", EX. . . . . \$6,000.00 B

Cardboard, cut out, model with a bottle and a colorful parasol, easel back, 1930s, 10"x18½", G. . . . \$1,000.00 D

Cardboard, cut out, orchid festoon component, 1939, 30"x18", G . . . . \$225.00 D

Cardboard, cut out, sign with elves and a bottle on sled, 12"x20", EX . . . . \$180.00 C

Cardboard, cut out stand up of Eddie Fisher, 1954, 19", EX. . . . . \$225.00 D

Cardboard, cut out, Toonerville, 1930, EX . \$95.00 D

Cardboard, cut out, Toy Town, 1927, EX . . \$75.00 C

Cardboard, die cast 3-D, featuring Claudette Colbert, 1933, 10"x20", EX . . . . \$5,500.00 C

Cardboard, die cut, embossed, easel back Victorian sign promoting Coca-Cola chewing gum, girl in woods, Kaufmann and Strauss Company, New York, framed and matted, 1903–05, 4½"x10½", NM. . . . . \$15,500.00 C

Cardboard, die cut, festoon centerpiece featuring soda jerk, scarce, 1931, G. . . . . \$1,600.00 C

Cardboard, die cut, hand in bottle, "Take Enough Home," companion piece at top, 1952, 11"x14", NM. . . . . \$180.00 D

Cardboard, die cut, French Canadian string hanger with great graphics featuring woman with a Coke, 1939, 15"x22", G . . . . \$1,600.00 B

Cardboard, die cut of lady's face with actual scarf, EX. . . . . \$125.00 D

Cardboard, die cut sailor girl, 1952, 11"x7", NM. . . . . \$350.00 D

Cardboard, die cut, sailor girl, framed under glass, 1952, 11"x7", EX. . . . . \$325.00 C

Cardboard, die cut six-pack, 1954, EX. . . . \$650.00 B

Cardboard, die cut, "Take Enough Home," bottle in hand, 1952, VG . . . . \$160.00 B

Cardboard, die cut, two sided, girl and a glass, 1960s, 13"x17", EX. . . . . \$425.00 B

Cardboard, die cut 6-pack, 1954, 12", NM \$700.00 C

Cardboard, die cut 6-pack with "6 for 25¢" on carton, 1950, 12", NM . . . . \$575.00 C

Cardboard, die cut, string hanger featuring Sprite Boy with bottle cap hat, "Drink Coca-Cola, Be Refreshed," Canadian, 1950s, 11" wide, NM. . . . . . . \$2,200.00 D

Cardboard, die cut window display, 15 piece Toonerville, EX. . . . . \$375.00 D

Cardboard die cut with an ice bucket scene and a glass and bottle in front, 1926, EX. . . . . $550.00 C

Cardboard, die cut, woman 5' tall, holding six-pack, EX. . . . . $95.00 C

Cardboard display, "Pick Up The Fixins, Enjoy Coke," 1957, 20"x14", NM. . . . . $35.00 D

Cardboard, double sided, Canadian, horizontal poster, featuring woman serving Coca-Cola on one side and a bottle in snow bank on reverse, 1950s, 36"x20", G . . . . $180.00 D

Cardboard, double sided, Canadian poster featuring woman with bottle on both sides, different backgrounds, 1950s, 56"x27", G. . . . . $220.00 C

Cardboard, "Drink Coca-Cola Delicious and Refreshing" sign with tin frame featuring 1915 bottle on each side, 1910s, 60"x21", NM. . . . . $1,450.00 C

Cardboard easel back, boy and girl under mistletoe, "Things Go Better With Coke," 1960s, 16"x27", EX . . . . $35.00 D

Cardboard, easel back French Canadian sign "Coke Convient," 1948, 18"x24", NM. . . . . $200.00 D

Cardboard easel back, girls on a bicycle built for two, "Extra Fun Takes More than One," 1960s . $35.00 D

Cardboard easel back, Kit Carson advertising bottle sales and Rodeo Tie promotion, 1953, 16"x24", G. . $275.00 C

Cardboard, easel back Kit Carson promotional sign, promoting kerchief, 1950s, 16"x24", EX. . . . . . $200.00 C

Cardboard, easel back or hanging sign featuring a glass of Coke, Canadian, 1949, 12' x 12", EX . . $120.00 D

Cardboard, easel back, Shopping Girl, 1956, 2½'x5', EX. . . . . $900.00 C

Cardboard, easel back sign "thirst asks nothing more" featuring bottle in hand, 1939, 12"x16", NM. . . $1,800.00 D

Cardboard featuring Eddie Fisher on radio, 1954, 12"x20", EX . . . . $75.00 C

Cardboard festoon backbar display, girl's head, five pieces, 1951, NM . . . . $1,250.00 C

Cardboard, festoon elements featuring man and woman with magnolias, great graphics, 1938, G . . . . $600.00 C

Cardboard, festoon unit "Shop Refreshed" featuring couple with a glass of Coke, 1950s, 29"x14", EX . . . . $210.00 C

Cardboard, French Canadian, girl in front of box cooler with bottle in hand, original easel back stand, 1940s, 12"x17", EX . . . . $225.00 C

Cardboard, French Canadian poster, woman shopper, 1950s, EX . . . . $150.00 C

Cardboard, French Canadian sign featuring bottle in snow bank, 1950s, 22"x50", EX. . . . . $150.00 D

Cardboard, horizontal, "Accepted Home Refreshment," couple with popcorn and Coca-Cola in front of fireplace, "Drink..." button lower right, 1942, 56"x27", VG . . . . $225.00 C

Cardboard, horizontal, "Accepted Home Refreshment," couple with popcorn and Coca-Cola in front of fireplace, "Drink..." button lower right, 1942, 56"x27", G. . . . . $175.00 B

Cardboard, horizontal, "Be Really Refreshed," scene of couple in boat on pond, 1960s, 36"x20", EX. . $100.00 D

Cardboard, horizontal, "Be Really Refreshed," scene of couple in boat on pond, 1960s, 36"x20", G. . . . . $85.00 B

Cardboard, horizontal, "Enjoy the quality taste," girl in swim suit at beach, 1956, 36"x20", EX . $255.00 C

Cardboard, horizontal, "For the taste you never get tired of," beside "Drink..." button, couple in pool, 1960s, 36"x20", EX . . . . $175.00 C

Cardboard, horizontal "Have a Coke," young cheerleader with megaphone and a bottle, "Coca-Cola" button on right, 1946, 36"x20", G . . . . $225.00 B

Cardboard, horizontal "Have a Coke," young cheerleader with megaphone and a bottle, "Coca-Cola" button on right, 1946, 36"x20", VG, ... $235.00 D

Cardboard, horizontal, "Here's Something Good!," woman with crown, man in clown suit with bottle, 1950s, 56"x27", VG. . . . . $225.00 C

Cardboard, horizontal, "Here's Something Good!", woman with crown, man in clown suit with bottle, 1950s, 56"x27", G . . . . $200.00 B

Cardboard, horizontal, "Home Refreshment," woman holding a bottle with flowers in the background, 1950s, 50"x29", G . . . . $200.00 C

Cardboard, horizontal, in original wooden frame, "Coke is Coca-Cola," 1949, 36"x20", EX . $675.00 C

Cardboard, horizontal, "Inviting you to refreshment," EX . . . . $650.00 B

Cardboard horizontal lettered, button right side, "Fountain Service," 1950, 30"x12" . . . . . . $450.00 B

Cardboard, horizontal poster "Coke is Coca-Cola" in original gold frame, 1949, EX . . . . $500.00 B

Cardboard, horizontal poster "Coke time" featuring three women at table, 1943, EX, ... $475.00 B

Cardboard, horizontal poster featuring artwork of woman at microphone with a bottle of Coke "Entertain your thirst," 1941, 36"x20", EX . . . . . $500.00 B

Cardboard, horizontal poster featuring bottle in ice "Have a Coke," 1944, 36"x20", NM . . . . . $300.00 B

Cardboard, horizontal poster featuring Coke crossing guard, "Let's watch for 'em," 1950s, 66"x32", NM . . . . $800.00 B

Cardboard, horizontal poster, featuring a lunch counter scene, "A great drink with food," Canadian, 1942, 36"x20", G . . . . $525.00 B

Cardboard, horizontal poster featuring people in a picnic scene with a cooler, 1954, 36"x24", EX . . . . $400.00 B

Cardboard, horizontal poster in original Kay Displays frame featuring two couples by fire, 1954, 36"x24", G . . . . $400.00 B

Cardboard, horizontal poster, "Play Refreshed" girl in cowboy hat, 1951, EX . . . . $325.00 B

Cardboard, horizontal poster with circus scene "Here's Something Good" in original repainted frame without applied detail, 1951, EX . . . . $350.00 B

Cardboard, horizontal, "Refreshing," woman in white dress at counter with a bottle, 1949, 56"x27", VG . . . . $375.00 B

Cardboard, horizontal, "Refreshing," woman in white dress at counter with a bottle, 1949, 56"x27", VG. . . . . $375.00 D

Cardboard, horizontal sign featuring girl with bottle and menu, 1960s, 66"x32", NM . . . . $650.00 B

Cardboard, horizontal, "Sparkling" bottle in Q of quality in yellow background, original frame, 1957, 36"x20", EX . . . . $450.00 D

Cardboard, horizontal, "That taste-good feeling," man drinking from bottle, "Drink Coca-Cola Delicious and Refreshing" button left, 1939, 56"x27", VG . . . . $1,000.00 B

Cardboard, horizontal, "The best of taste," "Drink..." button on right, woman in green suit, 1957, 36"x20", G. . . . . $300.00 D

Cardboard, horizontal, "12 oz. ice cold," head shot of woman with a bottle, promoting sale of king size products, 1959, 36"x20", EX . . . . $225.00 D

Cardboard, horizontal, "Welcome aboard," shore scene with "Drink..." button upper right, 1957, 36"x20", EX . . . . $275.00 D

Cardboard, horizontal, "Welcome," man in uniform and woman in yellow dress seated on couch with a bottle, 1943, 56"x27", EX. . . . . $450.00 C

Cardboard, Italian horizontal poster with a woman and a Coke bottle, 1940s, 36"x20", NM . . . . . . $425.00 B

Cardboard, "it's Twice Time, Twice the value," 1960s, 66"x32", NM. . . . . $800.00 D

Cardboard, large horizontal poster, cowgirl with bottle, 1951, G . . . . $375.00 C

Cardboard, large horizontal poster, double sided with a young couple on one side and a fishing girl on the other, 1950s, F. . . . . $230.00 C

Cardboard, large horizontal poster featuring hot dog roast, "Coca-Cola belongs," 1942, EX. . . . $400.00 C

Cardboard, large horizontal poster featuring sailor girl in original frame, 1940, F . . . . $400.00 C

Cardboard, large horizontal truck side poster featuring mod couple on a motor scooter, 1960s, 67"x32", NM. . . . . $210.00 D

Cardboard, large vertical poster featuring girl on diving board, 1939, G . . . . $450.00 C

Cardboard, large vertical poster featuring girl with horse, 1938, EX . . . . $1,000.00 B

Cardboard, large vertical poster featuring ice skater, 1940s, F. . . . . $80.00 D

Cardboard, "Let's watch for 'em," silhouette of running girl, 1950s, 66"x32", NM. . . . . $800.00 B

Cardboard light pulls with original strings advertising King Size Coca-Cola, two sided, 1950–60s, M, $35.00; in six pack, "puts you at your sparkling best," round, M. . . . . $30.00 C

Cardboard litho of circus performers, framed, 1936, 18"x27", EX . . . . $250.00 D

Cardboard, "New Family Size too!", Sprite Boy advertising Coca-Cola all on yellow background, 1955, 16"x 27", VG. . . . . $155.00 D

Cardboard, "New Family Size too!," Sprite Boy advertising Coca-Cola all on yellow background, 1955, 16"x27", NM. . . . . $175.00 C

Cardboard oval, string hung, denoting price, German, 1930s, EX . . . . $100.00 D

Cardboard oval, string hung, denoting price, German, 1930s, F. . . . . $65.00 D

Cardboard page, heavy, from a salesman's manual, rare and somewhat unusual, 12½"x18½", EX . . . . $450.00 D

Cardboard, panoramic view poster of couple in front of touring car, 1924, 32½"x18", EX . . . . . $800.00 D

Cardboard, "Party Pause," woman in clown suit, 1940s, 36"x20", G. . . . . $350.00 D

Cardboard, "Party Pause," woman in clown suit, 1940s, 36"x20", VG. . . . . $395.00 C

Cardboard, "Popcorn Delicious with Ice Cold Coca-Cola," open box of popcorn on its side with Coca-Cola bull's-eye at right, 1950s, 15"x12", EX . . . . $200.00 D

Cardboard poster, "At Ease... for refreshment," military nurse in uniform holding a bottle, in original wooden frame, 1942, NM. . . . . $1,000.00 B

Cardboard poster, Bathing Girl on rocks at beach, 1938, 30"x50", G . . . . $2,300.00 B

Cardboard, poster, "Big Refreshment," girl with bowling ball, 1960s, 66"x32", NM. . . . . $650.00 B

Cardboard poster, "Big Refreshment," girl with bowling ball, 1960s, 66"x32", EX . . . . $500.00 C

Cardboard poster, bird on bell and bottle, in aluminum frame, 1954, EX . . . . $250.00 D

Cardboard, poster, "Coke Time," cover girl with original frame, 1950s, 16"x27", NM. . . . . $750.00 B

Cardboard poster, "Coke Time," cover girl with original frame, 1950s, 16"x27", G . . . . $525.00 C

Cardboard poster, "Coke Time," woman in cowboy hat and western neck scarf with bottle in hand framed by brands, 1955, G . . . . $225.00 C

Cardboard poster, couple advertising six pack, framed and matted, 1940s, 16"x27", F . . . . $350.00 C

Cardboard poster, die cut with food scene and bottles, 1939, 31"x42", VG . . . . $350.00 D

Cardboard, poster, double sided, "Have A Coke" and Skater Girl on one side with "Refresh Yourself" with horses and riders, 1955, 16"x27", VG . . . . $200.00 D

Cardboard poster, double sided, "Have A Coke" and Skater Girl on one side with "Refresh Yourself" with horses and riders, 1955, 16"x27", EX . . . . $225.00 D

Cardboard poster, double sided, one side "the Best of Taste," the other side "Enjoy the Quality Taste," 1956, 56"x27", VG . . . . $275.00 C

Cardboard poster, easel back, "Refresh Yourself," girl on chair with glass, 1926, 16"x29½", EX . . . . . $1,500.00 B

Cardboard poster, "Easy To Take Home," 1941, EX . . . . $350.00 B

Cardboard, poster, "Easy To Take Home," 1941, NM . . . . $400.00 C

Cardboard poster, Elaine with glass, same artwork that was used on the calendar of this year, 1915, EX . . . . $3,000.00 C

Cardboard, poster featuring ballerinas, "entertain your thirst," 1942, 16"x27", F . . . . $125.00 C

Cardboard, poster featuring cartoon spaceman, 1960s, NM . . . . $160.00 C

Cardboard, poster featuring cheerleader "Refresh yourself," 1944, 16"x27", NM . . . . $1,150.00 C

Cardboard, poster featuring elves with a carton on wagon, "Take enough Home," 1953, 16"x27", G . . . . $170.00 C

Cardboard, poster featuring girl at refrigerator, 1940, 16"x27", EX . . . . $700.00 C

Cardboard, poster featuring Hostess Girl, artwork by Hayden, 1935, 29"x50", NM, $2,100.00 C

Cardboard poster, 5¢, framed under glass, 1930, 15"x12", EX . . . . $225.00 D

Cardboard, poster, girl against a rock wall, resting from bicycle riding, from Niagara Litho, 1939, VG . $375.00 C

Cardboard poster, girl with a menu and a bottle, 1960s, 66"x32", NM . . . . $650.00 B

Cardboard poster, "Have A Coke," a bottle against an iceberg, 1944, 36"x20", EX . . . . $325.00 D

Cardboard, poster, "Have A Coke," a bottle against an iceberg, 1944, 36"x20", G . . . . $275.00 C

Cardboard poster, horizontal, "All set at our house," with boy holding cardboard six pack carrier, 1943, P . . . . $100.00 C

Cardboard poster, horizontal, "Be Really Refreshed," 1950s, EX . . . . $90.00 C

Cardboard poster, horizontal, "Coca-Cola belongs," featuring couple with a picnic basket and a bucket of iced Coca-Cola, 1942, EX . . . . $750.00 B

Cardboard poster, horizontal, "Coke belongs," 1940s, 36"x20", EX . . . . $150.00 C

Cardboard poster, horizontal, "Coke for me, too," couple with bottles and a hot dog, 1946, 36"x20", EX . . . . $185.00 B

Cardboard poster, horizontal, "Coke knows no season," snow scene with a bottle in foreground and a couple of skiers in the background, framed, 1946, 62"x33", G. . . . . $200.00 C

Cardboard, poster, horizontal, "Face your job refreshed," woman wearing visor beside a drill press, 59"x30", F. . . . . $350.00 D

Cardboard poster, horizontal, "Got enough Coke on ice?," three girls on sofa, one with phone receiver, framed, Canadian, 1945, VG. . . . . $300.00 C

Cardboard, poster, horizontal, "Got enough Coke on ice?" three girls on sofa, one with phone receiver, framed, Canadian, 1945, G . . . . $250.00 C

Cardboard poster, horizontal, "Have a Coke," 1944, 36"x20", EX . . . . $175.00 C

Cardboard poster, horizontal, "Have a Coke," a bottle in snow, 1945, 36"x20", G. . . . . $175.00 C

Cardboard poster, horizontal, "Have a Coke," cheerleader and a bottle, 1946, EX . . . . $375.00 D

Cardboard poster, horizontal, "Hello – Coke," couple with bottles, 1944, 36"x20", EX . . . . $350.00 D

Cardboard poster, horizontal, "Hello Refreshment," woman in swimsuit coming out of swimming pool, 1940s, 36"x20", EX. . . . . $1,700.00 B

Cardboard poster, horizontal, "Here's to our G.I. Joes," 1944, VG. . . . . $750.00 B

Cardboard poster, horizontal, "He's Coming Home Tomorrow," woman in head scarf and coat with a picnic basket and a bottle, 1944, NM . . . . $1,250.00 C

Cardboard, poster, horizontal, "Hospitality Coca-Cola," girl lighting a candle with a bottle in foreground, 1950, 59"x30", VG. . . . .$700.00 D

Cardboard poster, horizontal, "Hospitality in your hands," woman serving four bottles from tray, 1948, 36"x20", EX. . . . .$250.00 B

Cardboard, poster, horizontal, "Hospitality in your hands," woman serving four bottles from tray, 1948, 36"x20", F. . . . .$100.00 C

Cardboard poster, horizontal, "I'll bring the Coke," girl on phone at the foot of stairs, 1946, 36"x20", EX . $300.00 D

Cardboard poster, horizontal, Italian, woman with a bottle, 1940s, 36"x20", EX . . . .$425.00 C

Cardboard, poster, horizontal, "Lunch Refreshed," 1943, G. . . . .$750.00 C

Cardboard, poster, horizontal, majorette, "Refresh," 1952, 36"x20", F . . . .$125.00 C

Cardboard poster, horizontal, majorette, "Refresh," 1952, 36"x20", VG . . . .$475.00 C

Cardboard poster, horizontal, "Now! for Coke," trapeze artist reaching for a bottle, framed, 1959, 27"x21", VG . . . .$300.00 C

Cardboard, poster, horizontal, "Now! for Coke," trapeze artist reaching for bottle, framed, 1959, 27"x21", P. . . . .$75.00 C

Cardboard, poster, horizontal, "Play refreshed," woman in cap with fishing rig and a bottle, 1950s, 36"x20", G. . . . .$225.00 C

Cardboard poster, horizontal, "Refreshing," pretty girl holding sunglasses and a bottle, in a reproduction frame, 1948, EX. . . . .$675.00 B

Cardboard, poster, horizontal, "The rest-pause that refreshes," three women in uniform, 1943, 36"x20", G . . . .$225.00 D

Cardboard poster, horizontal, "Shop refreshed," 1948, EX. . . . .$1,400.00 B

Cardboard poster, horizontal, "The answer to thirst," 1945, 36"x20", G. . . . .$100.00 C

Cardboard, poster, horizontal, "The drink they all expect," couple getting ready to entertain with finger sandwiches and iced bottles, 1942, G . . . . .$325.00 C

Cardboard, poster, horizontal, "The pause that refreshes," girl on a chaise holding a bottle, 1942, 36"x20", F. . . . .$95.00 C

Cardboard poster, horizontal, "The pause that refreshes," girl on a chaise holding a bottle, 1942, 36"x20", VG . . . .$300.00 D

Cardboard poster, horizontal, "Thirst knows no season," woman drinking from a bottle in front of skis, framed, 1940, 56"x27", G . . . .$300.00 C

Cardboard, poster, horizontal, "What I want is a Coke," girl on sandy beach in swim suit reaching for bottle, in original wooden frame, hard to find, 1952, F . . . . .$750.00 C

Cardboard poster, horizontal, "Why grow thirsty," 1945, 36"x20", VG . . . .$150.00 D

Cardboard, poster, horizontal, "Why grow thirsty," 1945, 36"x20", G. . . . .$100.00 C

Cardboard poster, horizontal, with Coke cap, 66"x32", EX. . . . .$800.00 B

Cardboard poster, horizontal, "Zing together with Coke," party scene and cooler on table, 1962, 37"x21", G. . . . .$200.00 D

Cardboard, poster, horizontal, "Zing together with Coke," party scene, cooler on table, 1962, 37"x21", P. . $100.00 C

Cardboard poster, "It's a Family Affair," family holding Coca-Cola, 1941, 36"x20", EX . . . .$675.00 C

Cardboard poster, "It's Twice the Time, Twice the Value," 1960, 66"x32", NM. . . . .$800.00 D

Cardboard poster, Jeff Gordon Coca-Cola 600, 23"x33", M . . . .$10.00 D

Cardboard poster, "Just a Drink But What a Drink," girl in bathing attire on lifeguard stand, 1929, 17"x29¾", F . . . .$300.00 C

Cardboard poster, large horizontal, "a Coke belongs," young boy and girl with a bottle, in original Coke frame, 1944, EX . . . .$950.00 C

Cardboard poster, large horizontal, "Accepted Home Refreshment," couple in front of warm fireplace, 1942, G. . . . . $725.00 D

Cardboard poster, large horizontal, couple at open refrigerator with bottles, "Welcome Home," 1944, EX. . . . . $450.00 D

Cardboard poster, large horizontal, girl on beach in original Coke frame, 1953, EX. . . . . . . $1,250.00 D

Cardboard poster, large horizontal, "Good Pause Drink Coca-Cola in Bottles," 1954, 36"x20", EX . . . $650.00 C

Cardboard poster, large horizontal, "The pause that refreshes at home," framed, 1940s, 56"x27", G. . . . . $250.00 C

Cardboard poster, large vertical, a soldier and a girl with bicycles and bottles, in original wooden frame, 1943, G. . . . . $525.00 C

Cardboard poster, large vertical, couple and man in navy uniform, 1943, G. . . . . $775.00 C

Cardboard, poster of woman with straw hat in water , 1960s, 36"x20", F . . . . $75.00 C

Cardboard poster, "On The Refreshing Side," 1941, 30"x50", VG . . . . $375.00 D

Cardboard, poster, one part of a series, "Through the years" with Victorian era advertising, 1939, 16"x27", NM . . . . $950.00 C

Cardboard poster, part of "Through the Years," Victorian advertising series, 1939, 16"x27", G. . . . . $750.00 D

Cardboard poster, "Play Refreshed," tennis girl sitting on drink box holding a bottle, in reproduction frame, 1949, 16"x27", G. . . . . $475.00 D

Cardboard poster, Reece Tatum of the Harlem Globetrotters holding a basketball with a bottle on top of the ball, 1952, 16"x27", EX. . . . . $700.00 C

Cardboard poster, "Refreshing," girl in water, 1960, 36"x20", EX . . . . $95.00 C

Cardboard poster, seated Chinese girl, 1936, 14½"x22", NM. $1,300.00 D

Cardboard poster, "Serve Coke At Home," 1949, EX. . . . . $300.00 C

Cardboard poster, "So Delicious," snow ski scene, 1954, 36"x20", VG . . . . $600.00 C

Cardboard poster, "So Refreshing," boy and girl by pool, 1946, 30"x50", EX . . . . $675.00 D

Cardboard poster, Sprite Boy of Woolworth, PA, 11"x14", EX . . . . $75.00 D

Cardboard poster, "The Best of Taste," girl being offered a bottle, 1956, EX . . . . $225.00 C

Cardboard, poster "Things go better with Coke" in original frame, 1960s, 16"x27", F . . . . . . $250.00 D

Cardboard poster, "Tingling Refreshment," girl with a glass waving, 1931, 21"x38", VG. . . . . . . $350.00 D

Cardboard poster, vertical, "And Coke Too," 1946, 16"x27", EX . . . . $325.00 D

Cardboard poster, vertical, "Coke headquarters," 1947, EX. . . . . $350.00 D

Cardboard poster, vertical, "Coke Time," in original wooden frame, 1943, G. . . . . $600.00 C

Cardboard poster, vertical, couple, woman in swim suit with large brim hat, 1934, 29"x50", EX . . . . $2,700.00 C

Cardboard poster, vertical, "Extra-Bright Refreshment," couple at party holding bottles, 33"x53", P. . . . $75.00 D

Cardboard, poster, vertical, "Face the sun refreshed," pretty girl in white dress shielding her eyes from the sun with one hand while holding a bottle with the other, 1941, 30"x53½", G . . . . $500.00 C

Cardboard poster, vertical, "For People on the Go," 1944, 16"x27", G. . . . . $275.00 D

Cardboard, poster, vertical, "For the party," soldier and woman on bicycle for two, 29"x50½", F . . . . . $175.00 C

Cardboard poster, vertical, French Canadian, 1947, 16"x27", VG . . . . $250.00 D

Cardboard poster, vertical, "Happy Ending to Thirst," 1940s, 16"x27", VG. . . . . $275.00 D

Cardboard, poster, vertical, "Happy Ending to Thirst," 1940s, 16"x27", G . . . . $250.00 D

Cardboard poster, vertical, "Have a Coke, Coca-Cola," couple at masquerade ball, framed under glass, rare item, F . . . . $550.00 C

Cardboard, poster, vertical, "Have a Coke, Coca-Cola," couple at masquerade ball, framed under glass, rare item, EX. . . . . $750.00 C

Cardboard poster, vertical, "Home Refreshment," framed under glass, EX. . . . . $1,800.00 C

Cardboard poster, vertical, "Just Like Old Times," 1945, 16"x27", EX. . . . . $375.00 C

Cardboard poster, vertical, "Let's have a Coke," cooler and majorette, 1946, 16"x27", EX. . . . . $300.00 D

Cardboard poster, vertical, man and woman advertising bottle sales, 1930–40s, 18"x36", VG . . $625.00 C

Cardboard poster, vertical, man in uniform and girl walking, each with a bottle, 1944, NM. . $1,250.00 D

Cardboard poster, vertical, mother and daughter at table opening bottle, French Canadian, 1946, 16"x27" . . . . $250.00 C

Cardboard poster, vertical, "Play Refreshed," 1949, EX. . . . . $750.00 D

Cardboard, poster, vertical, "Refreshment," pretty girl in fancy dress at a pool setting with bottles on table, 1949, 33½"x54", EX . . . . $525.00 D

Cardboard poster, vertical, "Right off the ice," girl at ice skating rink, 1946, 16"x27", G . . . . . . $210.00 D

Cardboard poster, vertical, same scene that appears on the 1936 serving tray, the Hostess, framed and under glass, 1935, Hayden, G . . . . $700.00 C

Cardboard, poster, vertical, "Start Refreshed," couple at roller skating rink, 1943, 16"x27", VG . . . . $300.00 C

Cardboard poster, vertical, "Take some home today," in original wooden frame, 1950s, 16"x27", VG . . . . $600.00 B

Cardboard poster, vertical, "Talk about refreshing," girl in rain with umbrella in front of cooler holding a bottle, 1942, 16"x27", NM . . . . $700.00 D

Cardboard poster, vertical, "The drink they all expect," similar to horizontal poster of this year but showing full length artwork of couple preparing for entertaining, 1942, P . . . . $75.00 C

Cardboard, poster, vertical, "Thirst knows no season," couple building a snowman, graphics are great, 1942, 30"x50", G . . . . $350.00 D

Cardboard poster, vertical, two sided, bottle on one side and target and bottle on the other side, French Canadian, 1951, EX . . . . $200.00 D

Cardboard, poster, vertical, two sided, bottle on one side and target and bottle on the other side, French Canadian, 1951, G. . . . . $100.00 C

Cardboard poster, vertical, with large bottle in foreground and places and events in background, "58 Million a Day," 1957, 17½"x28½", P . . . . $50.00 D

Cardboard poster, "Welcome Aboard," nautical theme, 1958, 36"x20", NM . . . . $375.00 C

Cardboard, poster, "Wherever thirst goes," great graphics of girl in row boat with a bucket of iced Coca-Cola, 1942, G . . . . $475.00 C

Cardboard poster, "Wherever you go," travel scenes in background, 1950s, G . . . . $150.00 D

Cardboard, poster, woman sitting wearing a broad brimmed hat with flowers, holding a Coca-Cola 5¢ bamboo fan and a glass, framed, 1912, F. . . . . $2,000.00 C

Cardboard, poster, "Yes," girl on beach with bottle, 1946, 56"x27", G. . . . . $225.00 C

Cardboard rack display, vertical, "Take more than one," 1960s, 16"x27", EX . . . . $110.00 C

Cardboard, red-haired woman in yellow scarf with cup of Coca-Cola, in original aluminum frame, 1951, 13"x11", NM. . . . . $650.00 D

Cardboard, "Serve Yourself," hand in cup, in original aluminum frame, 1951, 13"x11", NM . . . . $350.00 C

Cardboard, sign featuring girl with bowling ball, 1960s, 66"x32", NM . . . . $650.00 D

Cardboard six-pack bottle display with motorized hand in bottle that moves up and down, "Take Enough Home," 1950s, EX . . . . $395.00 D

Cardboard, small vertical, "So refreshing" with woman in white spotlight, 1941, EX . . . . $750.00 C

Cardboard, sports favorite, hanging, complete set consists of 10 signs; individual signs go in the $85.00 – $110.00 range, 1947, G . . . . $1,200.00 C

Cardboard, St. Louis Fair, woman sitting at table with a flare glass that has a syrup line, 1909, F . . . $4,000.00 C

Cardboard, stand up, Jeff Gordon & Coke, 1995, NM. . . . . $110.00 D

Cardboard store display, inside, featuring girl in roses, 1937, 52"x34", Hayden Hayden, EX . . . $5,000.00 C

Cardboard, "Things go better with Coke" sign with gold frame, 1950s – 60s, 24"x20", F . . . . . $160.00 D

Cardboard, 3-D, "Boy oh Boy," pictures boy in front of cooler with a bottle in hand, 1937, 36"x34", EX . . . . $1,500.00 C

Cardboard, 3-D cut-out sign featuring a sandwich and a glass, 1958, 17"x20", EX. . . . . $95.00 D*

Cardboard, 3-D, "On Your Break," self-framing, 1950s, F. . . . . $85.00 D

Cardboard, 3-D, "On Your Break," self-framing, 1950s, VG. . . . . $115.00 C

Cardboard, trolley car sign, "Delicious and Refreshing Drink Coca-Cola At Fountains Everywhere 5¢", 1905, 20½"x10¾", F. $1,850.00 B

Cardboard trolley car sign featuring a woman sitting off the side of a hammock holding a glass, 1912, EX . $3,400.00 C

Cardboard, trolley car sign featuring a woman sitting off the side of hammock holding glass, 1912, F . . . . . $2,100.00 C

Cardboard trolley car sign, "Tired? Coca-Cola Relieves Fatigue," young man at dispensers, 1907, VG. . . . . $1,800.00 C

Cardboard, trolley sign, double long, "Yes," 1946, 28"x11", NM. . . . . $750.00 C

Cardboard, trolley sign, "Drink Coca-Cola Delicious and Refreshing," 21"x11", P . . . . $675.00 C

Cardboard, truck poster, hard to find, girl in water, 1960s, 67"x32", NM . . . . $120.00 C

Cardboard, truck poster, "Refreshing new feeling," 1960s, 67"x32", EX. . . . . $110.00 C

Cardboard, truck poster, "Yield to the Children," hard to find, NM. . . . . $350.00 C

Cardboard, vertical, "Be Really Refreshed...Enjoy Coke!," woman at beach picnic with a bottle, 1959, 16"x27", EX . . . . $195.00 D

Cardboard, vertical, "Be Really Refreshed," girl in party dress, "Drink..." button in lower left, 1960s, 16"x27", EX . . . . $195.00 D

Cardboard, vertical, "Coke Time," bottle in hand with woman's face, "Drink..." button in lower center, 1954, 16"x27", EX . . . . $300.00 D

Cardboard, vertical, "Come and get it," farm bell and a bottle, "Drink..." button in lower right, in original wooden frame, 1954, 16"x27", EX. . . . . . . $350.00 C

Cardboard, vertical, "Come and get it," western dinner gong behind a bottle, "Drink..." button in lower right, 1952, 16"x27", EX. . . . . $275.00 C

Cardboard, vertical double sided sign, "The best of taste" on one side "Enjoy the quality taste" on the other, 1956, 56"x27", G . . . . $220.00 D

Cardboard, vertical, "For Holiday Entertaining," six bottle carton 36¢, featuring Christmas decor, Canadian, 1950, 12½"x18½", G. . . . . $85.00 D

Cardboard, vertical, "For Holiday Entertaining," six bottle carton 36¢, featuring Christmas decor, Canadian, 1950, 12½"x18½", EX. . . . . $95.00 C

Cardboard, vertical, "Now Coke in handy Plastic Cartons," eight pack, easel back, 1960s, 16"x27", EX . . . . . $65.00 D

Cardboard, vertical poster featuring bathing beauty, great graphics, 1934, 29"x50", EX . . . . . $2,700.00 B

Cardboard, vertical poster featuring fishing girl, 1953, 16"x27", EX . . . . $600.00 C

Cardboard, vertical poster featuring girl at beach, framed under glass, 1930s, G . . . . $1,150.00 C

Cardboard, vertical poster featuring girl on sidewalk, "So easy to carry home," 1942, 16"x27", EX. . . . . $800.00 C

Cardboard, vertical poster featuring girl standing beside a cooler with an umbrella, 1942, EX . . . . $475.00 D

Cardboard, vertical poster featuring girl with a tennis racquet, 1945, EX . . . . $525.00 D

Cardboard, vertical poster featuring girl with umbrella in front of cooler, "Talk about refreshing," 1942, 16"x27", G. . . . . $475.00 C

Cardboard, vertical poster featuring woman in yellow dress, walking in rain with an umbrella, 1942, G. . . . . $425.00 C

Cardboard, vertical poster with a couple at "Coke Time" and a six-pack in spotlight at bottom, 1943, EX. . . . . $900.00 D

Cardboard, vertical poster with girl on ping pong table, framed under glass, Canadian, 14"x28", VG . . . . $600.00 D

Cardboard, vertical poster, with girl on ping pong table, framed under glass, Canadian, 14"x28", EX . . $625.00 C

Cardboard, vertical, "So Refreshing," Autumn Girl in art work, 1940, 16"x27", VG. . . . . $425.00 C

Cardboard, vertical, "So Refreshing," Autumn Girl in artwork, 1940, 16"x27", G. . . . . $450.00 D

Cardboard, vertical, "The pause that refreshes," couple with bottles, "Drink..." button over woman's head, in original wooden frame, 1959, 16"x27", G . . . . $375.00 D

Cardboard, "Welcome friend," red and white lettering on simulated oak background, 1957, 14"x12", G. . . . . $175.00 C

Cardboard, window display, cameo fold out, 1913, F . . . . $3,000.00 D

Cardboard, window display, die cut, depicting a circus, large center piece is 4' x 3', a separate girl and ring master are approx. 30" tall, three scenes, clown at big top, vendors and tents, ringmaster and girl, 1932, G . . . . $3,500.00 D

Cardboard window display, die cut, depicting a circus, large center piece is 4'x3', a separate girl and ring master is approx. 30" tall, three scenes, clown at big top, vendors and tents, ringmaster and girl, 1932, EX . . . . $5,000.00 D

Cardboard, window display, trifold, Wallace Beery and Jackie Cooper sitting in director's chairs with a bottle in between them, 1934, 43"x31½", G . . . . $1,800.00 D

Cardboard window display, tri-fold, Wallace Berry and Jackie Cooper sitting in director's chairs with a bottle in between them, 1934, 43"x31½", VG. . . . . $2,750.00 B

Celluloid bottle, "Drink Coca-Cola Delicious and Refreshing," 1900, 6"x13¼", F . . . . $1,800.00 C

Celluloid, hand in bottle, foreign, 6½"x16", VG . . . . $250.00 C

Celluloid over tin, "Refresh Yourself Drink Coca-Cola," probably manufactured in the U.S.A. for use in Canada, yellow & white on red with green frame, 1930s, 11¾"x6", EX . . . . $1,800.00 C

Celluloid, round, "Coca-Cola," white lettering on top of a bottle in center with red background, 1950s, 9" dia., EX . . . . $325.00 C

Celluloid, round, hanging on easel back, "Delicious Coca-Cola Refreshing," white and black lettering on red background, 1940, EX. . . . . $180.00 D

Celluloid sign, "Delicious and Refreshing," red, 1940s, 9" dia., G. . . . . $225.00 D

Coca-Cola fashion girl, one of four fashion girls, framed and under glass, 1932, F. . . . . $4,000.00 C

Decal, bottle in hand, EX $30.00

Decal, "Drink Coca-Cola Ice Cold," 1960, EX . . . . $40.00 D

Decal, "Drink Coca-Cola Ice Cold," 1960, G . . $25.00 D

Decal, "Drink Coca-Cola In Bottles," mounted on glass, 1950s, 15"x9", NM . . . . $85.00 C

Decal, "Drink Coca-Cola in Bottles," on glass, framed, 1950s, 15"x18", EX . . . . $85.00 C

Decal, "Drink Coca-Cola In Bottles," red background with white and yellow lettering, 1950s, 16"x8", EX . . . . $80.00 C

Decal, "Drink" emblem on triangle, "Ice and Cold" by bottle, 1934, 15"x18", NM . . . . $150.00 D

Decal, "Drink," fishtail logo, foil, NM . . . . $20.00 D

Decal, "Enjoy That Refreshing New Feeling," fishtail logo, M . . . . $35.00 D

Decal, fishtail logo with sprig of leaves, EX . . $35.00 C

Decal for window, featuring bottle on blue background with original envelope, blue, 1940s, 8"x13½", EX. . . . . $25.00 D

Decal, Sprite Boy looking around a large bottle, 13"x13", EX . . . . $300.00 C

Decal, "Thank You Come Again," on bow tie emblem, foil, 1950s, NM. . . . . $25.00 D

Decal, "Things Go Better With Coke," 1960, NM. . . . . $30.00 D

Decal, white background, has been sanded down and reworked, 1950s, 24", NM. . . . . $275.00 B

Die cut bottle sign, 1953, 3' tall, EX . . . . . $275.00 D

Die cut original artwork of boy with Coke glass, framed under glass, 1940s, 8" x14", EX . $1,375.00 C

Dispenser sign featuring stainless band around border, red on white, 1950s, 27"x28", EX . . . . $900.00 B

"Drink Coca-Cola, Cures Headache... Relieves Exhaustion at Soda Fountains 5¢," framed under glass, 1890 – 1900s, VG. . . . . $1,000.00 C

Festoon, autumn leaves, 1922, NM . . . . $1,800.00 C

Festoon, leaf pattern with girl in center, five pieces with original envelope, 1927, NM . . . . . $4,500.00 C

Festoon, locket, five pieces with original envelope, 1939, NM. . . . . $1,800.00 C

Festoon, petunia, five pieces with original envelope, 1939, NM. . . . . $1,800.00 C

Festoon, snow bough and icicle, five pieces, in original envelope, 1937, NM . . . . $4,500.00 B

Festoon, swan, five pieces with original envelope, 1938, EX . . . . $1,800.00 C

Festoon, theme of parasols, 1918, NM . . $1,800.00 C

Festoon, three pieces of a five piece back bar display featuring girls' heads, 1951, F . . . . $725.00 C

Festoon, wild rose, five pieces with original envelope, 1938, VG . . . . $1,250.00 C

Festoon, wood flower, three pieces with original envelope, 1934, NM . . . . $1,500.00 C

Fountain service sign, two sided, features early dispenser, red on yellow background, 1941, 25"x26", NM. . . . . $2,200.00 B

Glass and metal frame menu board with fishtail logo at top center, 1960s, 37"x20", G . . . . $450.00 D

Glass and metal light-up, "work safely, work refreshed," 1950s, 16"x16", G . . . . $450.00 C

Glass, decal mounted on glass and framed, Sprite Boy, advertising bottles sales, note bottle cap hat as opposed to fountain hat, 13"x13", NM . . . . $375.00 D

Glass framed sign featuring a bell shaped glass with diminishing logo at top, hard-to-find piece, 1930s, 6"x9½", M . . . . $2,000.00 C

Glass front light-up, "Have a Coke" with cup at right, 1950s, 17"x10", EX. . . . . $1,425.00 C

Glass front light-up, metal frame, "Lunch With Us," 1950s, 18"x8", EX . . . . $750.00 C

Glass front light-up, "Please Pay When Served," located on top of courtesy panel, 1950s, 18"x8", G. . . . . $575.00 D

Glass front light-up, "Please Pay When Served," located on top of courtesy panel, 1950s, 18"x8", EX . . $625.00 C

Glass light-up, hand and bottle, probably an independent sign made by a bottler, unusual, 14"x10½", EX . . . . $1,200.00 D

Glass light-up, hanging, "Have A Coca-Cola," 1948, 20"x12", EX . . . . $525.00 D

Glass light-up, "Have A Coke, Refresh Yourself" with red arrow, 1950s, 10"x17", NM . . . . . . $1,275.00 C

Glass light-up, "Have A Coke, Refresh Yourself" with red arrow, 1950s, 10"x17", EX . . . . $1,200.00 C

Glass light-up, NOS, Coca-Cola Beverage Department, fishtail, 1960s, 50"x14", M. . . . . $350.00 C

Glass light-up, 20 oz. bottle, 1994, EX . . . $150.00 C

Glass, round mirror, "Drink Carbonated Coca-Cola 5¢ in Bottles," EX . . . . $600.00 C

Kay Displays sign "Quick Service" with die cut metal filigree, 1930s, 36"x10", EX . . . . $2,400.00 C

Light-up "Beverage Department" with fishtail logo, 1960s, 50"x14", EX . . . . $425.00 C

Light-up "Beverage Department" with fishtail logo, 1960s, 50"x14", G. . . . . $300.00 D

Light-up, cash register top, "Drink Coca-Cola, Lunch With Us," 1940–50s, 11"x6", NM. . . . . . . $350.00 D

Light-up counter sign featuring 20 oz. bottle, NOS in original box, 1990s, 12"x13", EX. . . . . . . $190.00 C

Light-up counter sign with dispenser, 1959, 12"w x 27"t x 15"d, G . . . . $950.00 B

Light-up counter top, motion wheel behind "Pause" at left of "Drink Coca-Cola" with "Please Pay Cashier" at bottom, 1950s, M . . . . $925.00 C

Light-up counter top sign, "Please Pay When Served," red and white, 1948, 20" x 12", EX. . . . . $2,800.00 B

Light-up, lantern on stand with four panels, "Have a Coke Here" on two panels and fishtail "Drink Coca-Cola" on other panels, 1960s, NM . . . . . . $125.00 C

Light-up, plastic and glass, "Pause and Refresh," "Quality carries on" on right side with bottle in hand, same art work as appears on fans of this vintage, 1940s, 19"x15½", G . . . . $560.00 C

Light-up, plastic and metal display, "Always a Party, Always Coca-Cola," for Superbowl XXVII, NM . . . . . . $45.00 C

Light-up, plastic and metal display, "Always a Party, Always Coca-Cola," for Superbowl XXVII, EX. . . . . $40.00 D

Light-up, plastic, double sided, hanging, 1950s, 16" dia, EX . . . . $475.00 D

Light-up, plastic with metal base, "Shop Refreshed," "Drink Coca-Cola," 1950s, VG . . . . $375.00 D

Light-up, plastic with metal base, "Shop Refreshed," "Drink Coca-Cola," 1950s, EX. . . . . $450.00 D

Light-up, red two-sided globe hanger, 1950–60, 16" dia., EX. . . . . $400.00 D

Masonite, "Delicious & Refreshing," girl with bottle, 1940s, F. . . . . $50.00 D

Masonite, "Delicious & Refreshing," girl with bottle, 1940s, EX . . . . $110.00 D

Masonite, diamond-shaped "Drink Coca-Cola" sign with bottle in spot light at bottom, yellow and white on red background, 1946, 42" sq., EX . . . $900.00 D

Masonite, "Drink," featuring bottle, 1940s, 54"x19", EX. . . . . $500.00 C

Masonite, horizontal, "Drink Coca-Cola Fountain Service," fountain heads on outside of lettering, 1930 – 40s, 27"x14", NM . . . . $1,800.00 D

Masonite, Kay Displays sign featuring the silhouette girl, white on red, 1939, 17" dia., F. . . . . . $175.00 D

Masonite, oval, "Drink Coca-Cola," white lettering on red, 1940, 13"x5½", EX. . . . . $250.00 C

Masonite, Sprite Boy in arrow through cooler, 1940s, G. . . . . $700.00 D

Masonite with metal arrow, 1940s, 17", EX . . . . $800.00 D

Metal and glass light-up, motion, red "Drink Coca-Cola" button in center with motion appearance between button and gold case, 1960s, 11¼" dia, VG . . . . $450.00 C

Metal, bag holder, painted, "For Home Refreshment Coca-Cola," Sprite Boy, 36"x17", NM . . . $675.00 C

Metal, building sign, "Drink Coca-Cola," 1950–60s, 48" dia, EX . . . . $225.00 D

Metal button, 12", with wings, Sprite Boy on ends and lettering of Sundaes and Malts in between, 1950s, 12"x78", VG . . . . $1,100.00 C

Metal, button, 12", with wings, Sprite Boy on ends and lettering of Sundaes and Malts in between, 1950s, 12"x78", F . . . . $775.00 D

Metal, Canadian cartoon rack, features sign at top advertising "Take home a carton 30¢," 1930s, 5' tall, EX . . . . $425.00 D

Metal, die cut radiator script sign "Drink Coca-Cola In Bottles," 1920s, 17", NM . . . . $400.00 D

Metal, double sided, "In any weather Drink Coca-Cola," thermometer on one side fits on outside of screen door, while the "Thanks, Call Again" fits on the inside of the door, rare, 1930s, NM . . . . $3,500.00 D

Metal double sided sidewalk sign, 30"x60", EX . . . . $775.00 D

Metal, double sided sidewalk sign featuring an early dispenser, difficult to find, 1940s, 25' x 26", NM . . . . $2,500.00 B

Metal, "Drink Coca-Cola, Delicious and Refreshing," bottle on left side, "The Icy-O Company Inc., Charlotte, N.C," F . . . . $450.00 D

Metal, "Drink Coca-Cola Ice Cold," original four type bracket, 1930s, NM . . . . $500.00 D

Metal, "Drink Coca-Cola in Bottles," original bent wire frame and stand, white lettering on red background wire is painted white, 1950s, EX . . $250.00 C

Metal, fishtail, painted "Drink Coca-Cola," white lettering on red, 1960s, 14"x8", VG . . . . $125.00 D

Metal fountain service sign, 1936, 27"x14", EX . . . . $425.00 C

Metal, French Canadian carton rack, advertising 25¢ cartons, sign has French on one side and English on the reverse side, 1930s, 5' tall, EX . . . . . . $475.00 D

Metal, French Canadian sidewalk sign, "Buvez Coca-Cola," 1949, 58"x28", EX . . . . $375.00 D

Metal light-up sign, "Drink Coca-Cola" on disc, wall basket, 1950s, EX . . . . $300.00 C

Metal pilaster, bottle under a 16" "Drink Coca-Cola" button, 1950, VG . . . . $575.00 D

Metal pilaster, six-pack being sold with a 16" "Sign of good taste" button on top, 1947, NM . . . . $725.00 D

Metal policeman, unusual paint on shield that reads "Stop Emergency Vehicles Only," 1957, 5" tall, EX . . . . $1,500.00 D

Metal rack, round, "Take home a Carton," 1930 – 40s, EX . . . . $225.00 D

Metal sidewalk, "Coca-Cola Ice Cold Sold Here," for curb service, 1931, 20"x28", VG . . . . $225.00 C

Metal sidewalk fishtail, "Ice Cold," 1960s, NM . . . . $195.00 D

Metal sidewalk with case of drinks, 1957, EX . $225.00 D

Mobile, red disc, double sided, 1950s, 19", EX . $600.00 D

Neon, "Coca-Cola in bottles," great colors, metal base, 1950s, VG . . . . $1,800.00 D

Neon, "Coke with Ice," three colors, 1980s, G . . . $250.00.

Neon, "Coke with Ice," three colors, 1980s, EX . . . . $375.00 C

Neon, "Coca-Cola," dynamic wave logo, M . . $650.00 D

Neon, "Coca-Cola In Bottles," on original base, rare, 1930–1940, EX . . . . $4,500.00 C

Neon counter top, "Drink Coca-Cola in Bottles" on a wrinkle paint base with rubber feet on bottom, 1939, 17"x13½", VG . . . . $1,850.00 C

Neon disc, "Drink...Sign of Good Taste," 1950s, 16" dia., EX . . . . $525.00 D

Neon disc, "Drink...Sign of Good Taste," 1950s, 16" dia., G . . . . $375.00 D

Neon, "Enjoy Coca-Cola," two-color red and white, NOS, M . . . . $375.00 D

Neon, girl drinking from a can, pink, red, and yellow, in original box, new, 20"x20", EX . . . . . . $300.00 D

Neon, "The Official Soft Drink of Summer," 1989, EX . . . . $1,000.00 D

Neon, "The Official Soft Drink of Summer," 1989, G . . . . $700.00 B

Neon script sign on two glass rods with the transformer hooked up in a separate location, red, 1930s, 27"x12", EX . . . . $1,200.00 B

Neon sign featuring three colors of girl drinking from can, yellow, red & pink, recent, 20"x20", NM . . . . $225.00 D

Neon window unit, "Drink Coca-Cola," two colors, 1940s, 28"x18", EX . . . . $600.00 D

Oil cloth, Lillian Nordica, "Coca-Cola at Soda Fountain 5¢," "Delicious Refreshing," rare, 1904, 25"x47", G . . . . $7,500.00 B

Oil painting by Hayden Hayden, original, rosy cheeked woman holding a glass, framed, 1940s, 24"x28", EX . . . . $4,500.00 C

Oil painting, girl with mittens holding a glass, 1940, 24"x28", Hayden, NM . . . . $4,500.00 C

Original artwork depicting actors taking a break from work on a western movie, signed by Verne Tossey, 1950s, 22"x14", NM . . . . $1,000.00 B

Oval, string hung, "Drink Coca-Cola Evegerkuhlt," German, 1930s, 12½"x8¼", G . . . . $50.00 D

Paper advertising, "See adventures of Kit Carson," 1953, 24"x16", G . . . . $75.00 C

Paper advertising, "See adventures of Kit Carson," 1953, 24"x16", EX . . . . $95.00 D

Paper, Autumn Girl, in original wooden frame, 1941, 16"x27", VG . . . . $850.00 C

Paper, bell-shaped glass with logo at top, in original black frame, 1930, 6"x9½", EX . . . . $2,200.00 C

Paper, bottler's calendar advance print, Garden Girl on a golf course, rare, 1919, G . . . . $5,000.00 C

Paper, calendar top, girl sitting on slat back bench wearing a large white hat with a red ribbon and drinking from a bottle with a straw, 1913, 16"x24", F . . . . $3,800.00 C

Paper, China girl sitting with a glass of Coke, matted and framed, 1936, 14¼"x22", NM . . . . . $1,800.00 C

Paper, "Cold" with bottle and button logo on iceberg, 1930s, EX . . . . $575.00 C

Paper, "Drink Coca-Cola Delicious and Refreshing," bottle on front of hot dog, framed and under glass, EX . . . . $150.00 C

Paper, "Drink Coca-Cola Delicious and Refreshing," bottle in front of hot dog, F . . . . $65.00 C

Paper, "Drink Coca-Cola, Quick Refreshment," bottle in front of hot dog, G . . . . $100.00 C

Paper, "Drink Coca-Cola, Quick Refreshment," bottle in front of hot dog, framed under glass, EX . . . . $150.00 C

Paper, Edgar Bergen and Charlie McCarthy, CBS Sunday Evenings, 1949, 22"x11", G . . . . . $165.00 D

Paper, Gibson Girl, matted and framed, 1910, 20"x30", P . . . . $1,800.00 D

Paper, girl in white dress with large red bow in back with a bottle and a straw, matted and framed under glass, 1910s, P . . . . $1,800.00 D

Paper, "Home Refreshment," three pieces of products, 1940s, NM . . . . $215.00 D

Paper, horizontal, "Cold Drink Coca-Cola," framed under glass, 1939, 58"x20", VG . . . . $600.00 C

Paper, instruction for hand in bottle outdoor painted signs, matted and framed, EX . . . . $100.00 B

Paper, "Let Us Put A Case In Your Car," with red carpet, 36"x20", EX . . . . $250.00 C

Paper, Lupe Valez in swim suit holding a bottle, framed and under glass, 1932, 11"x21½" NM . . . . $1,800.00 C

Paper, "Plastic Cooler For Picnics & Parties," 1950s, NM. . . . . $50.00 D

Paper poster featuring flapper girl with a bottle of Coke, 1920s, 12"x2", G . . . . $475.00 C

Paper poster, flapper girl holding a bottle, 1927–28, 12"x20", VG . . . . $550.00 C

Paper poster, man and woman with flare glasses and the globe sitting, very rare, under glass, 1912, 38"x49", VG . . . . $16,500.00 C

Paper poster, "Now! King Size Too!," Sprite Boy between two six-packs, 1955, 36"x20", NM. . . . . $100.00 C

Paper poster, "Ritz Boy," first time Ritz Boy was used, framed under glass, 1920s, EX. . . . . $975.00 C

Paper poster, vertical, "Drink Coca-Cola Delicious and Refreshing," 1927–28, 12"x20", F . . . . $275.00 C

Paper, Sprite Boy, "Come In Have a Coke," framed under glass, EX . . . . $150.00 C

Paper, Sprite Boy, "Come In, Have a Coke," framed under glass, F . . . . $75.00 D

Paper "That taste-good feeling," boy with Coca-Cola and hot dog, 1920s, F . . . . $175.00 D

Paper, two women drinking from bottles sitting in front of an ocean scene with clouds in the sky, 1912, 16"x22", F . . . . $1,875.00 D

Paper, "Take Along Coke In 12oz. Cans, Buy A Case," men beside boat, 1960s, 35"x19", EX . . . . $135.00 D

Paper, textured, travel exhibition promoting travel in France, matted and framed, 1970–80s, 24"x32", NM. . . . . $160.00 D

Paper, "That Taste-Good Feeling," 1920s, 14"x20", VG . . . . $275.00 D

Paper, "Treat Yourself Right, Drink Coca-Cola," 1920s, 12"x20", VG . . . . $675.00 B

Paper, "We have Coca-Cola 5¢," Sprite Boy, rare, soda fountain hat on Sprite Boy, 1944, 22"x7", NM. $600.00 C

Paper, "which" Coca-Cola or Goldelle Ginger Ale, 1905, VG . . . . $5,000.00 D

Paper window set for bottle sales, three piece, "Home Refreshment," 1941, 31" tall, G . . . . $275.00 C

Paper window set for bottle sales, three piece, "Home Refreshment," 1941, 31" tall, VG . . . . $300.00 D

Paper window sign, "Let Us Put A Case In Your Car," case of Coca-Cola, 36"x20", G . . . . $200.00 D

Paper window sign, "Let Us Put A Case In Your Car," case of Coca-Cola, 36"x20", EX . . . . $275.00 D

Plastic and metal light-up die cut sign, shaped like a paper serving cup, 1950-60s, 16"x17", G . . . . $1,300.00 D

Plastic, curved barrel, "Be really refreshed Coca-Cola," 1960, 17"x8", EX . . . . $35.00 D

Plastic, "Delicious With Ice Cold Coca-Cola," popcorn box overflowing with popcorn, 24"x7", G. . . . . $40.00 D

Plastic, "Delicious With Ice Cold Coca-Cola," popcorn box overflowing with popcorn, 24"x7", EX. . . . $55.00 D

Plastic, "Drink Coca-Cola" on red oval, Canadian, 1940–50s, 11"x9", NM . . . . $275.00 D

Plastic front light-up sign that gives a movement illusion when lit, "Drink Coca-Cola In Bottles" in red center, 1960s, 11" dia., EX . . . . $725.00 D

Plastic hanging light-up sign, "Leo's Fountain," 1950s, 24"x28", EX . . . . $475.00 D

Plastic, "Here's the real thing. Coke," wave logo, 1970s, 51"x7", M. $25.00 D

Plastic light-up, "Work Safely," "Safety is a job" cardboard insert, shows a Coca-Cola paper cup in lower left, 1950s, 15½" sq., EX. . . . . $700.00 D

Plywood and metal, Kay Displays sign, black lettering on yellow background, 1930s, 37" x 10", G . . . . $1,550.00 D

Plywood, double sided, "Slow School Zone Enjoy Coca-Cola, Drive Safely," 1950–60s, F . $575.00 C

Porcelain bottle button, 3' dia., M. . . . . $550.00 D

Porcelain bottle button, 3' dia., EX . . . . $495.00 C

Porcelain, bottle button with "Coca-Cola" across bottle front, 24", EX . . . . $450.00 D

Porcelain bottle, die cut, 16" tall, NM. . $300.00 D

Porcelain bottle, die cut, 1940s, 12", G . $150.00 D

Porcelain bottle, die cut, 1940s, 12", VG . . $175.00 C

Porcelain bottle, die cut, 1950s, 16", EX. . . $275.00 D

Porcelain button, candy, film with Coke in center, 1950, 18"x30", NM. . . . . $300.00 D

Porcelain button, "Drink Coca-Cola" considered to be the plain version of this piece, white on red, 1950s, 24", NM. . . . . $375.00 C

Porcelain button, "Drink Coca-Cola in Bottles," white on red, 1950s, 24", NM . . . . $425.00 C

Porcelain button, NOS, 1940s, 24", M . $800.00 C

Porcelain button with bottle, "Coca-Cola," red, 24", EX. . . . . $550.00 C

Porcelain button with bottle only, white, 1950s, 24", NM. . . . . $750.00 D

Porcelain button with bottle, white on red, 1950s, 48" dia., VG . . . . $250.00 C

Porcelain, "Buvez Coca-Cola," French Canadian sign, 1956, 29"x12", EX. . . . . $150.00 C

Porcelain, Canadian button with flat edge, "Drink Coca-Cola Ice Cold," 1940s, 3' dia., G . $165.00 D

Porcelain, Canadian "Coca-Cola Sold Here Ice Cold," white & yellow on red, 1947, 29"x12", G. . . . . $250.00 D

Porcelain, Canadian "Drink Coca-Cola," 1946, 28"x20", EX . . . . $220.00 D

Porcelain, Canadian "Drink Coca-Cola" button, 1954, 4' dia., NM . . . . $500.00 D

Porcelain, Canadian "Drink Coca-Cola" sign, red, yellow, and white, 1955, 29"x12", EX. . . $250.00 B

Porcelain, Canadian flange "Iced Coca-Cola Here," 1952, 18"x20", NM . . . . $575.00 C

Porcelain, Canadian fountain service sign, 1937, 8' x 4', NM . . . . $1,800.00 B

Porcelain, "Come In! Have A Coca-Cola," yellow and white, 1940s, 54", NM. . . . . $1,100.00 D

Porcelain cooler, die cut, white with black trim, 1930s, 18", EX . . . . $700.00 D

Porcelain, "Delicious & Refreshing," white background, 1950s, 24"x24", EX . . . . $275.00 D

Porcelain, delivery truck cab, "Ice Cold," red, white, and yellow, arched top, 1930s, NM . . . . $700.00 C

Porcelain delivery truck cab, "Ice Cold," red, white, and yellow, arched top, 1930s, NM . . . . $700.00 B

Porcelain, die cut bottle sign, 1950s, 16" tall, EX. . . . . $275.00 C

Porcelain, die cut bottle sign, 12' tall, G $175.00 D

Porcelain, die cut script "Drink Coca-Cola" sign, white, 18"x5½", M. . . . . $775.00 B

Porcelain, double sided, "Drink Coca-Cola" on one side, "Isenhower Cigar Store" on other side, 1930, 30"x40", EX . . . . $375.00 C

Porcelain, double sided, "Drink Coca-Cola" on one side, "Isenhower Cigar Store" on other side, 1930, 30"x40", G . . . . $250.00 D

Porcelain, double sided, "Drink Coca-Cola" with bottle in yellow circle at bottom of sign, 1939, 5'x4', G. . . . . $350.00 C

Porcelain, "Drink Coca-Cola Delicious & Refreshing," 1930s, EX. $500.00 D

Porcelain, "Drink Coca-Cola Delicious & Refreshing," self framing, 1930s, 4'x8', NM . . . $700.00 C

Porcelain, "Drink Coca-Cola, Ice Cold," fountain dispenser, 1950s, 28"x28", EX . . . . $750.00 D

Porcelain, "Drink Coca-Cola, Ice Cold," fountain dispenser, 1950s, 28"x28", G . . . . $500.00 C

Porcelain, "Drink Coca-Cola in bottles" sign with curved ends, white lettering on red, 1950s, 44"x16", EX . . . . $125.00 C

Porcelain, "Drink Coca-Cola" on button over bottle, 1950s, 18"x28", NM . . . . $500.00 C

Porcelain, "Drink Coca-Cola" on fishtail, 1950–60s, 44"x16", VG . . . . $225.00 D

Porcelain, "Drink Coca-Cola" on fishtail, 1950–60s, 44"x16", NM . . . . $300.00 D

Porcelain, "Drink Coca-Cola" sign, 1910s, 45"x18", EX . . . . $1,000.00 B

Porcelain, "Drink Coca-Cola," trademark in C tail, white lettering on red background, 1910–20s, 30"x12", VG . . . . $600.00 D

Porcelain, double sided flange, "Coca-Cola Here," colorful in yellow, red, and white, Canadian, 1952, 18"x20", VG . . . . $200.00 C

Porcelain, "Drug Store" over "Drink Coca-Cola Delicious & Refreshing," red, white, and green, 1930s, 90"x60", F . . . . $325.00 D

Porcelain, "Drug Store" over "Drink Coca-Cola Delicious & Refreshing," red, white, and green, 1930s, 90"x60", EX . . . . $750.00 C

Porcelain, "Drugs, Soda," 1950s, 18"x30", NM . . . . $950.00 D

Porcelain, featuring hand pulling dispenser top, 1930, 24"x26", EX . . . . $475.00 D

Porcelain flange, die cut, "Rafraichissez vous Coca-Cola," foreign, VG . . . . $400.00 D

Porcelain flange, double sided, "Refresh yourself! Coca-Cola Sold Here, Ice Cold," 1930s, EX . . . . . $800.00 C

Porcelain, flange "Drink" sign, Canadian, yellow and white on red, 1930s, 17"x20", EX . . $500.00 D

Porcelain, flange, "Enjoy Coca-Cola In Bottles," very rare and hard to find, 1948, VG . . . $850.00 B

Porcelain flange, "Enjoy Coca-Cola In bottles," very rare, 1948, EX . . . . $950.00 D

Porcelain, flange French Canadian, "Prenez un Coca-Cola," 1950s, 17"x19", EX . . . . . $200.00 D

Porcelain, flange mount, "Iced Coca-Cola Here," yellow and white lettering on red background with yellow trim around outside of sign, 1950s, NM . . . . $600.00 C

Porcelain, fountain service, diagonal, "Drink Coca-Cola," 1933, 22"x26", NM . . . . $1,100.00 C

Porcelain, fountain service, double sided, red and white fountain head and glass, 1950s, 28"x28", NM . . . . $1,600.00 D

Porcelain, fountain service, "Drink Coca-Cola Fountain Service," white and yellow lettering on red and black background framed by fountain heads, 27"x14", EX . . . . $1,200.00 D

Porcelain, "Fountain Service, Drink Coca-Cola" on button, 1950s, 34"x12", NM . . . . $400.00 C

Porcelain, "Fountain Service, Drink Coca-Cola" on button, 1950s, 34"x12", G . . . . $275.00 D

Porcelain fountain service, green lettering on white background with red decoration and "Drink Coca-Cola" in red bull's-eye at right, 1950s, 30"x12", EX . . . . $400.00 C

Porcelain, fountain service sign, "Fountain Service, Drink Coca-Cola," red, green, white, 1950s, 28"x12", EX . . . . $800.00 D

Porcelain, fountain service sign, 1935, 27"x14", NM . . . . $1,800.00 D

Porcelain fountain service, two sided, dispenser with stainless steel banding around the edge of the sign, 1950s, 27"x28", VG . . . . $325.00 C

Porcelain, French Canadian door kick plate, 1939, 29"x12", NM. . . . . $210.00 C

Porcelain, French Canadian double sided flange sign, 1940, EX . . . . $500.00 B

Porcelain, French Canadian sidewalk sign, both message and legs are porcelain, 1941, 27"x46", F . . . . $250.00 B

Porcelain, French Canadian sign, because of its construction it resembles the smaller door push, 1930s, 18"x54", G. . . . . $400.00 B

Porcelain, French Canadian sign, "Buvez Coca-Cola," white, red, & yellow, 1955, 29"x12", G. . . . . $150.00 C

Porcelain, horizontal, "Coca-Cola Sold Here Ice Cold," red background trimmed in yellow with white lettering, 1940s, 29"x12", EX. . . . $325.00 C

Porcelain, kick plate for screen door "Drink Coca-Cola Sold Here Ice Cold," 1930s, 31"x12", G. . . . . $450.00 C

Porcelain outdoor, "Drink Coca-Cola Delicious and Refreshing," white and yellow lettering on red background, 1938, 8'x4', NM . . . . $1,300.00 D

Porcelain, outdoor, "Drink Coca-Cola Delicious and Refreshing," white and yellow lettering on red background, 1938, 8' x 4', P . . . . $200.00 B

Porcelain outdoor, "Drink Coca-Cola, Delicious and Refreshing," white lettering on red background, 1932, 5'x3', G . . . . $500.00 D

Porcelain, round bottle unit, probably part of a larger sign, features the 1923 bottle, 18", NM. . . . . $250.00 D

Porcelain, sidewalk, double sided, courtesy panel over a 24" button, NOS, 1950s, 2'x5', EX . . . . $3,200.00 B

Porcelain, sidewalk, double sided, "Drink Coca-Cola In Bottles," 1940–50s, 4'x4½', VG $650.00 C

Porcelain, sidewalk, double sided vertical, "Stop Here Drink Coca-Cola," Canadian, 1941, 26"x36", G. . . . . $250.00 B

Porcelain sidewalk, double sided vertical, "Stop Here Drink Coca-Cola," Canadian, 1941, 26"x36", EX. . . . . $325.00 C

Porcelain, square sign featuring button in center, Italian, 22" sq, NM . . . . $525.00 B

Porcelain, square sign with bottle, "Delicious Refreshing," green on white, 1950s, 24" sq, NM. . . . . $300.00 C

Porcelain truck cab, "Drink Coca-Cola Ice Cold," yellow and white lettering on red background trimmed in yellow, 1950s, G . . . . $375.00 D

Porcelain, truck sign , "Drink Coca-Cola Ice Cold," yellow & white lettering on red, 1940s, 50"x10", G . . . . $130.00 B

Porcelain, truck cab, "Drink Coca-Cola in Bottles," red lettering on white background, 1950, EX. . . . . $250.00 C

Porcelain, 24" button "Drink Coca-Cola, Sign of Good Taste," white lettering on red, 1950s, 24", NM. . . . . $400.00 C

Porcelain wall, one sided, advertising fountain service, red and green background with yellow and white lettering, 1934, G. . . . . $650.00 C

Reverse glass, "Drink Coca-Cola," for back bar mirror, 1930s, 11" dia., EX. . . . . $625.00 D

Reverse glass light-up, "Drink Coca-Cola In Bottles," by Cincinnati Advertising Products Co, rare, 1920s, 15"x7"x5", EX. . . . . $2,000.00 D

Reverse glass mirror, "Please Pay when Served, Drink Coca-Cola, Thank You," 1920–1930, 11¼" dia., EX. . . . . $300.00 C

Reverse painted glass, "Refresh Yourself Drink Coca-Cola," Canadian, 1927, 11½"x5½", G. . . . . $325.00 B

Rice paper napkin with Oriental scene, VG . . . . $350.00 C

Rice paper napkin with Oriental scene, EX. . . . . $375.00 B

Rice paper napkin with girl and bottle with arrow, framed and matted under glass, G . . . . . . $50.00 D

Rice paper napkin with girl and bottle with arrow, framed and matted under glass, EX . . . . . $65.00 D

"Sign of Good Taste," ribbon attachments on both streamers, 1957, 3'x4', NM . . . . $150.00 C

Stainless steel from dispenser, "Drink Coca-Cola," horizontal lettering, 1930s, 6½"x3¼", EX . . . . $95.00 C

Tin, arrow, "Ice Cold Coca-Cola Sold Here," white lettering on red and green background, 30", G . . . . $250.00 D

Tin, bottle, oval, "Drink A Bottle of Carbonated Coca-Cola," rare, 1900s, 8½"x10½", F . $2,000.00 B

Tin arrow, "Ice Cold Coca-Cola Sold Here," white lettering on red and green background, 30", G . . . . $250.00 C

Tin bottle, die cut, 1951, 3' tall, EX . . . $275.00 D

Tin bottle, die cut, 1954, 20"x6', NM . . $575.00 C

Tin bottle, die cut, 1956, 16", NM . . . . $300.00 D

Tin bottle, die cut embossed, from a larger sign, 38" tall, EX . . . . $350.00 C

Tin, bottle, embossed die cut, with original silver and black wooden frame, 2'x4', NM . . . $525.00 C

Tin, bottle in original frame, on white background, 1950s, 36"x18", EX . . . . $250.00 C

Tin, bottle rack, double sided, round, "Take Home a Carton," yellow and white lettering on red background, 1930–1940, EX . . . . $240.00 D

Tin, bottle sign with original wooden frame, 1950s, 18"x36", EX . . . . $195.00 C

Tin, bottle sign with original wooden frame, 1948, 18"x36", F . . . . $100.00 D

Tin, bottle, vertical, in original silver wood frame, full-color bottle on white background, 1950s, 1½'x3', EX . . . . $350.00 C

Tin button, "Drink Coca-Cola Sign of Good Taste," yellow and white lettering, 1950s, 16", NM . . . . $375.00 D

Tin button, showing bottle on white, 1940–1950, 24", EX . . . . $325.00 D

Tin button with arrow, red lettering on white, all original hardware, 1950s, 16" dia., EX . . $500.00 C

Tin, button with circle and earlier arrow, with framework on back, red & white, 1953, 12" dia., EX . . . . $475.00 D

Tin, button with large arrow and original connecting hardware, red on white, 16" dia., NM . . . . $500.00+ D

Tin, Buvez Coca-Cola, embossed, painted, foreign, 17¼"x53", G . . . . $125.00 C

Tin, Canadian "Drink Coca-Cola Ice Cold," 1938, 5'x3', G . . . . $400.00 B

Tin, Canadian "Drink Coca-Cola" sign, G, bright colors, 1956, 28"x20", EX . . . . $450.00 D

Tin, Canadian six-pack in spotlight "Take home a carton," 1940, 36"x60", EX . . . . $475.00 C

Tin, Canadian six-pack in spotlight, "Take home a carton," 1942, 18"x54", EX . . . . $500.00 B

Tin, Canadian vertical "Refresh yourself" sign with 6 oz. bottle, 1920s, 18"x54", G . . . . $600.00 B

Tin, "Candy-Cigarettes" over fishtail logo, self-framed, 1960s, 28"x20", EX . . . . $250.00 C

Tin, "Candy-Cigarettes" over fishtail logo, self-framed, 1960s, 28"x20", G . . . . $175.00 D

Tin, "Coca-Cola," red background with green and yellow border, bottle centered, 1930s, 45" dia., EX . . . . $375.00 D

Tin, "Cold Drinks," 1960s, 24"x15", NM . . $200.00 D

Tin, "Cold Drinks" with "Drink" fishtail, "With Crushed Ice," 1960s, 24"x15", NM . . . . $275.00 D

Tin, "Cold Drinks" with "Drink" fishtail, "With Crushed Ice," 1960s, 24"x15", G . . . . . $200.00 C

Tin, "Cold Drinks" with fishtail in center, 1960s, 24"x15", NM. $200.00 D

Tin, Dasco bottle with 1923 bottle, 1931, 4½"x12", M . . . . $625.00 C

Tin, "Deli" with "Drink Coca-Cola" on dot at right, 1950s, 50"x15", NM . . . . $425.00 D

Tin, diamond shaped, with bottle spotlighted at bottom, in original black wooden frame, "Drink Coca-Cola" at top, 1940, 42"x42", NM . . . . . $500.00 C

Tin, diamond shaped, with bottle spotlighted at bottom, "Drink Coca-Cola" at top, 1940, 42"x42", G. $300.00 D

Tin, die cut bottle sign, 1930s, 39" tall, G. . $550.00 C

Tin, die cut bottle sign, 1949, 20"x72", NM. $625.00 D

Tin, die cut bottle sign, 1951, 16" tall, G . . $140.00 D

Tin, die cut, double sided, "Drink & Take Home A Carton," 1930s, 10"x13", EX. . . . . $200.00 D

Tin, die cut fishtail "Coca-Cola" sign, white on red, 1962, 24"x12", VG . . . . $425.00 D

Tin, die cut fishtail sign "Coca-Cola," white on red, 1962, 26"x12", NM . . . . $500.00 B

Tin, die cut six-pack sign, 6 for 25¢, 1950s, 11"x13", G. . . . . $600.00 D

Tin, die cut triangle sign with the original bracket and mounting hardware, 1934, EX . . . $1,750.00 B

Tin, die cut 12-pack sign, 1954, 20"x14", NM. . . . . $1,700.00 B

Tin, die-cut, two sided hanger, 1930s, 60"x48", EX . . . . $275.00 D

Tin, door kickplate sign, "Drink Coca-Cola" with bottle in spotlight, yellow & white on red, 1946, 34"x11", EX . . . . $175.00 D

Tin, double sided arrow sign "Coca-Cola Sold Here Ice Cold," red, green & white, 1927, F . $300.00 B

Tin, double sided rack sign, "Take home a Carton," yellow, white on red, 1930s, 13", G . . . . $200.00 C

Tin, double sided triangle "Ice Cold" with bottle at bottom, filigree work at top, 1936, 23"x23", F . . . . $675.00 B

Tin, "Drink Coca-Cola Enjoy that Refreshing New Feeling," self-framed, painted, fishtail design, 1960s, 28"x12", VG. . . . . $185.00 D

Tin, "Drink" button with '40s style arrow attachment at back of fixture with original hardware, 1948, 16", NM . . . . $900.00 C

Tin, "Drink..." button with wings, 1950s, 32"x12", NM. . . . . $275.00 C

Tin, "Drink Coca-Cola," American Artworks with scalloped top and filigree, 1936, G. . . . . $700.00 C

Tin, "Drink Coca-Cola," American Artworks with scalloped top and filigree, 1936, EX . . . $900.00 C

Tin, "Drink Coca-Cola," bottle at right, self framing, 1951, 28"x10", EX . . . . $195.00 C

Tin, "Drink Coca-Cola" button next to bottle, green border, 1950s, 28"x20", EX . . . . . $400.00 D

Tin, "Drink Coca-Cola" button with small arrow and original hardware, white on red, 1950s, 12" dia., EX. . . . . $475.00 C

Tin, "Drink Coca-Cola" button with small arrow, 1950s, 12" dia., VG . . . . $250.00 C

Tin, "Drink Coca-Cola Delicious & Refreshing," couple with a bottle, 1940s, 28"x20", G. $550.00 D

Tin, "Drink Coca-Cola Delicious & Refreshing," couple with a bottle, 1940s, 28"x20", EX . . . . $575.00 C

Tin, "Drink Coca-Cola Delicious & Refreshing," couple with bottle, self-framing, 1940s, NM. . . . . $800.00 D

Tin, "Drink..." button with wings, 1950s, 32"x12", NM. . . . . $275.00 D

Tin, "Drink Coca-Cola" fishtail, "Refreshes You Best," self-framing, 1960s, 28"x20", EX . $225.00 D

Tin, "Drink Coca-Cola" fishtail, white lettering on red fishtail against white sign background, 7½"x3½", NM . . . . $50.00 D

Tin, "Drink Coca-Cola 5¢ Ice Cold," self framing, tilted bottle, 1930s, 54"x18", G . . . . . . $250.00 C

Tin, "Drink Coca-Cola 5¢ Ice Cold," self framing, tilted bottle, 1930s, 54"x18", EX . . . . . $400.00 C

Tin, "Drink Coca-Cola 5¢ Ice Cold," white and yellow lettering on red background with vertical bottle in yellow bull's-eye, 1938, NM . . . . $375.00 C

Tin, "Drink Coca-Cola Fountain Service," red, green, and white lettering on yellow, red, and white background, 1950s, 28"x12", NM . . . . . $575.00 C

Tin, "Drink Coca-Cola Ice Cold" on red disc with bars, 1930s, 28"x20", EX . . . . $275.00 C

Tin, "Drink Coca-Cola Ice-Cold" over "Delicious & Refreshing" on bottles with green background, 1940s, 28"x20", EX . . . . $200.00 C

Tin, "Drink Coca-Cola in Bottles" button, all white lettering, 1955, 12", NM . . . . $295.00 C

Tin, "Drink Coca-Cola In Bottles" button with arrow shooting from right to left at about 2 and 8 o'clock, 1954, EX . . . . $375.00 C

Tin, "Drink Coca-Cola In Bottles" button with arrow shooting from right to left at about 2 and 8 o'clock, 1954, EX . . . . $550.00 C

Tin, "Drink Coca-Cola" in left and center with yellow dot bottle at lower right, 1940s, 28"x20", EX . . . . $350.00 D

Tin, "Drink Coca-Cola" lettered in white over dynamic wave logo, 1980s, 24"x18", G . . $55.00 D

Tin, "Drink Coca-Cola" lettered in white over dynamic wave logo, 1980s, 24"x18", EX . $75.00 D

Tin, "Drink Coca-Cola," marching bottles to left side of sign, 1937, 54"x18", VG . . . . $800.00 D

Tin, "Drink Coca-Cola" over yellow dot bottle, "5¢ Ice Cold" below, self framing, 1940s, 54"x18", EX . . . . $600.00 D

Tin, "Drink Coca-Cola," red background with yellow and white lettering featuring three receding bottles, 1930s, 54"x18", EX . . . . $750.00 C

Tin, "Drink Coca-Cola Sign of Good Taste," white and yellow on red, 1950s, 12" dia., EX . $275.00 D

Tin, "Drink Coca-Cola Sign of Good Taste," white and yellow lettering, 1950s, 24", G . . . . $300.00 D

Tin, "Drink Coca-Cola Sign of Good Taste," white and yellow lettering, 1950s, 24", EX . . . $450.00 D

Tin, "Drink Coca-Cola," 24" iron frame, one side has a 16" button while the opposite side as a 10" plastic button with a small light which creates a back light, VG . . . . $975.00 B

Tin, "Drink Coca-Cola," white on red with bottle at right on white background, self framing, 1956, NM . . . . $165.00 D

Tin, "Drink Coca-Cola," with smiling girl, self framing, 1940s, 28"x20", NM . . . . $450.00 D

Tin, "Drink" over bottle, "Coca-Cola" under bottle, 1930s, 5"x13", EX . . . . $350.00 C

Tin, "Drink," white on red with silver frame, 1950s, 34"x18", EX . . . . $195.00 D

Tin, embossed, "Drink Coca-Cola," 1920, 18"x5¾", VG . . . . $475.00 C

Tin, embossed, "Drink Coca-Cola Delicious and Refreshing," 14"x10", F . . . . $225.00 C

Tin, embossed, "Drink Coca-Cola Delicious and Refreshing," 14"x10", EX . . . . $325.00 D

Tin, embossed, "Drink Coca-Cola in Bottles 5¢," 1920, 23"x6", EX . . . . $450.00 C

Tin, embossed, "Drink Coca-Cola in Bottles 5¢," 1920, 23"x6", G . . . . $375.00 B

Tin, embossed "Drink Coca-Cola In Bottles 5¢" sign, red & white, 1930s, 23"x6", EX . . . $325.00 C

Tin, embossed, "Drink Coca-Cola" lettered in white on red with green border, 1920s, NM . . . . $825.00 B

Tin, embossed "Drink" sign by Dasco, in original wrapping paper, 1930s, 18"x6", NM . . . $350.00 D

Tin, embossed "Drink" sign with 1923 bottle on left side of sign,, 1931, 27½"x10", NM . . . $1,600.00 B

Tin, embossed "Gas Today" sign with good colors, 1929, 28"x20", G. . . . . $675.00 C

Tin, embossed, "Ice Cold Coca-Cola Sold Here," 1923 bottle inset at left, 1931, 28"x20", M. . . . . . $950.00 D

Tin, embossed, "Ice Cold Coca-Cola Sold Here," featuring 1916 bottle, 1926, 28"x20", F . $200.00 B

Tin, embossed, "Ice Cold Coca-Cola Sold Here," green and white trim, 1933, 19½" dia., EX. . . . . . . $475.00 C

Tin, embossed "Ice Cold Coca-Cola Sold Here," yellow & white on red, 1932, 29"x19", F . . . . $375.00 C

Tin, embossed over cardboard with string holder, "Drink Coca-Cola," 1922, 8"x4", EX. . . $900.00 C

Tin, embossed sign "Drink Coca-Cola In Bottles 5¢," white lettering on red, 1920s, 23"x6", EX. . . . . $450.00 B

Tin, embossed sign featuring 1915 bottle, 1927, F . . . . $325.00 C

Tin, embossed sign featuring the 1923 bottle, 1920s, 28"x20", F. . . . . $275.00 D

Tin, "Enjoy Coca-Cola All the Year Round," with giant earth, 1982, 33"x24", EX . . . . $175.00 C

Tin, "Enjoy Coca-Cola All the Year Round," with giant earth, 1982, 33"x24", G . . . . $125.00 C

Tin, "Enjoy that Refreshing New Feeling," fishtail logo with rolled frame, 1960s, 54"x18", NM. . . . . $325.00 D

Tin, "Enjoy That Refreshing New Feeling" on fishtail, self-framing, 1960s, 32"x12", NM . $225.00 D

Tin, featuring artwork of straight sided bottle on left side of sign, 1914, 27"x19", G. . . . $1,700.00 B

Tin, featuring Elaine holding a glass, 1916, 20"x30", G . . . . $4,000.00 B

Tin, fishtail, Coca-Cola fishtail in center with bottle at right hand, red, green, and white, vertical, 1960s, 56"x32", NM. . . . . $250.00 D

Tin, fishtail die cut, 1960s, 12"x26", VG. . $275.00 C

Tin, fishtail die cut, 1960s, 12"x26", EX . . $300.00 D

Tin, fishtail, "Enjoy that Refreshing New Feeling," bottle to right of fishtail, 1964, 28"x20", NM . . $225.00 D

Tin, fishtail flange, "Enjoy that Refreshing New Feeling," 1962, 18"x15", EX . . . . $275.00 D

Tin, fishtail flange, "Enjoy that Refreshing New Feeling," 1962, 18"x15", G . . . . $200.00 C

Tin, fishtail horizontal, "Cold Drinks Drink Coca-Cola," with crushed ice, 1960, 24"x15", NM. . . . . $225.00 D

Tin, fishtail, horizontal, "Sign of the Good Taste," full-color bottle at right side of sign, all on white background with green trim on frame, 1959, 54"x18", G . . . . $175.00 C

Tin, fishtail, horizontal, "Sign of the Good Taste," full-color bottle at right side of sign, white background with green trim on frame, 1959, 54"x18", NM. . . . $275.00 D

Tin, fishtail, horizontal, with bottle on right sign with "Ice Cold" beside bottle, 1958, 54"x18" . . . $275.00 D

Tin, fishtail, self-framed with bottle on right, "Drink Coca-Cola Enjoy that Refreshing new Feeling," horizontal, 1960s, 32"x12", NM . . $225.00 D

Tin, fishtail sign "Drink Coca-Cola," horizontal, white lettering on red, 12"x6", NM . . . . $195.00 C

Tin, fishtail sign with bottle on left and 12 oz. can on right, red, white, and green, 54"x18", EX . . . . $300.00 D

Tin, fishtail, vertical, "Drink Coca-Cola" with bottle at bottom of sign, 1960, 18"x54", NM . $250.00 D

Tin, flange, "Drink Coca-Cola," 1941, 24"x21", G. . . . . $400.00 C

Tin, flange, "Drink Coca-Cola," 1941, 24"x21", EX . . . . $475.00 D

Tin, flange, "Drink Coca-Cola, Ice Cold," flange forms arrow point, 1956, 18"x22", M. . . $500.00 C

Tin, flat, "Refresh Yourself," 1927, 29"x28", VG . . . . $350.00 D

Tin, French "Buvez" sign featuring Sprite Boy in spotlight on right side, 1948, 54"x18", NM . . . . $850.00 B

Tin, French Canadian bottle sign, with 1916 bottle, 1920s, 28"x20", F . . . . $150.00 C

Tin, French Canadian sign featuring 6 oz. bottle on right side, 1930s, 28"x20", G . . . . $700.00 B

Tin, French six-pack in spotlight, 1940s, 36"x60", F . . . . $140.00 C

Tin, French, six-pack in spotlight, 1942, 18"x52", F . . . . $150.00 D

Tin, "Gas & Oil" on bottle side of fishtail logo, self framing, 1960s, 96"x16", NM . . . . $475.00 D

Tin, girl with glass, gold beveled edge, 1920s, 8"x11", EX . . . . $900.00 D

Tin, girl with glass, gold beveled edge, 1920s, 8"x11", G. . . . . $750.00 B

Tin, "Grocery" over bottle with fishtail logo, 1960s, 28"x20", VG . . . . $150.00 C

Tin, "Grocery" over bottle with fishtail logo, 1960s, 28"x20", F. . . . . $75.00 C

Tin, "Have a Coke," showing a spotlighted bottle in center with "Coca-Cola" at bottom all on red background, vertical, 1948, 18"x54", EX. . . . $375.00 C

Tin, "Have a Coke," tilted bottle on yellow dot, 1940s, 54"x18", EX . . . . $400.00 C

Tin, heavy embossed,1923 bottle at each end, "Drink Coca-Cola" in center in white on red background, 1930s, EX . . . . $475.00 C

Tin, heavy embossed,1923 bottle at each end, "Drink Coca-Cola" in center in white on red background, 1930s, VG. . . . . $425.00 B

Tin, Hilda Clark, considered rare due to the fact this artwork is rarely found in the tin version, 1903, 16¼"x19½", NM . . . . $4,500.00 C

Tin, Hilda Clark, round, "Coca-Cola Drink Delicious and Refreshing," 1903, 6" dia., VG . . . . . $5,000.00 C

Tin, Hilda Clark, showing her drinking from a glass while seated at a table with roses and stationery, very rare, 1899, G. . . . . $13,000.00 B

Tin, horizontal, "Drink Coca-Cola In Bottles," 1916 bottle at left of sign, 1920s, 35"x12", G . . . $175.00 D

Tin, horizontal, "Drink Coca-Cola Ice Cold," with bottle at right, red and white, 1957, 28"x20", EX . . . . $175.00 D

Tin, horizontal, "Drink Coca-Cola," red background, silver border on self frame, bottle in spotlight in lower right hand corner, 1946, 28"x20", F . . . . $250.00 D

Tin horizontal "Drink Coca-Cola" with bottle to right, red & white, 1954, 54"x18", EX. . $170.00 C

Tin, horizontal embossed, "Drink Coca-Cola," 1923 bottle on left side, 35"x12", EX . . $375.00 D

Tin, horizontal "Enjoy Coca-Cola" with bottle to right of message in white square, red & white, 1960s, 54"x18", NM . . . . $250.00 C

Tin, horizontal, "Things go better with Coke," self framing, 1960s, 32"x12", NM . . . . $200.00 C

Tin, horizontal, "Things go better with Coke," self framing, 1960s, 32"x12", G . . . . $100.00 B

Tin, horizontal, "Things go better with Coke," self framing with full-color bottle on right, all on white background, 1960s, 54"x18", EX . . . . . . $210.00 B

Tin, "Ice Cold Drinks," disc logo and cup, "Serve Yourself," 1960s, 27"x22", NM . . . . $250.00 C

Tin, "Ice Cold Drinks Enjoy Coca-Cola," with cup of Coke and snowflakes, 1960, 27"x22", NM. . . . . $275.00 D

Tin, "Ice Cold" featuring '60s cup, white on blue, 1960s, 28"x20", NM . . . . $65.00 D

Tin, "It's A Natural! Coca-Cola In Bottles," over bottle on red background, 1950s, 16" dia., EX . . . $375.00 D

Tin, "It's A Natural! Coca-Cola In Bottles," over bottle on red background, 1950s, 16" dia., G . . . . $275.00 C

Tin, Kay Displays sign, cardboard back plate, stand up featuring "Drink Coca-Cola," 1930s, 9"x10", EX. . . . . $650.00 C

Tin, "Let us put a Coke in your car," EX$125.00 C

Tin, Lillian Nordica, oval framed, "Coca-Cola Delicious and Refreshing," featuring Coca-Cola table and oval "Drink Coca-Cola 5¢," rare, 1904, 8½"x10¼", F . . . . $3,500.00 C

Tin, Lillian Nordica, self framed, embossed, promoting both fountain and bottle sales, 1904 – 05, G . . . . $4,000.00 C

Tin, octagonal, "Drink Coca-Cola" over bottle in circle, 1930s, 10" dia., EX . . . . $500.00 D

Tin, oval, with French lettering "Buvez Coca-Cola Glace," Canadian, 1950s, 3'x2', EX . . . . $225.00 D

Tin, over cardboard, featuring a straight sided bottle, rare and hard to find, white background, 1908, 6"x13", F . . . . $1,250.00 C

Tin, over cardboard, "Treat Yourself To A Coke," 1950–60s, EX . . . . $155.00 D

Tin, over cardboard, with "Drink Coca-Cola," featuring 1915 bottle, red lettering on white background, 1920s, 6"x13", G . . . . $1,400.00 D

Tin, painted litho, "Drink Coca-Cola In Bottles 5¢," bottle on each side, framed, 1907, 34½"x12", F . . $400.00 C

Tin, painted, "Take a case home today $1.00 deposit," 19½"x27¾", VG. . . . . $175.00 D

Tin, painted, "Take a case home today, $1.00 deposit," 19½"x27¾", EX . . . . $275.00 C

Tin, "Pause Drink Coca-Cola" on bottle in yellow center dot, 1940s, 54"x18", EX . . . . . . $175.00 D

Tin, "Pause, Drink Coca-Cola," tilted bottle on yellow dot, self framing, 1930s, 54"x18", EX . . . . . $250.00 D

Tin, "Pause Drink Coca-Cola," white lettering on red and yellow background, vertical, 1930s, 18"x54", G . . . . $150.00 D

Tin, "Pause Drink Coca-Cola," white lettering on red and yellow background, vertical, 1930s, 18"x54", EX . . . . $250.00 D

Tin, pilaster sign, with six-pack artwork and 16" button at top, 1948, 16"x54", EX. . . . . $675.00 C

Tin, rack sign with Sprite Boy decal, yellow on red, 1940s, 16"x23", EX . . . . $325.00 C

Tin, raised frame "Drink" sign with 1923 bottle, 1942, 28"x20", G . . . . $550.00 B

Tin, rectangular, man and woman with a bottle, "Drink Coca-Cola Delicious & Refreshing," all on red background, 1941, 28"x20", NM . . . $850.00 D

Tin, "Refresh Yourself, Drink Coca-Cola, Sold Here Ice Cold," 1927, 29"x30", EX. . . . $275.00 D

Tin, "Refresh Yourself, Drink Coca-Cola, Sold Here Ice Cold," 1927, 29"x30", G . . . . . $225.00 C

Tin, "Refresh Yourself Drink Coca-Cola Sold Here Ice Cold," trimmed in red and green, 1920s, 28"x29", EX . . . . $400.00 D

Tin, ribbon, die cut, "Sign of Good Taste," 1957, 3', NM. . . . . $275.00 C

Tin, ribbon, die cut, "Sign of Good Taste," 1957, 3', EX . . . . $225.00 D

Tin, round sign with bottle and logo, red, 1937, 46", NM . . . . $1,000.00 D

Tin, self-framing "Drink" sign with couple holding bottle, woman in spotlight, 1942, 28"x20", EX . . . . $550.00 D

Tin, self-framing, horizontal oval, "Coca-Cola," girl in foreground of lettering offering a bottle, 1926, 11"x8", F. . . . . $250.00 D

Tin, "Serve Coca-Cola at home," six pack highlighted at center of sign all on red background, vertical, 1950, 18"x54", EX. . . . . $450.00 D

Tin, "Serve Coca-Cola At Home," yellow dot six-pack, 1950s, 54"x18", G. . . . . $175.00 C

Tin, "Serve Coca-Cola At Home," yellow dot six-pack, 1950s, 54"x18", NM. . . . . $275.00 D

Tin, sidewalk, embossed, "Take home a carton," 1942, 20"x28", EX. . . . . $375.00 B

Tin, sidewalk sign "Big King Size" featuring fishtail over bottle all on green and white background, 1960s, 20"x28", G. . . . . $150.00 D

Tin, sidewalk sign "Delicious and refreshing," 1930s, 20"x28", F . . . . $150.00 D

Tin, sidewalk sign "Drink Coca-Cola Ice Cold, Delicious and Refreshing," yellow, white, red, and green, 1939, 20"x28", NM. . . . . $275.00 B

Tin, sidewalk sign, big King Size, fishtail design with bottle, 1958–1960, 20"x28", EX . . $150.00 D

Tin, sidewalk sign featuring fishtail over bottle on green and white striped background, 1960s, NM. . . . . $225.00 D

Tin, sign featuring straight sided bottle with wooden frame, 1914, 28"x20", F . . . . $275.00 C

Tin, "Sign of Good Taste" button, white & yellow on red, 1950s, 12" dia., F. . . . . $175.00 C

Tin, "Sign of Good Taste," fishtail logo, with raised border, 1960s, 32"x11", EX. . . . . $225.00 D

Tin, "Sign of Good Taste, Ice Cold," fishtail logo and bottle, 1960s, 56"x32", EX . . . . . . $275.00 D

Tin, "Sign of Good Taste" in fishtail with bottle at bottom on green and white striped background, 1960s, 16"x41", EX . . . . $300.00 C

Tin, "Sign of Good Taste," vertical fishtail, green rolled frame, 1960s, 18"x54", NM. . . . . $275.00 D

Tin, sign with man and woman in spotlight "Drink Coca-Cola," 1942, 56"x32", NM. . . . . . $525.00 D

Tin, sign with woman with a bottle of Coca-Cola, "Drink Coca-Cola," 1942, 56"x32", EX . . $475.00 D

Tin, six-pack, die cut, "King Size, Coca-Cola," 1960s, EX . . . . $325.00 C

Tin, six-pack, die cut, "King Size, Coca-Cola," 1960s, G . . . . $200.00 D

Tin, six-pack, die cut, red wire handle, 1950s, EX . . . . $400.00 D

Tin, six-pack, die cut, "6 for 25¢," 1950s, EX . . . . $500.00 D

Tin, six-pack sign featuring six-pack, "Take home a Carton," with fishtail "Coca-Cola" at top of sign, 1958, 20"x28", EX. . . . . $550.00 B

Tin, "Take A Case Home Today, Quality Refreshment," red carpet with a yellow Coke case on it, 1950s, 28"x20", NM . . . . $375.00 D

Tin, "Take a case home today," white and yellow lettering on red background, vertical, 1949, 20"x28", NM. . . . . $250.00 C

Tin, "Take Home A Carton," fishtail green border, 1960s, 28"x20", EX. . . . . $250.00 D

Tin, "Take Home A Carton" over six-pack, Canadian, 1950s, 53"x35", NM . . . . $575.00 D

Tin, "Take Home A Carton" over six-pack, Canadian, 1950s, 53"x35", F. . . . . $100.00 C

Tin, "Take Home a Carton" sign, with six-pack featured artwork, 1954, 20"x28", NM. . . . . $600.00 B

Tin, "Things Go Better With Coke" left of bottle, raised border, 1960s, 24"x24", EX. . . . . $225.00 D

Tin, "Things Go Better With Coke" on right, with disc logo at left, 1960s, 21"x11", VG. . . $250.00 C

Tin, "Things Go Better With Coke" on right, with disc logo at left, 1960s, 21"x11", EX . . . $275.00 D

Tin, "Things Go Better With Coke," red border, 1960s, 32"x12", EX. . . . . $200.00 D

Tin, "Things Go Better With Coke" with bottle, disc logo on both sides raised border, 1960s, 54"x18", EX . . . . $300.00 D

Tin, "Things Go Better With Coke" with bottle, disc logo on both sides raised border, 1960s, 54"x18", VG . . . . $250.00 C

Tin, twelve-pack, die cut, 1954, 20"x13", NM . $550.00 D

Tin, two sided die cut triangle with hanging bracket, "Drink Coca-Cola" at top, white lettering on red background with "Ice Cold" at bottom over bottle, 1937, G. . . . . $575.00 D

Tin, two sided flange, "Ice Cold Coca-Cola Sold Here," white lettering on red and green background, 1920s, 12½"x10", G . . . . $400.00 C

Tin, two sided flange with attached 16" buttons at top of arrow, 1950s, G. . . . . $725.00 D

Tin, two sided rack, "Six bottles for 25¢, Take Home a Carton," 1937, 13"x10", EX. . . $300.00 D

Tin, vertical "Enjoy that Refreshing new taste" in fishtail with bottle at bottom on green & white stripe background, 1960s, 16"x41", NM $325.00 D

Tin, vertical "Gas Today" sign, 1937, 18"x54", F. . . . . $300.00 D

Tin, vertical "Gas Today" sign, 1931, 18"x54", EX . . . . $1,300.00 C

Tin, vertical "Pause" sign featuring bottle in spotlight in center, 1940, 18"x54", VG . . . . $350.00 D

Tin, vertical, "Sign of Good Taste," fishtail logo at top over bottle, 1960s, 18"x54", EX. . . . $200.00 C

Tin, vertical, "Take Home A Carton, Big King Size," six pack of big Cokes, self framing, 1962, 20"x28", EX . . . . $250.00 D

Tin, with button and bottle, Canadian, 1956, 28"x20", EX. . . . . $450.00 B

Window decal, "Drink Coca-Cola" with fretwork top, 1940, 25"x12", M . . . . $110.00 B

Window decal, "Drink Coca-Cola" with fretwork top, 1940, 25"x12", M. . . . . $110.00 D

Wood and masonite, "Beverage Department" with Sprite Boy, 1950s, NM . . . . $1,200.00 C

Wood and masonite, "Beverage Department" with Sprite Boy, 1950s, G . . . . $575.00 B

Wood and masonite, hanging, "Drink Coca-Cola. Delicious... Refreshing," with silhouette on left-hand side, 1941, 3'x1', NM . . . . $950.00 C

Wood and masonite, hanging, "Drink Coca-Cola. Delicious... Refreshing," with silhouette in left-hand side, 1941, 3'x1', G . . . . $700.00 B

Wood and masonite, Kay Displays industry work refreshed sign, 1940s, EX . . . . $300.00 C

Wood and masonite, Kay Displays, refreshed communication sign, 1940s, EX. . . . . $200.00 C

Wood and masonite, Kay Displays refreshed communication sign, 1940s, EX. . . . . $275.00 C

Wood arrow, "Drink Coca-Cola Ice Cold," silver painted bottle and arrow, 17" dia., F . . . $400.00 B

Wood, figural, die cut, "Coca-Cola" cooler, probably part of another sign, 1950s, EX . . . . $275.00 C

Wood, "Here's Refreshment," bottle and horseshoe on plank, 1940s, F . . . . $100.00 C

Wood and masonite, Kay Displays transportation, work refreshed, 1940s, EX. . . . . $325.00 D

Wood and masonite, Kay Displays work refreshed, agriculture, 1940, EX . . . . $250.00 D

Wood and masonite, Kay Displays work refreshed, science, 1940, EX . . . . $200.00 C

Wood and masonite, work refreshed, highlighting education, 1940, EX . . . . $200.00 C

Wood and plastic, "Drink Coca-Cola," advertising bar for Roden Soda Bar, unusual Canadian piece, 1940–1950s, 11"x9", NM. . . . . $260.00 C

Wood bottle, 3-D, silver bottle, red background, 1940s, 2'x4', EX. . . . . $250.00 C

Wood, "Drink Coca-Cola" above gold bottle and leaf designs, 1930s, 23"x23", EX . . . . . . $900.00 B

Wood, Kay Displays, "Drink Coca-Cola," two glasses on top of red emblem, 1930s, 9"x11", M. . . . . $875.00 B

Wood, Kay Displays, metal at top showing glasses of Coca-Cola, 1930, EX . . . . $900.00 D

Wood, Kay Displays, "Please Pay Cashier," filigree on ends, 1930s, 22"x12", EX. . . . . . . $1,500.00 B

Wood, Kay Displays "Please Pay Cashier" with Coca-Cola at bottom, 22"x12½", 1950, EX . . . . $375.00 D

Wood, Kay Displays, "Quick Service," 1930, 3"x10", VG. . . . . $2,100.00 B

Wood, "Quick Service" on board with red "Drink Coca-Cola" emblem below, 1930s, 10"x3" EX . . . . $2,000.00 D

Wood, "Quick Service" on board with red "Drink Coca-Cola" emblem below, 1930s, 10"x3", F . . . . $500.00 B

Wood, Kay Displays sign, "Take some home today" double sided with button in center, 1940s, 3' x 1', F . . . . $550.00 C

Wood, Kay Displays, "While Shopping" with "Drink Coca-Cola" at center, 1930, 3"x10", VG . . . . $1,500.00 B

Wood, Kay Displays, "While Shopping" with red "Drink Coca-Cola" below, 1930s, 10"x3", EX . . . . $1,700.00 B

Wood, Kay Displays, "Ye What Enter Here" on board above emblem, 1940s, 39"x11", EX . . . . $475.00 D

Wood, "Please Pay Cashier," cut out rope hanger, 1950s, 15"x19", EX . . . . $275.00 C

Wood, "Quick Service" on board with red "Drink Coca-Cola" emblem below, 1930s, 10"x3", EX . . . . $2,000.00 D

Wood, "Resume Speed/Slow School Zone" two sided on diamonds, 1960s, 48", EX . . . . $875.00 B

Wood, Silhouette Girl, metal hanger, 1940, P . . . . $100.00 D

Wood, Silhouette Girl, metal hanger, 1940, F . . . . $200.00 C

Wood, "Slow School Zone," silhouette girl running, "Resume Speed" on back, 1957, 16"x48", EX. . . . . $525.00 C

Wood, Sprite Boy Welcome Friend, 1940, 32"x14", F . . . . $200.00 C

Wood, Sprite Boy Welcome Friend, 1940, 32"x14", NM. . . . . $725.00 C

Wood, "Sundae/Malt," button logo and Sprite Boy, 1950s, 12"x78", EX . . . . $975.00 C

Wood, "Yes," swimming girl miniature billboard, F . . . . $95.00 C

Wood, "Yes," swimming girl miniature billboard, EX. . . . . $150.00 C

Wooden, Kay Displays sign "Please Pay Cashier" on two bars above "Drink" display, 1930s, 22"x12½", G . . . . $1,950.00 B

Wooden, Kay Displays sign with metal filigree at top with artwork of glasses in center, 1930s, 9"x11½", NM . . . . $900.00 B

Wooden, Kay Displays, "While Shopping" with metal filigree at top and bottom, 1930s, 36"x10", EX . . . . $1,500.00 B

Wooden, outdoor sign, weathered and worn advertising supplies, red and white on green, 1910s, 38"x90", F. . . . . $150.00 C

Wooden, School Zone sign, one side has silhouette girl running, other side has bottle over button, 1957, 16"x48", NM . . . . $2,000.00 C

Calendar top, missing the bottom pad area, 1909, 11"x14", EX, $5,500.00 B.

Muddy River Trading Co./Gary Metz.

Calendars, 75th Anniversary bottlers calendar from Jackson, TN, 1980, EX, $25.00 C. Al & Earlene Mitchell.

"Drink Coca-Cola," brass perpetual desk, EX, $150.00 C. Mitchell Collection.

Perpetual desk showing day, month, and year, 1920, EX, $375.00 D.

Tin, calendar holder with daily tear sheets at bottom featuring tin button at top, red & white, 1950s, 8"x19", EX, $400.00 B.

Muddy River Trading Co./Gary Metz.

1891, from ASA Chandler & Co. featuring girl in period dress holding a sport racquet with full pad moved to reveal full face of sheet, rare, EX, $12,500.00 C.

1897, "Coca-Cola at all Soda Fountains," all monthly pads displayed at once, 7"x12", EX, $10,000.00 C.

1900, Hilda Clark at table with glass, all month pads displayed on front sheet, rare, 7"x12", EX, $10,000.00 D.

1901, "Drink Coca-Cola at all Soda Fountains 5¢" with full monthly pad, framed, matted, and under glass, rare, EX, $5,500.00 C.

1902, "Drink Coca-Cola 5¢" with wrong month sheet, EX, $5,500.00 C.

1904, Lillian Nordica standing by table with a glass, 7"x15", EX, $4,000.00 D.

1905, Lillian Nordica standing beside table holding fan, table has a glass, framed, matted, and under glass, 7"x15", EX, $5,000.00 C.

1906, Juanita, "Drink Coca-Cola Delicious Refreshing," framed, matted, under glass, 7"x15", $5,000.00 D.

1907, "Drink Coca-Cola Delicious Refreshing, Relieves Fatigue Sold Everywhere 5¢" featuring woman in period dress holding up a glass of Coca-Cola, EX, $6,000.00 C.

1908, "Drink Coca-Cola Relieves Fatigue Sold Everywhere 5¢," top only, double this price if calendar is complete, 7"x14", EX, $2,500.00 C.

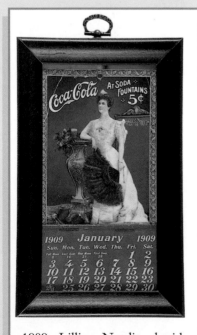

1909, Lillian Nordica beside tall table with a glass, full pad, framed under glass, 3¾"x7", EX, $1,200.00 C. Mitchell Collection.

111

1910, the Coca-Cola Girl with partial month pad matted, framed under glass, 8"x17", King, EX, $5,000.00 C.

1911, the Coca-Cola Girl, "Drink Delicious Coca-Cola," framed under glass, 10"x17", Hamilton King, M, $4,500.00 C. Mitchell Collection.

1912, "Drink Coca-Cola Delicious Refreshing," wrong calendar pad, correct pad should be at bottom of picture, King, EX, $2,500.00 C.

1913, "Drink Coca-Cola Delicious Refreshing," girl drinking from flare glass with syrup line, 13"x22", King, EX, $3,500.00 C.

1913, top, girl in white hat with red ribbon, value would double if complete, rare piece matted and framed under glass, EX, $4,000.00 C. Mitchell Collection.

1914, Betty, top with monthly pad missing, this piece has the bottle featured which is rare, if it were intact and in G to EX condition value would increase to $5,000.00, G, as is, $2000.00 C. Mitchell Collection.

1914, Betty, full pad and original metal strip at top, VG, $1,000.00 B. Muddy River Trading Co./Gary Metz.

1915, Elaine, matted and framed with partial pad, VG, $1,300.00 B. Muddy River Trading Co./Gary Metz.

1916, Elaine with bottle, partial pad, under glass in frame, 13"x32", M, $2,000.00 C. Mitchell Collection.

1916, the World War I Girl holding a glass, she also appears holding a bottle of another version, wrong pad, framed, 13"x32", M, $2,000.00 C.

1917, Constance, with glass, full pad, framed and matted under glass, EX, $2,500.00 C. Mitchell Collection.

1918, June Caprice with glass, framed under glass, G, $375.00 C.

Mitchell Collection.

1919, Knitting Girl, great artwork of girl with bottle and a knitting bag, partial pad, framed under glass, 13"x32", EX, $3,000.00 C. Mitchell Collection.

1919, Marian Davis shown holding a glass, partial pad, framed, matted, under glass example of an early star endorsement, 6"x10½", EX, $3,000.00 C.

1920, Garden Girl with a bottle, actually at a golf course, framed under glass, 12"x32", M, $2,500.00 C. Mitchell Collection.

1921, model sitting beside flowers with a glass, known as the Autumn Girl, partial pad, framed under glass, 12"x32", M, $1,500.00 C.

Mitchell Collection.

1922, girl at baseball game with glass, framed under glass, 12"x32", NM, $2,000.00 C. Mitchell Collection.

1923, girl with shawl and a bottle with a straw, full pad, framed under glass, 12"x24", VG, $850.00 C. Mitchell Collection.

1924, Smiling Girl in period dress holding a glass with a bottle close by, framed under glass. 12"x24", M, $1,200.00 C. Beware: Reproductions exist. Mitchell Collection.

1925, Girl at Party with white fox fur and a glass, framed under glass, 12"x24", M, $1,000.00 C. Beware: Reproductions exist.

Mitchell Collection.

1926, girl in tennis outfit holding a glass, with a bottle, sitting by the tennis racquet, framed under glass, 10"x18", VG, $1,000.00 C.

Mitchell Collection.

1927, girl in sheer dress holding a glass, partial pad, framed under glass, Taylor's Billiard Parlor, 12"x24", M, $1,750.00 C.

Mitchell Collection.

1927, "The Drink that Makes The Whole World Kin," with bottle in oval frame at lower left, framed under glass, M, $1,000.00 C.

Mitchell Collection.

1928, model in evening wear holding glass, partial pad, framed under glass, 12"x24", M, $1,000.00 C. Mitchell Collection.

1929, girl in green dress with string of beads displaying both glass and bottle, full pad, framed under glass, 12"x24", M, $950.00 C.

Mitchell Collection.

1930, woman in swimming attire sitting on rock with canoe in foreground with bottles, display partial pad, framed under glass, 12"x24", M, $1,000.00 C. Mitchell Collection.

1931, boy at fishing hole with dog, sandwich, and a bottle, full pad, framed under glass, 12"x24", Rockwell, M, $850.00 C.

Mitchell Collection.

1932, boy sitting at well with a bucket full of bottles and a dog sitting up at his feet, full pad, framed and under glass, 12"x24", Rockwell, M, $775.00 C.

Mitchell Collection.

1933, the Village Blacksmith will full pad, framed and under glass, 12"x24", Frederic Stanley, M, $750.00 C. Mitchell Collection.

1934, girl on porch playing music for elderly gentleman with cane, full pad, framed under glass, 12"x24", Rockwell, M, $700.00 C.

Mitchell Collection.

1935, boy sitting on a stump fishing with a bottle, full pad, framed under glass, 12"x24", Rockwell, M, $650.00 C. Beware: Reproductions exist. Mitchell Collection.

1936, 50th Anniversary, older man at small boat and a young girl enjoying a bottle, full pad, framed under glass, 12"x24", N. C. Wyeth, M, $750.00 C. Mitchell Collection.

1937, boy walking with fishing pole over his shoulder holding a couple bottles, framed under glass, 12"x24", M, $650.00 C. Mitchell Collection.

1938, girl sitting in front of blinds with a bottle, full pad, framed under glass, Crandall, M, $675.00 C. Mitchell Collection.

1939, girl starting to pour Coca-Cola from bottle into glass, unmarked, full pad, framed under glass, M, $500.00 C. Mitchell Collection.

1940, woman in red dress with a glass and a bottle, full pad, framed and under glass, VG, $500.00 C. Mitchell Collection.

1941, girl sitting on a log with ice skates displaying a bottle, full pad that displays two months at once, EX, $375.00 C. Mitchell Collection.

1942, "America Love It or Leave It" from Brownsville, TN, featuring a drum & fife attachment with monthly pads, EX, $115.00 C. Mitchell Collection.

1942, boy and girl building snowman with a bottle, full pad displays two months at once, VG, $300.00 C. Mitchell Collection.

1943, pocket, "Tastes like Home," small, with all months shown on one front sheet, sailor drinking from a bottle, EX, $55.00 C. Mitchell Collection.

1943, pocket, "Here's to our GI Joes," two girls toasting with bottles, EX, $55.00 C.

Mitchell Collection.

1943, military nurse with a bottle, full pad displays two months at once, EX, $375.00 C.

Mitchell Collection.

1944, woman holding a bottle, full pad, EX, $250.00 C. Mitchell Collection.

1945, girl in head scarf with snow falling in the background, full pad, EX, $300.00 C. Mitchell Collection.

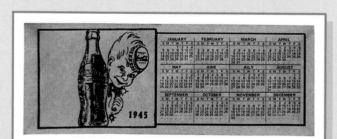

1945, pocket, with Sprite Boy looking around bottle on left side, EX, $45.00 C. Mitchell Collection.

1946, Sprite Boy on cover with two months and a scene on each page, framed under glass, EX, $1,250.00 C. Mitchell Collection.

1947, girl holding snow skis with mountains in background, full pad, EX, $325.00 C. Mitchell Collection.

1948, girl in coat and gloves holding a bottle, full pad, EX, $325.00 C. Mitchell Collection.

1949, girl in red cap with a bottle, full pad, M, $275.00 C. Mitchell Collection.

1950, woman with a serving tray full of bottles, full pad, M, $275.00 C. Mitchell Collection.

1951, girl at party holding a bottle, with colorful streamers in background, full pad, M, $150.00 C. Mitchell Collection.

1952, "Coke adds Zest," party scene with a girl serving bottles from tray, full calendar pad, M, $175.00 C.

Mitchell Collection.

1953, Boy Scout, Cub Scout, and Explorer Scout in front of the Liberty Bell, Coca-Cola Bottling Works, Greenwood, Mississippi, matted and framed under glass, Rockwell, EX, $375.00 D.

Mitchell Collection.

1953, "Work Better Refreshed," work scenes with woman in center in work scarf holding a bottle, full pad, M, $175.00 C. Mitchell Collection.

1954, "Me, too!" with 1953 Santa cover sheet, full pad, owner recorded high and low temperatures of each day, VG, $140.00 B. Muddy River Trading Co./Gary Metz.

1954, reference edition with full pad featuring Santa with a bottle, EX, $100.00 C. Mitchell Collection.

1954, sports scene in background with woman in foreground holding a bottle, full calendar pad, M, $175.00 C. Mitchell Collection.

1955, woman in hat holding a bottle, full pad, M, $175.00 C. Mitchell Collection.

1956, famous flower paintings, reference version, EX, $25.00 C. Mitchell Collection.

1956, "There's nothing like a Coke," full pad, featuring girl pulling on ice skates, M, $135.00 C. Mitchell Collection.

1957, reference edition of flower prints with Santa on front, M, $25.00 C. Mitchell Collection.

1957, "The pause that refreshes," girl holding ski poles and a bottle, EX, $85.00 C. Mitchell Collection.

1958, snow scene of a boy and girl with a bottle, "Sign of Good Taste," full pad, M, $175.00 C. Mitchell Collection.

1958, reference edition with "Sign of Good Taste" with flowers against a brick background, M, $20.00 C. Mitchell Collection.

1959, birds sitting on branch with a Coke button under branch, reference version, Athos Menaboni, M, $30.00 D. Mitchell Collection.

1959, girl being offered a bottle in front of a sports scene, full pad, G, $135.00 C. Mitchell Collection.

1960, "Be Really Refreshed," featuring man and woman holding skis each with a bottle, full pad, M, $75.00 C. Mitchell Collection.

1960, reference with puppies in Christmas stockings, EX, $25.00 C. Mitchell Collection.

1961, "Coke Refreshes You Best," woman being offered a bottle, full pad, M, $75.00 C. Mitchell Collection.

1961, reference with Santa sitting in an easy chair holding a glass that's being filled by an elf, M, $30.00 C. Mitchell Collection.

1962, "Enjoy that Refreshing New Feeling," boy holding bottle and offering other hand to dance with a young woman, M, $75.00 C. Mitchell Collection.

1962, reference of birds of America, M, $25.00 C.

Mitchell Collection.

1963, reference edition with Santa Claus, holding a bottle, in middle of electric train display in front of Christmas tree with helicopter flying around his head, M, $35.00 C. Mitchell Collection.

1963, "The Pause that Refreshes," with a woman looking at new clothes in a door mirror, M, $75.00 C. Mitchell Collection.

1964, reference featuring Santa standing by a fireplace with his list and a bottle, M, $25.00 C.

Mitchell Collection.

1965, reference edition with Santa and children, M, $25.00 C.

Mitchell Collection.

1964, "Things go better with Coke," featuring a woman reclining on a couch while a man is offering her a bottle, M, $85.00 C. Mitchell Collection.

1965, "Things go better with Coke," a couple relaxing by a log cabin, each with a bottle, $75.00 C. Mitchell Collection.

1966, man pictured holding serving tray with food and bottles over woman's head, full pad, "Things Go Better with Coke," M, $85.00 C. Mitchell Collection.

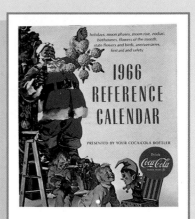

1966, Santa Claus standing on ladder with a bottle and a Christmas ornament in front of a Christmas tree, M, $25.00 C. Mitchell Collection.

1967, "For the taste you never get tired of," featuring five women with trophy, full pad, M, $55.00 C. Mitchell Collection.

1967, reference edition with Santa Claus sitting at desk with a bottle, EX, $20.00 C. Mitchell Collection.

1968, "Coke has the taste you never get tired of," girl looking at 45rpm record and holding a bottle, with full pad, M, $75.00 C. Mitchell Collection.

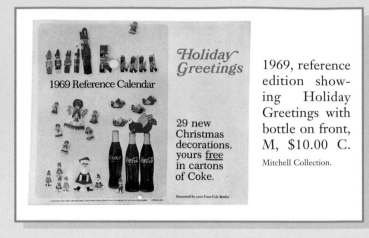

1969, reference edition showing Holiday Greetings with bottle on front, M, $10.00 C.
Mitchell Collection.

1969, "Things go better with Coke," featuring boy whispering into girl's ear while both are seated at a table enjoying a bottle, full pad, M, $75.00 C. Mitchell Collection.

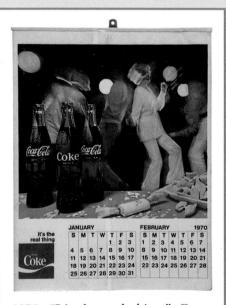

1970, "It's the real thing," Coca-Cola presented its new image here, one that many collectors don't care to collect, so demand for 1970 or newer calendars is not great — yet!, M, $20.00 C. Mitchell Collection.

1970, reference edition featuring Santa with a bottle, M, $15.00 C.
Mitchell Collection.

1972, cloth featuring Lillian Nordica, EX, $10.00 C.

1973, cloth with Lillian Nordica standing by Coca-Cola table, EX, $5.00 D.

1975, scenes of America showing backpackers, with full pad, M, $15.00 C. Mitchell Collection.

1976, "Look up America," "It's the real thing – Coke," with full pad, M, $30.00 C. Mitchell Collection.

1979 Olympic torch, full pad, M, $15.00 C. Mitchell Collection.

1981, "Have a Coke and a smile," full pad with scenes of America at top, EX, $15.00 C.
Mitchell Collection.

"Drink Coca-Cola," brass perpetual desk, MIN . . . . $300.00 C

Perpetual desk showing day, month, and year, 1920, P . . . . $35.00 D

Tin, embossed calendar holder with a new 1988 pad, with "Drink" fishtail at top, red and white, 1960s, 9"x13", EX. . . . . $135.00 C

Tin, fishtail calendar holder with daily tear sheets at bottom, red & white, 1960s, 9"x13", NM. . $175.00 C

1891, from ASA Chandler & Co. featuring girl in period dress holding sport racquet with full pad moved to reveal full face of sheet, rare, EX. . . . . . $10,500.00 B

1904, Lillian Nordica standing by table with a glass, 7"x15", F. . . . . $2,200.00 D

1905, Lillian Nordica standing beside table holding fan, table has a glass, framed, matted, and under glass, 7"x15", G. . . . . $3,500.00 C

1907, "Drink Coca-Cola Delicious Refreshing, Relieves Fatigue, Sold Everywhere 5¢," G . . . . . . $2,500.00 D

1908, "Drink Coca-Cola Relieves Fatigue Sold Everywhere 5¢," top only, double this price if calendar is complete, 7 x 14, G. . . . . $1,000.00 C

1911, the Coca-Cola Girl, "Drink Delicious Coca-Cola," framed, 10"x17", Hamilton King, F . . . . . . $1,800.00 C

1912, "Drink Coca-Cola Delicious Refreshing," large version of this year's calendar, 12"x30", King, EX . . . . $5,000.00 C

1912, "Drink Coca-Cola Delicious and Refreshing," King, P. . . . .$750.00 C

1913, top, girl in white hat with red ribbon, value would double if complete, rare piece matted and framed under glass, G . . . . $1,950.00 C

1914, Betty, with full pad, F . . . . $350.00 C

1916, Elaine with glass, pad, 13"x32", EX . $1,500.00 D

1916, World War I Girl holding a glass, she also appears holding a bottle of another version, wrong pad, framed, 13"x32", VG . . . . $1,000.00 C

1917, Constance, with glass, full pad, matted and framed under glass, G . . . . $1,500.00 C

1918, June Caprice with glass, framed under glass, P . . . . $75.00 C

1918, two women at beach, one with a bottle, the other has a glass, wrong pad, 13"x32", EX . . . . $4,000.00 C

1919, Knitting Girl, great artwork of girl with bottle and a knitting bag, partial pad, 13"x32", G . . . . $1,250.00 C

1920, Garden Girl with bottle, 12"x32", EX . $1,750.00 C

1921, Autumn Girl, 12"x32", EX . . . . . $1,000.00 C

1922, girl at baseball game with a glass, 12"x32", EX . . . . $1,500.00 C

1923, girl with shawl and a bottle with straw, full pad, 12"x24", G . . . . $700.00 C

1924, Smiling Girl holding a glass with a bottle close by, 12"x24", Beware: Reproductions exist. VG . . $900.00 B

1925, girl at party with white fox fur and a glass, 12"x24". Beware: Reproductions exist. EX . . . . $750.00 C

1926, girl in tennis outfit holding a glass, with a bottle sitting by the tennis racquet, 10"x18", G . . . $750.00 C

1927, "The Drink that Makes The Whole World Kin," G. . . . . $750.00 C

1927, "The Drink that Makes The Whole World Kin," with bottle in oval frame at lower left, VG . . $750.00 C

1928, model in evening wear holding glass, partial pad, 12" x 24", VG . . . . $850.00 C

1929, girl in green dress, string of beads, glass and bottle, full pad, 12" x 24", VG . . . . $725.00 C

1930, woman in swimming attire sitting on rock with canoe in foreground with bottles, partial pad, 12"x24", VG . . . . $695.00 D

1933, the Village Blacksmith with full pad, 12"x24", Frederic Stanley, G . . . . $600.00 C

1934, girl on porch playing music for elderly gentleman with cane, full pad, 12"x24", Rockwell, G. . . . . $425.00 C

1935, boy with a bottle sitting on a stump fishing, full pad, 12" x 24", Rockwell, Beware: Reproductions exist. EX. . . . . $500.00 C

1936, 50th Anniversary, older man at small boat and a young girl enjoying a bottle, full pad, 12" x 24", N. C. Wyeth, G, ... $425.00 C

1937, boy walking, fishing pole over his shoulder, holding bottles, 12" x 24", EX. . . . . $475.00 C

1941, girl wearing ice skates sitting on log, displaying a bottle, full pad displays two months at same time, G . . . . $200.00 C

1942, "America Love It or Leave It" from Brownsville, Tenn., featuring a drum & fife attachment, with monthly pads, G . . . . $65.00 C

1943, military nurse with a bottle, full pad displays two months at same time, G . . . . $275.00 C

1943, pocket, "Tastes like Home," small, with all months shown on one front sheet, sailor drinking from a bottle, G. . . . . $30.00 C

1945, Boy Scout in front of the Scout Oath, Rockwell, M . . . . $500.00 D

1945, girl in head scarf with snow falling in the background, full pad, VG. . . . . $225.00 C

1946, Boy Scout den chief showing younger Cub Scout how to tie a knot, Rockwell, VG. . . $400.00 D

1946, Sprite Boy on cover with two months and a scene on each page, G . . . . $825.00 C

1948, girl in coat and gloves, holding a bottle, full pad, G . . . . $175.00 C

1952, "Coke adds Zest," full calendar pad, VG . . . . $100.00 C

1953, Boy Scout, Cub Scout, Explorer Scout in front of Liberty Bell, Coca-Cola Bottling Works, Greenwood, Mississippi, Rockwell, G . . . . $200.00 C

1953, "Work Better Refreshed," full pad, G . $95.00 C

1954, "Me, too!" 1953 Santa cover sheet, full pad, G . . . . $75.00 C
1954, reference edition with full pad featuring Santa with bottle, VG . . . . $75.00 C

1955, reference edition with Santa holding a bottle, M . . . . $25.00 C

1956, "There's nothing like a Coke," full pad, EX . . . . $100.00 C

1957, "The pause that refreshes," girl holding ski poles and bottle, G . . . . $50.00 C

1958, snow scene of a boy and girl with a bottle, "Sign of Good Taste," full pad, EX . . . . $125.00 C

1960, "Be Really Refreshed," G . . . . $35.00 C

1960, reference with puppies in Christmas stockings, VG . . . . $12.00 D

1961, Santa reference calendar, VG . . . . . . $15.00 C

1963, reference edition with Santa Claus, holding a bottle, in middle of electric train display in front of Christmas tree with helicopter flying around his head, G . $15.00 C

1964, Japanese girl pictured on front, full pad, EX . . . . $375.00 B

1964, reference featuring Santa standing by a fireplace with his list and a bottle, VG . . . . $12.00 C

1964, "Things go better with Coke," featuring a woman reclining on a couch while a man is offering her a bottle, VG . . . . $65.00 C

1965, reference edition with Santa and children, VG . . . . $15.00 C

1967, "For the taste you never get tired of," featuring five women with trophy, full pad, VG . . . . $25.00 C

1967, reference edition with Santa Claus sitting at desk with a bottle, G . . . . $8.00 C

1968, "Coke has the taste you never get tired of," girl looking at 45rpm record and holding a bottle, with full pad, EX . . . . $60.00 C

1968, reference edition of Santa on ladder, M . . . . $25.00 D

1969, reference edition showing Holiday Greetings, bottle on front, EX . . . . $8.00 C

1970, "It's the real thing," Coca-Cola presented its new image here, one that many collectors don't care to collect, so the demand for 1970 or newer calendars is not great... yet!, G . . . . $5.00 C

1970, reference edition featuring Santa with a bottle, EX . . . . $10.00 C

1970s, tin holder with wave logo at top and tear-off day sheets on bottom, EX . . . . $65.00 D

1971, shadow box with full pad, M . . . . $25.00 D

1972, cloth featuring Lillian Nordica, VG . . $5.00 D

1972, "Featuring crafts & hobbies to enjoy with the real thing. Coke," M . . . . $20.00 D

1974, 1927 reproduction, reverse image, full pad, M . . . . $20.00 D

1978, air-borne snow skier, full pad, M . . . . $10.00 D

1980, sports scenes, full pad, M . . . . $10.00 D

1982, four women around piano, full pad, M . . . . $15.00 D

1983, iced down bottles in front of a bonfire, full pad, M . . . . $10.00 D

Candles TV tray, 1961, 18¾"x13½", EX, $15.00 D.

Change, "Drink a Bottle of Carbonated Coca-Cola," 1903, 5½" dia., EX, $5,000.00 C.

Top left: Change, "Drink Coca-Cola Delicious Refreshing," Juanita, 1900S, 4" dia., EX, $1,000.00 D. Top right: Change, World War I Girl, 1916, 4⅜"x6⅛", EX, $325.00 C. Bottom left: Change, "Drink Coca-Cola, Relieves Fatigue," 1907, EX, $725.00 C. Bottom right: Change, featuring Betty, 1914, EX, $425.00 C. Mitchell Collection.

Change, featuring Hilda Clark, round, 1903, 6" dia., VG, $2,300.00 B.

Muddy River Trading Co./Gary Metz.

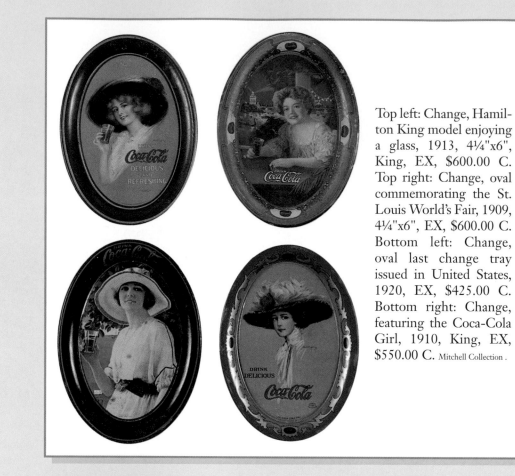

Top left: Change, Hamilton King model enjoying a glass, 1913, 4¼"x6", King, EX, $600.00 C. Top right: Change, oval commemorating the St. Louis World's Fair, 1909, 4¼"x6", EX, $600.00 C. Bottom left: Change, oval last change tray issued in United States, 1920, EX, $425.00 C. Bottom right: Change, featuring the Coca-Cola Girl, 1910, King, EX, $550.00 C. Mitchell Collection .

Change, featuring the Coca-Cola Girl by Hamilton King, 1909–10, 4⅜"x6⅛", King, VG, $350.00 B. Muddy River Trading Co./Gary Metz.

Change, Hilda Clark, 1901, 6" dia., VG, $1,250.00 B. Muddy River Trading Co./Gary Metz.

Change, Hilda Clark at table with stationery holding a glass in a glass holder, 1903, 6" dia., EX, $1,700.00 B.

Change, Hilda Clark, metal, 1903, 4" dia., EX, $2,300.00 D.

Change, Hilda Clark seated at table with glass, 1900, 6" dia., EX, $3,500.00 D.

Change, Hilda Clark with flowers, 1901, 6" dia., EX, $2,500.00 C.

Change receiver, ceramic, with dark lettering and red line outline "The Ideal Brain Tonic, For Headache and Exhaustion," 1899, EX, $5,500.00 C.

Change receiver, glass, "Drink Coca-Cola 5¢," 1907, 7" dia., EX, $1,100.00 C.

Change receiver, Griselda Change, 1905, 13"x13", EX, $875.00 D.

Change receiver, Hilda Clark, glass, 1900, 8½" dia., EX, $4,500.00 C.

Christmas serving tray, there are many variations of this tray, 1973, EX, $10.00 D.

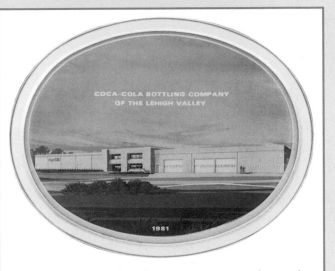

Commemorative bottlers serving tray from the Lehigh Valley with artwork of plant, 1981, EX, $12.00 C. Al & Earlene Mitchell.

Serving, Autumn Girl, this model is featured on the 1922 calendar, rectangular, 1920s, 10½"x13¼", EX, $900.00 C. Mitchell Collection.

Serving, Betty, manufactured by Stelad Signs, Passic New Jersey, oval, 1914, 12½"x15¼", EX, $825.00 C. Beware of reproductions. Mitchell Collection.

Serving, boy and dog, boy is holding sandwich and a bottle, 1931, 10½"x13¼", Rockwell, EX, $875.00 C. Mitchell Collection.

Serving, Canadian commemorative with the English version, with Lillian Nordica, 1968, 10½"x13¼", EX, $85.00 C. Mitchell Collection.

Serving, Coca-Cola Girl holding a glass, 1913, 10½"x13¼", King, EX, 900.00 C. Beware of reproductions. Mitchell Collection.

Serving, Coca-Cola Girl, oval, 1913, 12¼"x14¼", King, EX, $950.00 C. Mitchell Collection.

Serving, "Coca-Cola" with good litho by Western Coca-Cola Bottling Company of Chicago, Illinois, without the sanction of the Coca-Cola Company, 1908, VG, $4,500.00 B. Muddy River Trading Co./Gary Metz.

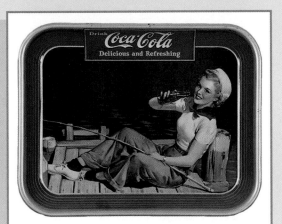

Serving, "Drink Coca-Cola, Delicious and Refreshing," girl on dock, Sailor Girl, 1940, 13¼"x10½", EX, $261.00 B. Buffalo Bay Auction Co.

Serving, "Drink Coca-Cola, Refreshing Delicious," featuring Hilda Clark, 1900, 9¼" dia., EX, $7,500.00 B.

Serving, "Drink Coca-Cola Relieves Fatigue," oval, 1907, 10½"x13¼", EX, $2,250.00 C. Mitchell Collection.

Serving, featuring a couple receiving curb service, 1927, 13¼"x10½", G, $700.00 C. <small>Mitchell Collection.</small>

Serving, featuring a pull cart with a picnic basket, 1958, 13¼"x10½", EX, $25.00 C. <small>Mitchell Collection.</small>

Serving, featuring Betty, rectangular, 1914, 10½"x13¼", EX, $775.00 C. Beware of reproductions. <small>Mitchell Collection.</small>

Serving, featuring birdhouse full of flowers, French version, 1950s, 10½"x13¼", EX, $110.00 C. <small>Mitchell Collection.</small>

Serving, featuring Elaine, manufactured by Stelad Signs Passaic Metal Ware Company, Passaic, New Jersey, rectangular, 1916, 8½"x19", EX, $575.00 C. Beware of reproductions.

Mitchell Collection.

Serving, featuring girl on arm of chair in party dress, Hostess, 1936, 10½"x13¼", EX, $400.00 C. Mitchell Collection.

Serving, featuring girl on beach in chair with a bottle, 1932, 10½"x13¼", EX, $650.00 C. Mitchell Collection.

Serving, featuring girl running on beach with bottles in each hand, 1937, EX, $300.00 C. Beware of reproductions. Mitchell Collection.

Serving, featuring girl on log with ice skates and a bottle, 1941, 10½"x13¼", EX, $325.00 C. Mitchell Collection.

Serving, featuring Lillian Nordica on Canadian commemorative, 1968, 10½"x3¼", EX, $85.00 C. Mitchell Collection.

Serving, featuring movie star Madge Evans, manufactured by American Art Works, Inc, Coshocton, Ohio, 1935, 10½"x13¼", EX, $400.00 D. Mitchell Collection.

Serving, featuring red-haired woman in yellow scarf with a bottle, 1950s, 10½"x13¼", EX, $125.00 C. Beware of reproductions. Mitchell Collection.

Serving, featuring the Coca-Cola Girl, this was the first rectangular tray used by the Coca-Cola Company by American Art Work, Inc., 1909, 10½"x13¼", King, EX, $1,200.00 C. Beware of reproductions. Mitchell Collection.

Serving, featuring the famous Maureen O'Sullivan and Johnny Weissmuller both holding bottles, 1934, 13¼"x10½", EX, $900.00 C. Beware of reproductions. Mitchell Collection.

Serving, featuring the girl at party, 1921, 10½"x13¼", EX, $475.00 C. Mitchell Collection.

Serving, featuring the movie star, Francis Dee, 1933, 10½"x13¼", EX, $550.00 C. Mitchell Collection.

Serving, featuring the Smiling Girl holding a glass, this tray can have either a brown or maroon border, add $200.00 for maroon tray, 1924, 10½"x13¼", EX, $700.00 C. Mitchell Collection.

Serving, featuring the Summer Girl, manufactured by the H. D. Beach Company, Coshocton, Ohio, 1922, 10½"x13¼", EX, $825.00 C. Mitchell Collection.

Serving, featuring woman in rain coat with umbrella and a bottle, French version, 1950s, 10½"x13¼", G, $150.00 C. Mitchell Collection.

Serving, Flapper Girl, 1923, 10½"x13¼", EX, $400.00 C.

Mitchell Collection.

Serving, French, featuring food and bottles on table, 1957, EX, $100.00 C. Mitchell Collection.

Serving, Garden Girl, 1920, 13¼"x16½", EX, $875.00 C. Mitchell Collection.

Serving, girl in afternoon with a bottle, produced by American Art Works Inc, Coshocton, Ohio, 1938, 10½"x13¼", EX, $275.00 C. Mitchell Collection.

Serving, girl in swimsuit holding bottle, promoting bottle sales, 1929, 10½"x13¼", EX, $700.00 C.

Serving, girl on a spring board, 1939, 10½"x13¼", EX, $300.00 C. Mitchell Collection.

Serving, Hilda Clark, "Drink Coca-Cola Invigorating, Refreshing, Delicious," 1899, 9¼" dia., EX, $10,500.00 D.

Serving, Hilda Clark, round, 1903, 9½" dia., NM, $3,200.00 B.

Muddy River Trading Co./Gary Metz.

Serving, "Here's a Coke for you," more than three versions of this tray, 1961, 13¼"x10½", EX, $25.00 C. Mitchell Collection.

Serving, Juanita, oval, "Drink Coca-Cola, In Bottles 5¢, at Fountains 5¢," 1906, 10½"x13¼", EX, $2,500.00 D.

Serving, Lillian Nordica, "Drink Coca-Cola at Soda Fountains, Delicious Refreshing," oval, 1905, 10½"x13", EX, $4,000.00 D.

Serving, Menu Girl, French version, 1955 – 60, 10½"x13¼", EX, $100.00 D.

Serving, Menu Girl holding a bottle in her hand, 1950s, 10½"x13¼", EX, $75.00 C. Mitchell Collection.

Serving, miscellaneous items, French version, 1950s, 10½"x13¼", G, $110.00 C.

Mitchell Collection.

Serving, picnic basket, 1958, 11¼"x10½", EX, $45.00 D.

Serving, promoting bottle sales, 1929, 10½"x13¼", F, $450.00 C.
Mitchell Collection.

Serving promoting bottle sales, bobbed hair girl drinking from bottle with a straw, 1928, 10½"x13¼", EX, $725.00 C. Mitchell Collection.

Serving, promoting bottle sales, girl in red swim cap and bathing suit with towel, 1930, EX, $450.00 C.
Mitchell Collection.

Serving, promoting fountain sales featuring girl in yellow swimsuit, produced by American Art Works Inc. of Coshocton, Ohio, 1929, 10½"x13¼", EX, $550.00 C.

Mitchell Collection.

Serving, promoting fountain sales, girl on phone, "meet me at the soda fountain," 1930, 10½"x13¼", EX, $475.00 C. Mitchell Collection.

Serving, promoting fountain sales with soda person (the term "soda jerk" wasn't used until much later), 1928, 10½"x13¼", EX, $650.00 C; G, $308.00 B. Mitchell Collection.

Serving, round, "Drink a Bottle of Carbonated Coca-Cola, The Most Refreshing Drink in the World," 1903, 9¾" dia., EX, $6,500.00 D.

Serving, sports couple, 1926, 10½"x13¼", EX, $800.00 C. Beware of reproductions. Mitchell Collection.

Serving, St. Louis Fair, oval, 1909, 13½"x16½", EX, $2,800.00 C. Mitchell Collection.

Serving, two women at car with bottles, because of metal needed in the war effort this was the last tray produced until after World War II, 1942, EX, $325.00 C; G, $104.00 B. Mitchell Collection.

Serving, Victorian Girl, "Drink Coca-Cola, Refreshing, Delicious," woman drinking from a glass, 1897, 9¼" dia., EX, $14,000.00 B.

Serving, with Garden Girl, 1920, 10½"x13¼", EX, $875.00 C.

Mitchell Collection.

Trays, Commemorative Alabama/Auburn tray, 1975, EX, $25.00 C. Al & Earlene Mitchell.

TV assortment, 1956, 18¾"x13½", EX, $15.00 D.

TV, Duster Girl, 1972, 10¾"x14¾", EX, $10.00 C.

TV, Thanksgiving, 1961, 187¾"x13½", EX, $20.00 C.

Canadian, 1957, 14¼"x10½", EX. . . . . . $150.00 C

Change, "Drink a Bottle of Carbonated Coca-Cola," 1903, 5½" dia., F . . . . $2,000.00 C

Change, featuring Hilda Clark, round, 1903, 6" dia., G . . . . $1,200.00 C

Change, featuring the Coca-Cola Girl, 1910, King, VG . . . . $375.00 C

Change, featuring the Coca-Cola Girl by Hamilton King, 1909 – 10, 4⅜"x6⅛", King, G . . . $175.00 C

Change receiver, ceramic, "The Ideal Brain Tonic" with red lettering, 1890s, 10½" dia., EX . . . . $4,500.00 C

Change receiver, ceramic, with dark lettering and red line outline "The Ideal Brain Tonic, For Headache and Exhaustion," 1899, F . . $2,500.00 C

Change receiver, glass, "Drink Coca-Cola 5¢," 1907, 7" dia., F . . . . $550.00 C

Change receiver, Griselda Change, 1905, 13"x13", NM . . . . $950.00 D

Change receiver, Hilda Clark, glass, 1900, 8½" dia., EX . . . . $4,500.00 D

Christmas serving tray, there are many variations of this tray, 1973, EX. . . . . $15.00 D

"Drink Coca-Cola, Delicious Refreshing," red background with yellow and white lettering, fairly rare, 1940 – 50s, 12¾" dia., EX . . . . $325.00 C

Serving, Autumn Girl, rectangular, 1920s, 10½"x13¼", VG . . . . $700.00 C

Serving, Betty, manufactured by Stelad Signs, Passaic, New Jersey, oval, 1914, 12½"x15¼". Beware of reproductions. P . . . . $125.00 C

Serving, boy and dog, boy is holding sandwich and a bottle, 1931, 10½"x13¼", Rockwell, VG. $750.00 C

Serving, Captain James Cook bicentennial, produced to celebrate the landing at Nootka Sound, B.C, "Coca-Cola" on back, 1978, EX . . . $25.00 D

Serving, Captain James Cook bicentennial, produced to celebrate landing at Nootka Sound, B.C, "Coca-Cola" on back, 1978, EX . . . . $25.00 D

Serving, "Coca-Cola" with good litho by Western Coca-Cola Bottling Company of Chicago, Illinois, without the sanction of the Coca-Cola Company, 1908, F . . . . $2,500.00 C

Serving, Coca-Cola Girl holding a glass, 1913, 10½"x13¼", King, Beware of reproductions. G . . . . $500.00 C

Serving, Curb Service for fountain sales, 1928, EX . . . . $700.00 B

Serving, "Drink Coca-Cola, Delicious and Refreshing," Sailor Girl, 1940, 13¼"x10½", F . . . $75.00 C

Serving, "Drink Coca-Cola Relieves Fatigue," oval, 1907, 10½"x13¼", EX . . . . $2,250.00 B

Serving, "Drive-In," "Drink Coca-Cola" in fishtail logo "Goes good with food" under logo "Drive in for Coke" on rim, a hard to find piece, 1959, VG . . . . . $125.00 C

Serving, Edmonton, rectangular, 1978, 10½"x13¼", EX . . . . $25.00 C

Serving, Elaine, 1916, 8½"x19", EX . . . $350.00 D

Serving, featuring a couple receiving curb service, 1927, 13¼"x10½", NM . . . . $875.00 C

Serving, featuring a pull cart with a picnic basket, 1958, 13¼"x10½", P . . . . $5.00 C

Serving, featuring Betty, rectangular, 1914, 10½"x13¼", Beware of reproductions. F . . $425.00 C

Serving, featuring birdhouse full of flowers, French version, 1950s, 10½"x13¼", F . . . . $25.00 D

Serving, featuring bottle of Coca-Cola with food, Mexican, 1970, 13¼", M . . . . $25.00 D

Serving, featuring Elaine, manufactured by Stelad Signs Passaic Metal Ware Company, Passaic, New Jersey, rectangular, 1916, 8½"x19". Beware of reproductions. P . . . . $200.00 C

Serving, featuring girl at party, 1921, 10½"x13¼", P . . . . $200.00 C

Serving, featuring girl on arm of chair in party dress, Hostess, 1936, 10½"x13¼", G . . . . $250.00 C

Serving, featuring girl on beach in chair with a bottle, 1932, 10½"x13¼", G . . . . $375.00 C

Serving, featuring girl running on beach with bottle in each hand, 1937. Beware of reproductions. P . . . . $100.00 D

Serving, featuring ice skater with bottle on log, 1941, 10½"x13¼", G . . . . $200.00 C

Serving, featuring Lillian Nordica on Canadian commemorative, 1968, 10½"x13¼", VG . $60.00 C

Serving, featuring movie star Madge Evans, manufactured by American Art Works, Inc., Coshocton, Ohio, 1935, 10½"x13¼", VG . . . . $350.00 C

Serving, featuring red-haired woman in yellow scarf with a bottle, 1950s, 10½"x13¼". Beware of reproductions. G . . . . $75.00 C

Serving, featuring the Coca-Cola Girl; this was the first rectangular tray used by the Coca-Cola Company by American Art Works, Inc., 1909, 10½"x13¼", King. Beware of reproductions. G . . . . $725.00 C

Serving, featuring the famous Maureen O'Sullivan and Johnny Weissmuller, 1934, 13¼"x10½". Beware of reproductions. P . . . . $300.00 C

Serving, featuring the movie star, Francis Dee, 1933, 10½"x13¼", G . . . . $325.00 C

Serving, featuring the Smiling Girl holding a glass, 1924, 10½"x13¼", EX . . . . $525.00 C

Serving, featuring the Summer Girl, 1922, 10½"x13¼", VG . . . . $675.00 C

Serving, Flapper Girl, 1923, 10½"x13¼", F . . . . $75.00 C

Serving, Garden Girl, 1920, 13¼"x16½", G . . . . $350.00 C

Serving, girl in afternoon with a bottle, produced by American Art Works Inc., Coshocton, Ohio, 1938, 10½"x13¼", VG . . . . $200.00 C

Serving, girl in swimsuit holding bottle, promoting bottle sales, 1929, 10½"x13¼", VG . . . . $575.00 C

Serving, girl on a spring board, 1939, 10½"x13¼", VG . . . . $200.00 C

Serving, girl with glass and bottle, Mexican, round, 1965, 13¼" dia., M . . . . $110.00 D

Serving, "Hambly's Beverage Limited," featuring World War I girl, 60th anniversary, 1977, EX . . . . . $25.00 D

Serving, "Here's a Coke for you," more than three versions of this tray, 1961, 13¼"x10½", F . $15.00 D

Serving, Juanita, bottle version, 1906, 10½"x13½", EX . . . . $2,500.00 D

Serving, Juanita, oval, "Drink Coca-Cola, In Bottles 5¢, at Fountains 5¢," 1906, 10½"x13¼", F . . . . $750.00 C

Serving, Lillian Nordica, "Drink Carbonated Coca-Cola in Bottles 5¢ Delicious Refreshing," oval, 1905, 10½"x13", EX . . . . $4,000.00 C

Serving, Menu Girl holding a bottle in her hand, 1950s, 10½"x13¼", G . . . . $35.00 D

Serving, oval, Hilda Clark, 1903, 15"x18½", EX. . . . . $5,100.00 B

Serving, pansy garden, 1961, 13¼"x10½", EX . . . . $30.00 B

Serving, promoting bottle sales, bobbed hair girl drinking from bottle with a straw, 1928, 10½"x13¼", VG . . . . $650.00 C

Serving, promoting bottle sales, girl in red swim cap and bathing suit with a towel, 1930, G. . $275.00 C

Serving, promoting fountain sales featuring girl in yellow swimsuit, produced by American Art Works Inc. of Coshocton, Ohio, 1929, 10½"x13¼", VG. . . . $475.00 C

Serving, promoting fountain sales, girl on phone, "meet me at the soda fountain," 1930, 10½"x13¼", VG . . . . $350.00 C

Serving, promoting fountain sales with soda jerk, 1928, 10½"x13¼", F . . . . $225.00 C

Serving, rectangular, covered bridge with "Coca-Cola" on side, Summer Bridge, 1995, Jim Harrison, EX. . . . . $10.00 D

Serving, rectangular, "Goodwill Bottling Std.," logo in lower right, 1979, EX . . . . $15.00 D

Serving, red-haired girl with wind in hair on solid background, 1950. Beware: Reproductions exist. EX. . . . . $175.00 C

Serving, round, "Drink a Bottle of Carbonated Coca-Cola, The Most Refreshing Drink in the World," 1903, 9¾" dia., NM. . . . . $7,000.00 C

Serving, round, featuring University of Indiana basketball, 1976, EX. . . . . $25.00 D

Serving, sports couple, 1926, 10½"x13¼". Beware of reproductions. VG . . . . $725.00 B

Serving, St. Louis Fair, oval, 1909, 13½"x16½", VG . . . . $1,800.00 C

Serving, two women at car with bottles, because of metal needed in the war effort this was the last tray produced until after World War II, 1942, NM . . . . $400.00 C

Serving, with Garden Girl, 1920, 10½"x13¼", G. . . . . $575.00 C

St. Louis Fair, 1909, 10½"x13¼", EX . $1,500.00 C

TV assortment, 1956, 18¾"x13½", EX . . $15.00 D

TV, Duster Girl, 1972, 10¾"x14¾", EX . $10.00 D

TV, Thanksgiving, 1961, 18¾"x13¾", EX $15.00 D

Victorian Girl, "Drink Coca-Cola, Refreshing, Delicious," woman drinking from a glass, 1897, 9¼" dia., F . . . . $3,500.00 C

Advertisement from the Chicago Daily News, full page, 1908, EX, $10.00 B.

Muddy River Trading Co./Gary Metz.

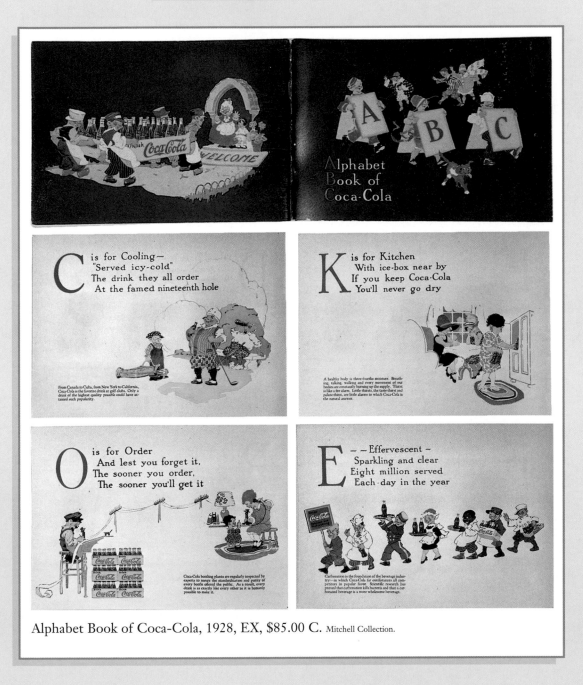

Alphabet Book of Coca-Cola, 1928, EX, $85.00 C. Mitchell Collection.

Book, 1942 advertising price list, 1942, EX, $190.00 B.

Muddy River Trading Co./Gary Metz.

Book, 1943 price list for advertising, 1943, EX, $225.00 B.

Muddy River Trading Co./Gary Metz.

Book, 1944 advertising price list, 1944, EX, $250.00 B. Muddy River Trading C./Gary Metz.

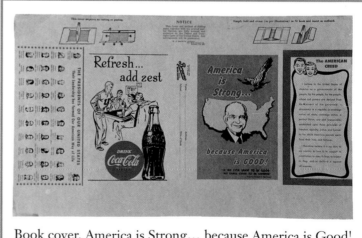

Book cover, America is Strong… because America is Good! with Dwight Eisenhower on front, 1950s, EX, $10.00 C.

Mitchell Collection.

Book cover for school book, 1940–50s, white and red, EX, $10.00 C.

Mitchell Collection.

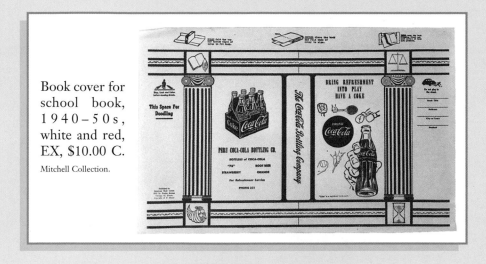

Book cover, national insignia of planes, 1940s, EX, $30.00 C. Mitchell Collection.

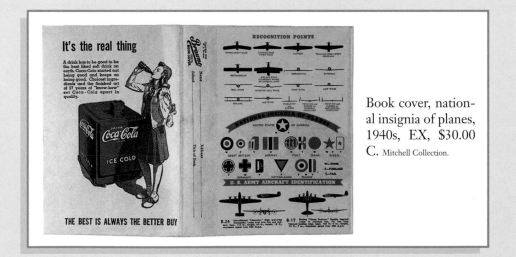

Book cover, Planets and the Stars, 1960s, EX, $20.00.

Mitchell Collection.

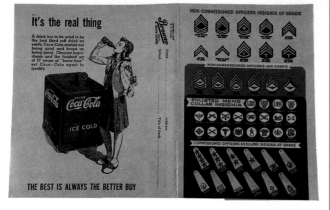

Book cover showing military rank insignias, 1940s, EX, $12.00 C. Mitchell Collection.

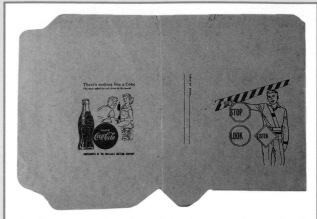

Book cover, "There's nothing like a Coke," school boy, 1940s, EX, $18.00 C. Mitchell Collection.

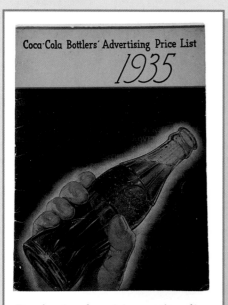

Bottlers' advertising price list, 1935, EX, $225.00 C. Mitchell Collection.

Booklet, *The Charm of Purity*, 1920s, $35.00. Mitchell Collection.

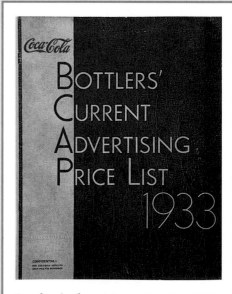

Bottlers' advertising price list, 1933, EX, $225.00 C. Mitchell Collection.

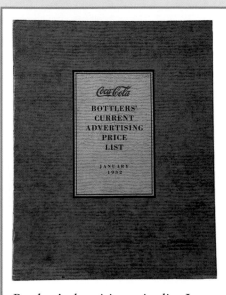

Bottlers' advertising price list, 50th Anniversary, 1936, EX, $300.00 C.

Mitchell Collection.

Bottlers' advertising price list, January 1932, 1932, EX, $225.00 C.

Mitchell Collection.

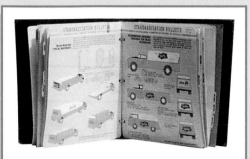

Bulletins book with Coca-Cola bulletins from the '50s and '60s featuring some great information, 1950s, G, $25.00 B. Muddy River Trading Co./Gary Metz.

Top: Check, Globe Bank and Trust Co., 1907, EX, $15.00. Center: Check, Coca-Cola Bottling Works with bottling plant on left side of check at Sixth and Jackson, Paducah, KY, 1915, EX, $50.00 C. Bottom: Check, Coca-Cola Bottling Works banner at top and Eagle on top of world globe on left side of check, 1905, EX, $20.00 C. Mitchell Collection.

Check, "Globe Bank & Trust Co., Paducah, Ky. signed by Paducah Ky. bottler Luther Carson, 1908. While most checks are valued in the $5.00 – 15.00 range this one is higher due to bottler's signature. EX, $100.00 C.

Mitchell Collection.

Coca-Cola News, 3rd edition, dated April 15, 1896, very hard to find, 1896, 6" x 8", NM, $125.00 D.

Muddy River Trading Co./Gary Metz.

Coupon for 5¢, EX, $15.00 C.

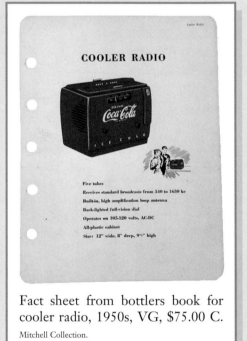

Fact sheet from bottlers book for cooler radio, 1950s, VG, $75.00 C.

Mitchell Collection.

Grier's Almanac featuring a large amount of advertising from Coca-Cola, and Asa Chandler, druggist, matted and framed, rare and hard to find, 1891, F, $1,300.00 B.

Muddy River Trading Co./Gary Metz.

Handbook used for sales preparation in retail stores, white lettering on red, 1950s, EX, $15.00 B. Muddy River Trading Co./Gary Metz.

Invitation to attend the opening of the Paducah, KY, Coca-Cola plant, with picture of the bottling plant at top of sheet, 1939, G, $25.00 C. Mitchell Collection.

Magazine ad featuring Lillian Nordica and a coupon at bottom, matted and framed and under glass, 1904, EX, $110.00 B. Muddy River Trading Co./Gary Metz.

Magazine cover, front and back, *The Housewife*, June 1910, framed, The A. D. Poster Co, Publisher, New York, 1910, G, $175.00 C. Mitchell Collection.

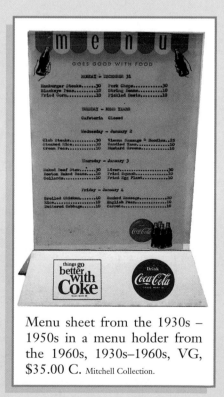

Menu sheet from the 1930s – 1950s in a menu holder from the 1960s, 1930s–1960s, VG, $35.00 C. Mitchell Collection.

Newspaper, *Paducah Sun-Democrat*, June 18, 1939, advertising the opening of a new bottling plant, F, $75.00 C. Mitchell Collection.

Paper adjustable, "Drink Coca-Cola," sun visor, red on white, NM, $5.00 D.

Rare Bird Antique Mall/ Jon & Joan Wright.

Paper, St. Louis Cardinals Official Score Card and Program, with art work of stadium vendor with Coke bottle, G, $15.00 C. Al & Earlene Mitchell.

Paper St. Louis Cardinals souvenir Score Card, art of woman vendor on back with St. Louis products that make the game more enjoyable, EX, $20.00 C. Al & Earlene Mitchell.

Price list with great colors and period graphics in book form, 1941, EX, $325.00 B. Muddy River Trading Co./Gary Metz.

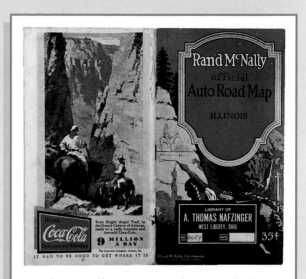

Rand McNally Auto Road Map of Illinois with a Coca-Cola advertisement on the back cover, 1920s, $40.00 C. Mitchell Collection.

Return ticket showing price of returned bottle deposit, G, $12.00 C. Mitchell Collection.

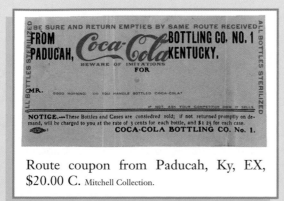

Route coupon from Paducah, Ky, EX, $20.00 C. Mitchell Collection.

Salesman merchandise book, hardback 5-ring binder, 1942, EX, $400.00 D.

Chief Paduke Antiques Mall.

School book cover with Sprite Boy, 1940–50s, EX, $8.00 C. Mitchell Collection.

Score pads, "Spotter," "Drink Coca-Cola Delicious and Refreshing," and military nurse in uniform, 1940, EX, $12.00 each C. Mitchell Collection.

Score card for St. Louis National League, Robison Field, 1916, EX, $20.00 C. Al & Earlene Mitchell.

Sheet music for "The Coca-Cola Girl," words and music by Howard E. Way, published by The Coca-Cola Company, Atlanta, Ga., U.S.A, framed, 1927, VG, $325.00 C. Mitchell Collection.

Sheet music of "My Old Kentucky Home," featuring Juanita on cover with a glass, 1906, EX, $850.00 B.

Sheet music, "Rock me to Sleep Mother," with Juanita on cover drinking from a glass, 1906, EX, $875.00 C.

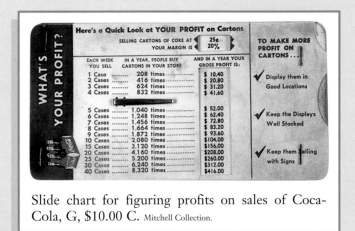

Slide chart for figuring profits on sales of Coca-Cola, G, $10.00 C. Mitchell Collection.

Slide information booklet, Kit Carson, 1950s, VG, $35.00 C. Mitchell Collection.

Wildflower study cards for schools, complete set consists of 20 cards and envelopes, 1920–30, VG, $65.00 set D.

Alphabet Book of Coca-Cola, 1928, G .... $45.00 C

Book, 1942 advertising price list, 1942, VG .. $175.00 C

Book, 1943 advertising price list, 1943, NM.. $250.00 C

Book, 1944 advertising price list, 1944, NM.. $275.00 C

Book cover, America is Strong... because America is Good! Dwight Eisenhower on front, 1950s, VG. $8.00 C

Book cover for school book, 1940 – 50s, white and red, NM............................... $12.00 C

Book, *100 Best Posters*, hard cover, 1941, EX... $55.00 D

Book, *Illustrated Guide to the Collectibles of Coca-Cola*, Cecil Munsey, 1972, EX .... $85.00 C

Book, *Illustrated Guide to the Collectibles of Coca-Cola*, Cecil Munsey, 1972,NM .... $100.00 C

Book, *Pause For Living*, bound copy, 1960s, red, EX.................................. $12.00 C

Book, six bottle carton with dealer info, 1937, EX.................................. $12.00 C

Book, sugar ration, 1943, EX .... $25.00 D

Book, *The 5 Star Book*, 1928, EX........ $35.00 D

Book, *The Six Bottle Carton for the Home*, illustrated, 1937, EX............................ $240.00 C

Book, *The Wonderful World of Coca-Cola*, NM . $75.00 D

Book, *When You Entertain*, by Ida Bailey Allen, 1932, EX.................................. $15.00 D

Booklet, *Easy Hospitality*, 1951, EX .... $12.00 D

Booklet, *Easy Hospitality*, 1951, VG........ $7.00 C

Booklet, *Facts*, 1923, EX .... $55.00 D

Booklet, *Flower Arranging*, 1940, EX...... $10.00 C

Booklet, *Homes and Flowers*, 1940, EX..... $10.00 C

Booklet, *Know Your War Planes*, 1940s, EX .... $45.00 C

Booklet, *Know Your War Planes*, 1940s, P... $25.00 D

Booklet, *Profitable Soda Fountain Operation*, 1953, EX.................................. $65.00 C

Booklet, *Profitable Soda Fountain Operation*, 1953, P................................... $20.00 D

Booklet, *Profitable Soda Fountain Operation*, with Sprite Boy logo on back, 1953, EX .... $75.00 D

Booklet, *Pure and Healthful*, 1915, G ...... $30.00 B

Booklet, *The Charm of Purity*, 1920s, EX... $30.00 C

Booklet, *The Coca-Cola Bottler*, 1940, EX... $35.00 C

Booklet, *The Coca-Cola Bottler*, 1940, P .... $10.00 C

Booklet, *The Romance of Coca-Cola*, 1916, EX $75.00 C

Booklet, *The Romance of Coca-Cola*, 1916, F.... $40.00 D

Booklet with woman in front of sun dial on front and bottle in hand on back cover, with original envelope, 1923, EX...........................$40.00 D

Bottlers' advertising price list, January 1932, 1932, F...................................$85.00 D

Bottlers' advertising price list, 1933, VG . $190.00 D

Bottlers' advertising price list, 1935, VG . $195.00 D

Bottlers' advertising price list, 50th Anniversary, 1936, P.....................................$100.00 D

Bottlers' magazine, *The Red Barrel*, 1940, EX.. $15.00 D

Bottlers' magazine, *The Red Barrel*, 1940, P ....$8.00 D

Bulletin book for route men, 1950–60s, VG...$25.00 D

Card hologram, Cal Ripken, McDonald's & Coke, 1991, NM...........................$15.00 D

Cap saver bag, for saving caps to redeem for cash from bottler at Bethlehem, Pa., red & white, 2½" x 5", EX.....................................$17.00 C

Carton wrap, "Holiday Hospitality," 1940s, M. $20.00 D
Catalog sheet, Roy G. Booker Coca-Cola jewelry from "Gifts In Fine Jewelry," 1940, NM.......$70.00 C

Catalog, The All-Star Mechanical Pencil Line, featuring Coca-Cola and other drink lines, 1941, M...............................$45.00 D

Christmas card with "Seasons Greetings" under silver ornament, 1976, red, M..............$10.00 D

Circus cut out for kids, still uncut in one piece, 1927, EX....................................$300.00 D

Circus cut out for kids, uncut in one sheet, 1932, NM...................................$200.00 D

Coca-Cola money roll, quarters, M, $6.00 C. Coca-Cola money roll, halves.................$6.00 C

Comic book, "Refreshment Through The Ages," 1951, EX..............................$25.00 D

Comic book, "Refreshment Through The Ages," 1951, P...............................$5.00 D

Comic trade card featuring woman in bathtub and serving bottles from a serving tray, 1905. Beware: Reproductions exist..................$800.00 D

Convention packet, 14th Annual Coca-Cola Convention at Philadelphia, 1988, MIB.........$30.00 C

Convention packet, 14th Annual Coca-Cola Convention at Philadelphia, 1988, F............$15.00 C

Coupon, 1900, EX ....$400.00 C

Coupon, featured 12-pack, 1950s, EX....$10.00 C

Coupon, featured 12-packs, 1950s, F......$5.00 D

Coupon for 5¢, EX...................$15.00 C

Coupon, for free six-pack with return of empty six-pack featuring Santa Claus, issued from bottling company in Youngstown, Ohio, white lettering on light green background with Santa in 4-color, 6" x 3", EX.............................$5.00 C

Coupon, for six free bottles of Coke with purchase of twelve-pack, red and green on white, 6" x 3½", G ....$5.00 C

Coupon, free bottle of Coke, 1920s, EX...$15.00 C

Coupon, Free Coke at soda fountain, 1908, EX..............................$225.00 B

Coupon, Free Coke with Sprite Boy, 1950s, VG.................................$15.00 D

Coupon, "Free 6 Bottles of Coca-Cola," pictures six-pack with wire handle, 1950s, EX.......$10.00 C

Coupon, good for six-pack of Coke when five are accumulated, red & green lettering on light green background, 3½" x 2", EX.............$5.00 C

Coupon, Hilda Clark, 1901, EX.......$500.00 D

Coupon, Lillian Nordica, 1905, 6½"x9¾", EX. $250.00 C

Coupon, "Refresh yourself," Free at Roberts & Echols, Glendale, Calif., 1920s, 5"x2", EX.................................$35.00 C

Coupon, "Take home a carton," 1930s, EX. $30.00 C

Coupon, "This card entitles an adult to one glass of Coca-Cola Free," 1890s, EX . . . . $250.00 B

Coupon, "This Card Entitles You To One Glass of Coca-Cola," 1903, EX . . . . $400.00 B

Coupon, "Wholesome Refreshment" with red headed boy drinking from a bottle with a straw, 1920s, EX . . . . $20.00 D

Coupons, "Refresh Yourself" with bottle in hand, 1920s, EX . . . . $20.00 C

Coupons, soda person "Refresh Yourself," 1927, 2¼"x4", EX . . . . $85.00 B

Display sheet for cartons, "Match The Brides... for Fun and Prizes," for 35-cap display, 1967, EX . . . . $20.00 C

Driver's license holder featuring bottle in hand from Terra Haute, Ind., dark blue lettering on light blue background, 2" x 3½", EX . . . . $20.00 C

Driver's route book, EX . . . . $10.00 D

Famous Doctors Series, set of six heavy folders, complete, of individual figure approximately $35.00 each, 1932, EX . . . . $250.00 C

Halloween promotional package for dealers, 1954, EX . . . . $20.00 C

Health record, My Daily Reminder, Compliments of Sanford Coca-Cola Bottling Co., Sanford, N.C. Phone 20, 1930s, EX . . . . $20.00 D

Health record, My Daily Reminder, Compliments of Sanford Coca-Cola Bottling Co., Sanford, N.C. Phone 20, 1930s, G . . . . $12.00 C

Holder for gas ration book, "Drink Coca-Cola in Bottles," G . . . . $20.00 D

Information kit, New York World's Fair, "The Coca-Cola Company Pavilion," 1964, NM . . . . . $50.00 D

Kit, merchandising for cooler, 1930, M . . . $85.00 D

Letter, Asa G. Chandler, matted and framed, 1889, EX . . . . $200.00 C

Magazine, *Pause for Living*, a single copy, 1960, EX . . . . $5.00 C

Magazine, *The Coca-Cola™ Bottler*, 1940s, EX . . . . $20.00 C

Magazine, vest pocket, complete set of 52, 1928, NM . . . . $500.00 D

Menu, for soda fountain, matted and framed, 1902, 4⅛"x6⅛", EX . . . . $600.00 B

Menu, Hilda Clark, rare, 1901, 11¾"x4", EX . . . . $1,200.00 B

Menu, Hilda Clark, soda menu, matted and framed, hard to find, 1903, 4⅛"x6⅛", EX . . . . . . $650.00 B

Menu, Lillian Nordica, matted and framed, 1904, 4⅛"x6½", EX . . . . $650.00 B

Menu sheet, "Today's Menu" featuring artwork of button and glass in lower page corners, green on white, 1950s, 6" x 11", EX . . . . $5.00 D

Menu sheet, "Today's Menu" featuring "goes good with food," artwork of glass in red banner at bottom, green on white, 1950s, 6" x 11", EX . . . . . $5.00 D

Napkin with Sprite Boy, 1950s, M . . . . $15.00 C

National Geographic Coca-Cola ads, full set, EX . . . . $300.00 C

Note pad, celluloid, 1902, 2½"x5", EX . . . $600.00 B

Note pad, green alligator cover, "Compliments the Coca-Cola Co." stamped on front in gold, 1906, EX . . . . $225.00 D

Note pad, Hilda Clark, matted and framed, 1903, 2½"x5", EX . . . . $600.00 C

Note pad holder, calfskin, 1946, EX . . . . . . $25.00 D

Note pad, leather covered, 1905, 2¾"x4½", EX . . . . $225.00 D

Note pad, pocket size, white lettering on red, 1943, 4" x 6", EX . . . . $15.00 D

Note pad with boy and dog, 1931, 10"x7", Rockwell, EX. . . . . $35.00 D

Notebook, "Coca-Cola Advertised Schedule," 1980, EX. . . . . $20.00 C

Olympiad Records wheel, 1932, EX . . . . . $100.00 D

Opera program presented by Columbus Coca-Cola Bottling Co., 1906, EX . . . . $100.00 C

Placemats, "Around The World," set of four, 1950s, EX. . . . . $15.00 C

Pocket secretary, hard bound, 1920s, EX . . $30.00 D

Punch card for a "Bottle Coke" Special, with punches of 1, 2, 3, 4, and 5 cents manufactured by W. H. Hardy Co., Eau Claire, Wisc., 1900, VG. . . . . $5.00 C

Report card holder with 1923 bottle, 1930s, EX . . . . $85.00 D

Report card holder with 1923 bottle, 1930s, P . $15.00 D

Return ticket showing price of returned bottle deposit, NM. . . . . $25.00 C

Route coupon from Paducah, Ky., VG . . . . $15.00 C

Sack for popcorn from Jungleland with "Drink Coca-Cola" logo in center featuring artwork of tiger face, orange, red, black, 4" x 15", EX . . . . $15.00 D

School book cover with Sprite Boy, 1940–50s, G . . . . $5.00 C

School kit, Man & His Environment, 1970s, EX . . . . $22.00 D

Score pad, American Women's Volunteer Service, 1940s, EX . . . . $15.00 C

Score pad, American Women's Volunteer Service, 1940s, F. . . . . $5.00 C

Score pad for playing cards, six pack in spotlight "easy to serve, good with food," green on white, 4" x 11", EX . . . . $5.00 D

Service manual and parts catalog for VMC, manufactured Vendolator Mfg. Co. in leatherette book, 1950s, 8" x 9", EX . . . . $300.00 D

Sheet music, cover and song sheet, "I'd Like to Buy the World A Coke™," 1971, 8½"x11½", EX . . . . $25.00 D

Sheet music, It's the Real Thing, 1969, EX. . $12.00 C

Sheet music, "It's the Real Thing," 1969, M $20.00 D

Sheet music, "Rum & Coca-Cola," Jeri Sullivan, EX. . . . . $20.00 C

Slide chart for figuring profits on sales of Coca-Cola, M . . . . $25.00 D

Souvenirs, Confederate Bank note, 1931, EX. . $75.00 D

Toonerville cut out still uncut and in one piece, 1930, M . . . . $55.00 C

Writing tablet featuring Sprite Boy and safety ABC's, 1950s, EX . . . . $10.00 D

Writing tablet featuring Sprite Boy and safety ABC's, 1950s, G $6.00

Writing tablet, flags, 1960s, EX . . . . $10.00 D

Writing tablet, landmarks of the U.S.A, 1960s, EX . . . . $10.00 D

Writing tablet, Pure As Sunlight, 1930s, EX . . $25.00 D

Writing tablet, Pure As Sunlight, 1930s, F . . . . $12.00 D

Writing tablet, wildlife of the United States, 1970s, EX. . . . . $10.00 D

Writing tablet, wildlife of the United States, 1970s, G. . . . . $5.00 D

Writing tablet, with Silhouette Girl, 1940s, EX . . . . $15.00 D

Writing tablet, with Silhouette Girl, 1940s, EX. . . . . $10.00 C

Bamboo with front and back graphics, "Keep Cool, Drink Coca-Cola," Oriental lady drinking a glass of Coca-Cola on opposite side, 1900, VG, $175.00 C. Mitchell Collection.

Cardboard fold out from the Atlanta Coca-Cola Bottling Company, EX, $55.00 C. Mitchell Collection.

Cardboard fold out from the Coca-Cola Bottling Co., Bethlehem, Pennsylvania, 1950s, EX, $55.00 C. Mitchell Collection.

Cardboard fold out with Sprite Boy from the Coca-Cola bottler at Memphis, Tenn., 1951, F, $65.00 C. Mitchell Collection.

Cardboard on wooden handle, "Enjoy Coca-Cola," 1960s, EX, $15.00 C. Mitchell Collection.

Cardboard on wooden handle, with Sprite Boy, "Have A Coke," 1950s, EX, $75.00 C. Mitchell Collection.

Cardboard with rolled paper handle, "Drink Coca-Cola the Pause that Refreshes," 1930, $175.00 C. Mitchell Collection.

Cardboard with rolled paper handle, with poem on cover, 1930s, EX, $175.00 C. Mitchell Collection.

Cardboard with wooden handle, "Buy by the carton, 6 for 25¢," Memphis, Tenn, 1930s, EX, $95.00 C. Mitchell Collection.

Cardboard with wooden handle, "Drink Coca-Cola" with bottle in spot light, 1930s, EX, $95.00 C. Mitchell Collection.

Cardboard with wooden handle from the Coca-Cola Bottling Works of Greenwood Mississippi, "Enjoy Coca-Cola," 1960s, EX, $25.00 C. Mitchell Collection.

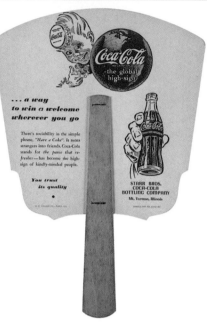

Cardboard with wooden handle, Sprite Boy, "A way to win a welcome whenever you go," Starr Bros. Coca-Cola Bottling Company, Mt. Vernon, Illinois, 1950s, $110.00 C. Mitchell Collection.

Cardboard with wooden handle, Sprite Boy, "Bottles, Bottles Who's got the Empty Bottles?," Paducah Coca-Cola Bottling Company, Inc, 1950s, EX, $125.00 C. Mitchell Collection.

"Drink Coca-Cola" featuring a spotlighted bottle with wooden handle, 1930s, EX, $75.00 C. Mitchell Collection.

Paper on wooden handle manufactured by Franklin-Cora Co Richmond, Va, "Chew Coca-Cola Gum," red lettering on white background, 1912–16, VG, $2,000.00 B.

Paper with wooden handle, spotlight on bottle in center, 1950s, EX, $65.00 C. Mitchell Collection.

Property of Church, donated by Ruston Coca-Cola Bottling Co, Ph 87, Ruston, La, 1920s, EX, $125.00 C. Mitchell Collection.

"Quality carries on, Drink Coca-Cola" with bottle in hand, 1950, EX, $50.00 C. Mitchell Collection.

Rolled paper handle, "Drink Coca-Cola The Pause That Refreshes," Coca-Cola Bottling Co. Martin, Tenn, Phone 411, EX, $100.00 C. Mitchell Collection.

Wicker, compliments of Waycross Coca-Cola Bottling Co, 1950s, EX, $65.00 C. Mitchell Collection.

Bamboo with front and back graphics, "Keep Cool, Drink Coca-Cola," Oriental lady drinking a glass of Coca-Cola on opposite side, 1900, F . . . . . $85.00 C

Cardboard and wood with picture of a mother and child, "Drive with care, protect our loved ones" . . . $125.00 D

Cardboard fold out from the Coca-Cola Bottling Co., Bethlehem, Pa., 1950s, F . . . . $20.00 C

Cardboard on wooden handle, with Sprite Boy, "Have A Coke," 1950s, G. . . . . $35.00 D

Cardboard with wooden handle, "Drink Coca-Cola" with bottle in spotlight, 1930s, G . . . . $30.00 D

Blotters

Left, from top: "So Refreshing, Keep on Ice," couple at ice box, 1927, M, $60.00 D; "Refresh Yourself," white haired gentleman in hat looking at bottle, 1928, $75.00 D; "Be Prepared, be Refreshed," Boy Scout at cooler with a bottle in each hand, 1940s, M, $15.00 D. Right, from top: "And one for you," girl on blanket holding bottle, 1934, $95.00 D; Boy with fishing pole and dog drinking from a bottle, 1930s, $100.00 D; "Good with food. Try It," plate of food with two bottles, 1930s, M, $50.00 C.

Canadian blotter with ruler and protractor markings on edges, hard to find piece, 1930s, NM, $275.00 B.

Muddy River Trading Co./Gary Metz.

"The Pause That Refreshes," 1930, EX, $40.00.

Muddy River Trading Co./Gary Metz.

50th Anniversary, 1936, EX . . . . $65.00 D

"A pure drink of natural flavors," 1929, G. . $50.00 C

"A pure drink of natural flavors," 1929, EX . . $150.00 B

"Be Prepared," 1950, EX . . . . $20.00 D

Bottle in hand over the earth, 1958, VG . . . . $5.00 C

Bottle in hand over the earth, 1958, EX . . . $15.00 D

Bottle, large, "Over 60 million a Day," 1960, VG . . . . $8.00 D

Bottle, large, "Over 60 million a Day," 1960, EX . . . . $12.00 D

Bottle, paper label, "The Most Refreshing Drink in the World," 1904, EX . . . . $350.00 B

Boy Scouts, "Wholesome Refreshment," 1942, VG . . . . $8.00 C

Boy Scouts, "Wholesome Refreshment," 1942, EX. . . . . $15.00 D

Canadian, 1940, NM. . . . . $30.00 D

"Carry A Smile Back To Work Feeling Fit," 1935, M. . . . . $95.00 B

Coca-Cola being enjoyed by a policeman, 1938, G. . . . . $20.00 D

Coca-Cola, policeman enjoying, 1938, EX$30.00 C

"Coke Knows No Season," snow scene, great graphics, 1947, EX . . . . $25.00 C

"Cold Refreshment," 1937, EX . . . . $30.00 C

"Completely Refreshing," with disc upper left, 1942, EX. . . . . $30.00 D

Couples at a party, Canadian, 1955, EX. . $20.00 D

"Delicious and Refreshing," fountain service, 1915, EX. . . . . $185.00 B

"Delicious, Refreshing, Invigorating," 1909, Red & White, EX. . . . . $110.00 B

"Delicious, Refreshing," Sprite Boy and a bottle, 1951, EX. . . . . $20.00 D

"Drink Coca-Cola," Atlanta, 1904, EX. . $400.00 B

"Drink Coca-Cola," Chicago, 1904, EX. $110.00 B

"Drink... Delicious & Refreshing All Soda Fountain 5 cents," 1915, EX . . . . $175.00 B

Fountain sales, 1913, EX . . . . $75.00 B

"Friendliest drink on earth," a bottle in hand, 1956, 4"x8", EX . . . . $20.00 C

Full set of six , different poses, 1970s, EX$250.00 B

Girl in boat, 1942, EX. . . . . $25.00 D

Girl laying on her stomach, 1942, EX . . . $20.00 D

"I Think It's Swell," 1944, 3½"x7½", EX . . $15.00 D

" I Think It's Swell," girl, 1942, EX. . . . . $15.00 D

Policeman with bottle, 1938, EX. . . . . . . $75.00 D

"Pure and Healthful," with a paper label on each side to promote bottle sales, 1913, EX. . . $75.00 D

"Pure and Healthful," with bottles on both sides, 1916, G. . . . . $55.00 D

"Refresh Yourself," 1926, EX. . . . . $75.00 D

"Refreshing & Delicious" disc, 1940, EX. $30.00 D

"Restores Energy," 1906, red and white, EX. . . . . $130.00 B

Sprite Boy, 1947, EX . . . . $90.00 B

Sprite Boy with a bottle in the snow, 1953, EX. . . . . $15.00 D

"The Drink Everyone Knows," 1939, EX $35.00 D

"The Greatest Pause On Earth," 1940, EX. $75.00 D

"The most refreshing drink in the world," 1905, EX. . . . . $200.00 B

"The Pause That Refreshes," 1929, EX . . $95.00 C

"The Pause That Refreshes," 1930, EX . . $65.00 C

"The Pause That Refreshes," 1931, EX . $225.00 B

Three girls with bottles, disc at right, 1944, NM . . . . $30.00 B

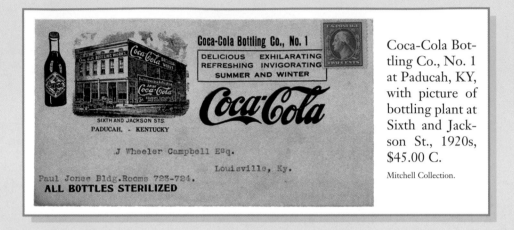

Coca-Cola Bottling Co., No. 1 at Paducah, KY, with picture of bottling plant at Sixth and Jackson St., 1920s, $45.00 C.

Mitchell Collection.

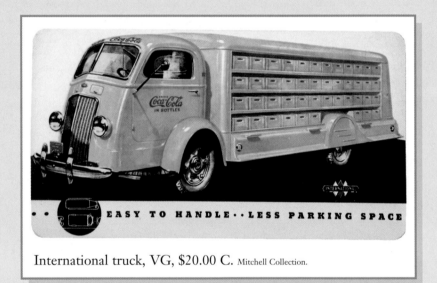

International truck, VG, $20.00 C. Mitchell Collection.

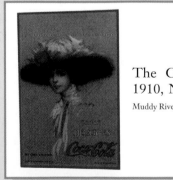

The Coca-Cola Girl, 1910, NM, $775.00 B.

Muddy River Trading Co./Gary Metz.

Auto delivery truck with an even loaded bed and five men on board, 1913, EX . . . . $135.00 B

Bobby Allison & Coke, 1970s, NM . . . . . . $12.00 D

Bottling plant showing interior, 1905, EX . $125.00 B

Coca-Cola™ girl, 1910, Hamilton King, EX . . . . $700.00 B

Duster girl, 1911, 3½"x5½", EX . . . . $700.00 B

Exterior of a bottling plant showing the truck fleet in front of building, 1906, EX . . . . $150.00 D

Folding, "Have You a Hobby?," showing a youngster on a rocking horse, 1910, EX . . . . $175.00 D

Folding, "Will You Have It – When They Call?," 1913, EX . . . . $150.00 D

Free six bottles with wire handled carton commemorating 65th Anniversary, 1950s, EX . . . . . . $15.00 D

Horse-drawn delivery wagon, 1900, EX . . $125.00 B

Horse-drawn delivery wagon with a Coca-Cola umbrella, 1913, EX . . . . $130.00 D

Interior of store, 1904, EX . . . . $100.00 B

International truck, 1940s, EX . . . . $20.00 D

International truck, 1940s, EX . . . . $8.00 C

Motorized delivery wagon with three men standing beside it, 1915, EX . . . . $125.00 B

Photo truck loaded with case of Coca-Cola in snow, framed, 1910, 8"x10", black and white, EX . . . . $125.00 D

Postcard featuring picture of DuQuoin, Illinois, bottling plant, NM . . . . $35.00 D

Postcard from Charleston, Ill., good for free bottle of Coke, red lettering on white, 5" x 3", G . . . . $9.00 D

Race car of Bobby Allison, 1973, EX . . . . . $10.00 D

Store showing bar with ceramic dispensers and pool table, 1904, EX . . . . $100.00 D

The Fulton Coca-Cola Bottling Co., 1909, EX . . . . $150.00 B

Trifold, showing profit for selling Coca-Cola, featuring a teacher at blackboard, 1910s, EX . . . $450.00 B

Trifold, showing profits sitting on top of globe, 1913, EX . . . . $200.00 D

Weldmech truck, 1930, EX . . . . $20.00 D

Magazine, "Even the bubbles taste better," 1956, VG, $5.00 D.

Magazine, Sprite Boy looking at Santa in front of opened refrigerator, 1948, EX, $30.00 C.

National Geographic, cover, back, "You Taste Its Quality," 1951, F, $5.00 D.

Magazine, Sprite Boy at soda fountain wearing
soda fountain hat, 1949, G, $30.00 C.

The Housekeeper cover, front and back, August 1909,
framed, 1909, VG, $150.00 C. Mitchell Collection.

American, man and woman toasting each other with flare glasses inside a large flare glass, NM... $8.00 D

"Baseball and Coke grew up together," young boy in uniform with a bottle, framed, 1951, 12"x15", NM................................. $10.00 D

Delineator featuring a city scene, 1921, EX .. $10.00 D

Delineator featuring a city scene, 1921, VG .. $5.00 D

"Drink," glass on ledge, 1917, EX........ $15.00 D

"Face the Day Refreshed," woman at table, "Drink..." button upper left, framed, 1939, 12"x15", EX. $15.00 D

"Get together with refreshment," couple at soda fountain, "Drink..." button upper right, matted and framed, 1941, 12"x15", NM .... $12.00 D

Girl with flare glass, 1910s, EX......... $20.00 D

Girl with muffler, 1923, NM........... $20.00 D

"Has Character," featuring soda person, 1913, VG .... $12.00 D

Human Life, color, lady in arrow, 1910, NM... $85.00 D

Human Life, color, lady in arrow, 1910, F ..... $15.00 D

Human Life, color, "Come In" with arrow encircling soda fountain, 1909, NM.................... $60.00 D

Ladies' Home Journal, "Enjoy Thirst," girl with straw and bottle, 1923, EX.................. $15.00 D

Ladies' Home Journal, "Enjoy Thirst," girl, straw and bottle, 1923, NM.................... $15.00 D

Ladies' Home Journal, girl with background showing golfers, 1922, EX.................... $20.00 D

Ladies' Home Journal, girl, background showing golfers, 1922, NM.................... $25.00 D

Ladies' Home Journal, snow scene and skiers with flare glass in hands, 1922, EX .... $12.00 D

Ladies' Home Journal, snow scene and skiers with flare glass in hand, 1922, NM .... $15.00 D

Ladies' Home Journal, "Thirst Knows No Season" with calendar girl, December, 1922, EX ...... $20.00 D

Ladies' Home Journal, "Thirst Knows No Season" with calendar girl, December, 1922, NM ..... $25.00 D

"Let's Get a Coca-Cola," featuring couple under a fountain service sign, framed, 1939, 12"x15", EX... $12.00 D

Magazine, buggy, 1906, EX............. $35.00 D

Magazine, featuring Lillian Nordica and a Coke, matted and framed, 1904, NM............. $110.00 B

Magazine, golfing couple, 1906, EX...... $110.00 B

Magazine, "Scorching Hot Day," arrow above test, 1909, EX............................ $45.00 D

Magazine, "Scorching Hot Day," arrow above test, 1909, VG............................ $30.00 D

Magazine, Sprite Boy at soda fountain wearing soda fountain hat, 1949, G .... $25.00 D

Massengale, lady and maid, 1906, EX .... $110.00 B

Massengale, lady and maid, 1906, G ..... $50.00 D

"Pause and refresh," three girls in car, "Drink..." button upper right, 1938, 12"x15", NM...... $20.00 D

"Pause... and shop refreshed," couple of ladies at table with glasses, 1940, 12"x15", NM......... $10.00 D

People waiting behind counter, matted and framed, 1905, 14"x10", EX..................... $120.00 B

"Refreshment through the years," "Drink..." button lower right, 1951, 12"x15", EX.......... $10.00 D

Saturday Evening Post, water skier, EX..... $10.00 D

Seated girl, 1915, 14"x19", EX.......... $140.00 B

"Through 65 Years," one side 1886 fountain service, other side 1951 fountain service, framed, 1951, 12"x15", NM........................ $10.00 C

Woman's World, 1920, EX .... $35.00 D

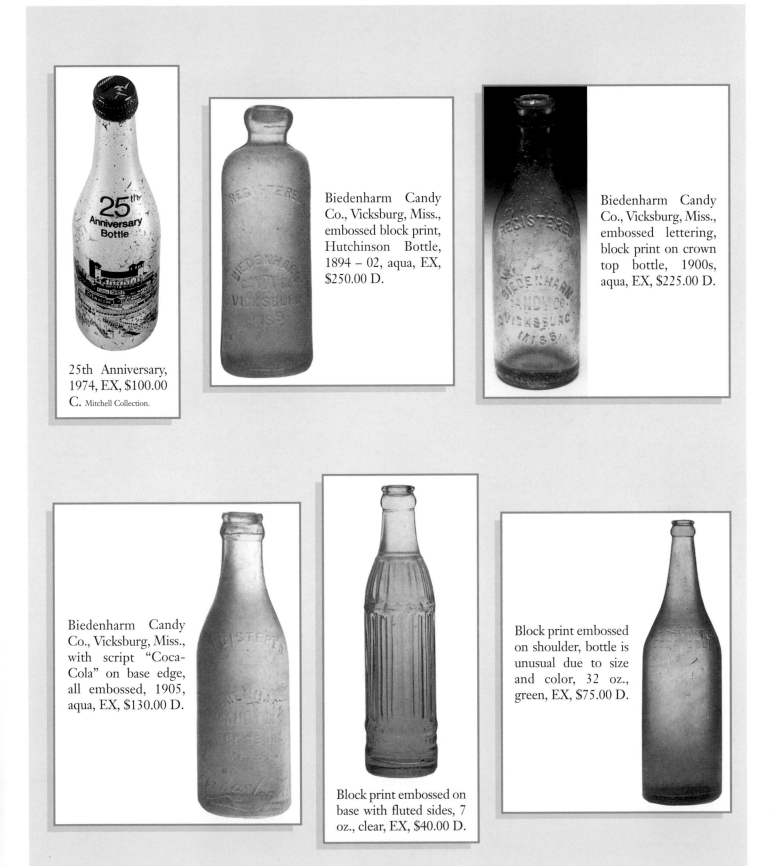

25th Anniversary, 1974, EX, $100.00 C. Mitchell Collection.

Biedenharm Candy Co., Vicksburg, Miss., embossed block print, Hutchinson Bottle, 1894 – 02, aqua, EX, $250.00 D.

Biedenharm Candy Co., Vicksburg, Miss., embossed lettering, block print on crown top bottle, 1900s, aqua, EX, $225.00 D.

Biedenharm Candy Co., Vicksburg, Miss., with script "Coca-Cola" on base edge, all embossed, 1905, aqua, EX, $130.00 D.

Block print embossed on base with fluted sides, 7 oz., clear, EX, $40.00 D.

Block print embossed on shoulder, bottle is unusual due to size and color, 32 oz., green, EX, $75.00 D.

Block print embossed on side in circle from S e d a l i a, MO, 6½", aqua, EX, $40.00 D.

Block print on base, embossed, 6½-oz., aqua, EX, $35.00 D.

Block print on shoulder, C.C.B. Co. from Raton, NM, embossed, 6-oz., aqua, EX, $25.00 D.

Bottles, six-pack of bottles with original carrier showing one year to go until the Olympics, 1995, 6-pack, EX, $35.00 D. Pleasant Hill Antique Mall & Tea Room/Bob Johnson.

Canadian with white lettering on clear glass with screw on top, 40-oz., clear, EX, $30.00 D.

Carbonation tester used before the introduction of premix, extremely hard to locate since normally only the bottlers had these items, EX, $500.00 B.

Ceramic syrup jug with paper label, tall, two-color stoneware, hardest to find, 1900s, 10" tall, VG, $2,600.00 B.

Muddy River Trading Co./Gary Metz.

Convention, 50th Anniversary National Soft Drink Association, 1969, EX, $100.00 C. Mitchell Collection.

Convention, 1976, EX, $45.00 C. Mitchell Collection.

Convention, 1981, EX, $40.00 C. Although not strictly a Coca-Cola item, these bottles are collected by most Coke collectors and I had several requests to include them here.

Mitchell Collection.

Convention, Anaheim, CA, 1985, EX, $40.00 C. Mitchell Collection.

Convention, Anaheim, CA, 1977, EX, $75.00 C. Mitchell Collection.

Convention, Atlanta, GA, 1978, EX, $45.00 C. Mitchell Collection.

Convention, Atlanta, GA, 1982, EX, $40.00 C. Mitchell Collection.

Convention, Atlanta, GA, 1988, EX, $30.00 C. Mitchell Collection.

Convention, Atlanta, GA, 1994, EX, $25.00 C. Mitchell Collection.

Convention, Atlantic City, NJ, 1952, EX, $125.00 C. Mitchell Collection.

Convention, Atlantic City, NJ, 1958, EX, $95.00 C. Mitchell Collection.a

Convention, Atlantic City, NJ, 1962, EX, $65.00 C. Mitchell Collection.

Convention, Atlantic City, NJ, 1966, EX, $50.00 C. Mitchell Collection.

Convention, Chicago, IL, 1953, EX, $100.00
C. Mitchell Collection.

Convention, Chicago, IL, 1964, EX, $55.00
C. Mitchell Collection.

Convention, Chicago, IL, 1972, EX, $45.00
C. Mitchell Collection.

Convention, Chicago, IL, 1980, EX, $40.00
C. Mitchell Collection.

Convention, Chicago, IL, 1984, EX, $40.00
C. Mitchell Collection.

Convention, Chicago, IL, 1987, EX, $30.00
C. Mitchell Collection.

Convention, Chicago, IL, 1990, EX, $25.00
C. Mitchell Collection.

Convention, Chicago, IL, 1992, EX, $25.00
C. Mitchell Collection.

Convention, Cleveland, OH, 1956, EX, $95.00 C. Mitchell Collection.

Convention, Dallas, TX, 1963, EX, $60.00 D. Mitchell Collection.

Convention, Dallas, TX, 1975, EX, $55.00 D. Mitchell Collection.

Convention, Dallas, TX, 1979, F.X, $45.00 C. Mitchell Collection.

Convention, Dallas, TX, 1986, EX, $35.00 C. Mitchell Collection.

Convention, Detroit, MI, 1960, EX, $80.00 C. Mitchell Collection.

Convention, Detroit, MI, 1968, EX, $50.00 D. Mitchell Collection.

Convention, Houston, TX, 1967, EX, $50.00 C. Mitchell Collection.

Convention, Houston, TX, 1971, EX, $45.00 C. Mitchell Collection.

Convention, Houston, TX, 1983, EX, $40.00 C. Mitchell Collection.

Convention, Las Vegas, NV, 1989, EX, $30.00 C. Mitchell Collection.

Convention, Miami, FL, 1955, EX, $95.00 C. Mitchell Collection.

Convention, Miami, FL, 1965, EX, $50.00 D. Mitchell Collection.

Convention, Miami, FL, 1973, EX, $45.00 C. Mitchell Collection.

Convention, Philadelphia, PA, 1954, EX, $95.00 C. Mitchell Collection.

Convention, Philadelphia, PA, 1970, EX, $50.00 C. Mitchell Collection.

Convention, San Francisco, CA, 1950, EX, $700.00 C. Mitchell Collection.

Convention, San Francisco, CA, 1961, EX, $70.00 C. Mitchell Collection.

Convention, St. Louis, MO, 1959, EX, $85.00 C. Mitchell Collection.

Convention, Washington, D.C., 1951, EX, $125.00 C. Mitchell Collection.

Convention, Washington, D.C., 1957, $90.00 C. Mitchell Collection.

From left: Double diamond with script "Coca-Cola" inside diamond from Toledo, Ohio, 1900–10s, 6-oz., amber, EX, $125.00 C; Script "Coca-Cola" on bottom edge of front side, on reverse "This bottle our private property & protected by registration under Senate Bill No. 130 approved June 7th, 1911," Dayton, Ohio, 1900 – 10, 6-oz., amber, EX, $200.00 C; Script "Coca-Cola" inside arrow circle, Louisville, Ky., 1910s, 6-oz., amber, EX, $95.00 C; Script "Coca-Cola" on shoulder of bottle with vertical arrow, Cincinnati, Ohio, registered on bottom in block print, 1910s, 6-oz., amber, EX, $125.00 C.

Embossed script "Coca-Cola" at edge of base with unusual shoulder, clear, EX, $65.00.

Glass display 1923 Christmas bottle with display cap, 1930s, 20" tall, F, $250.00 B. Muddy River Trading Co./Gary Metz.

Gold, 50th Anniversary 1899 – 1949, Everett Pidgeon in bottle cradle, 1949, EX, $200.00 C. Mitchell Collection.

Gold, 100th Anniversary, 1986, EX, $45.00 C. Mitchell Collection.

Miniature perfume bottle with glass stopper, 1930s, clear, EX, $65.00 D. Beware: Reproductions exist.

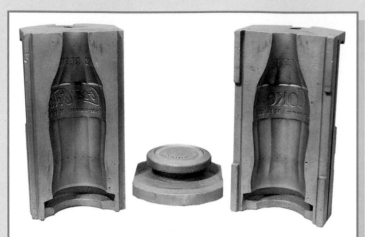

Mold made of solid iron, for 10-oz. no return bottle, very heavy, EX, $375.00 B. Muddy River Trading Co./Gary Metz.

National Convention, 75th Anniversary Hutchinson style bottle, fairly scarce, 1961, light aqua, EX, $250.00 D.

Left: Oklahoma Anniversary, regular capped, gold dipped with white lettering, dated 1903 – 1967 on reverse, only 1,000 made make this a fairly scarce item, 1967, 6½-oz., gold, EX, $135.00 C. Right: Regular capped gold dipped, embossed lettering, these were made for individual bottlers for special occasions, 6-oz., gold, EX, $35.00 D.

Original paper label with script "Coca-Cola Beverage," reproduction labels are available, 1900–10, aqua, EX, $225.00 C.

Premix, 1920s, green, EX, $65.00 C. Mitchell Collection.

"Property of Coca-Cola Bottling Co, La Grange, Texas," in block print on body with embossed ribbon on shoulder, 6-oz., aqua, EX, $40.00 C. Mitchell Collection.

"Root" commemorative bottle is a reissue of the original bottle design of 1915. The original bottle bottoms were plain, the reissue is so marked only 5,000 of the reissues were made, 1965, EX, $425.00 C. Mitchell Collection.

From left: Script "Coca-Cola" at bottom from any location, 1910s, 6-oz., amber, EX, $55.00 C; Script "Coca-Cola" on base edge, "Bottling WKS 2nd Registered" in block print at bottom of base, 1910s, 6½-oz., amber, EX, $110.00 C; Script "Coca-Cola" midway from any location, 1910s, 6-oz., amber, EX, $55.00 C; Script "Coca-Cola" on shoulder from any location, 1910s, 6-oz., amber, EX, $65.00 C.

Script "Coca-Cola" embossed on body with embossed art around name, 1910–20s, aqua, $85.00 C. Mitchell Collection.

Script "Coca-Cola" in shoulder from Verner Springs Water Co., Greenville, SC, 9", aqua, G, $30.00 C.

Syrup can with paper label, red & white, 1940s, one-gallon, EX, $275.00 B.

Muddy River Trading Co./Gary Metz.

Syrup keg with paper label on end, 1930s, 5-gallon, F, $100.00 B.

Muddy River Trading Co./Gary Metz.

Syrup, with applied label and original cap, $1,000.00 B. Muddy River Trading Co./Gary Metz.

Syrup, with original metal cap, 1920s, EX, $650.00 C. Mitchell Collection.

The Coca-Cola Bottling Company, six-sided body, 1920–30, aqua, EX, $65.00 C. Mitchell Collection.

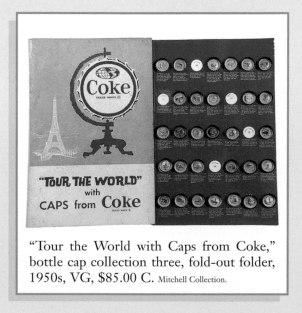

"Tour the World with Caps from Coke," bottle cap collection three, fold-out folder, 1950s, VG, $85.00 C. Mitchell Collection.

Tri-State Area Council Boy Scouts of America, 1953, green, EX, $230.00 C. Mitchell Collection.

White lettering on clear glass with tight fitting plastic top, used as a display piece, 1960s, 20" tall, clear, EX, $65.00 D.

75th Anniversary, Paducah Coca-Cola Bottling Company, Inc, 1978, 10-oz., clear, EX . . . . $20.00 D

75th Anniversary, Paducah Coca-Cola Bottling Company, Inc., 1978, 10-oz., clear, VG . . . . $15.00 D

75th Anniversary, Thomas Bottling Company, 1974, amber, G . . . . $50.00 D

75th Anniversary, Thomas Bottling Company, 1974, amber, EX . . . . $75.00 C

America's Cup, 1987, NM . . . . $45.00 D

American Airlines LE commemorative bottle, 8-oz., NM . . . . $150.00 D

Analyst-Portfolio Managers Meeting, limited edition of 408 bottles produced, 1996, M . . . . . . $225.00 C

Annie Oakley Days LE commemorative, 1985, NM . . . . $65.00 D

Atlanta Christian College, 1987, 10-oz., NM $8.00 D

Atlanta Falcons, NM . . . . $8.00 D

Atlanta Olympics, 1996, NM . . . . $5.00 D

Baskin Robbins LR commemorative bottle, NM . . . . $150.00 D

Biedenharm Candy Company with applied paper label and "Coca-Cola" in script on bottle shoulder, 1905, aqua, EX . . . . $250.00 D

Block print "Coca-Cola" in center of bottle body, fluted above and below name, EX . . . . $20.00 D

Brickyard 400 Nascar Inaugural at Indianapolis, NM . . . . $50.00 D

California State Fair LE commemorative bottle, 1995, NM . . . . $5.00 D

Cal Ripken, "The Record Breaking Year," NM . . . . $5.00 D

Can, alternating red and white diamonds, red "Coca-Cola" next to white "Coke" on center diamond, 1960s, VG . . . . $50.00 C

Can, experimental fashioned to feel like bottle, red and white Coca-Cola logo, not put into production, 1970s, 12-oz., NM . . . . $425.00 C

Can, fashioned to feel like a bottle, white with the dynamic wave logo, experimental only, not put into production, 1970s, 12-oz., NM . . . . $325.00 C

Carolina Panthers #1, NM . . . . $5.00 D

Casey's General Store 25th Anniversary 1968 – 1993, NM . . . . $145.00 D

Clear syrup with metal lid, "Drink Coca-Cola" with outline etched in bottle, 1920s, clear, VG. $475.00 D

Clemson, 1981, NM . . . . $5.00 D

Coca-Cola safe truck driving rodeo limited ed. commemorative, M . . . . $160.00 D

Commemorative Hutchinson style, "Coca-Cola 1894 – 1979," 1979, 7¼" h, M . . . . $50.00 D

Commemorative reproduction of 1927 bottle used on luxury liners, green glass with green and red label, foil covered neck and top, 1994, M . . . . $65.00 D

Cub Foods, NM . . . . $25.00 D

Dallas Cowboys silver season commemorative, 1984, 10-oz., M . . . . $75.00 D

Dallas Cowboys Superbowl XXX commemorative, 8-oz., M . . . . $65.00 D

Detroit Red Wings, NM. . . . . $5.00 D

Display bottle with cap and patent date, 1923, 20" tall, EX. . . . . $450.00 C

Domino's commemorative, M. . . . . $75.00 D

Easter Seals commemorative, M . . . . $28.00 D

Embossed 24 set, yellow wooden case with red lettering, 1920s, 24-bottle case, yellow, EX. . . . $175.00 D

England Royal Wedding, featuring Union Jack flag with screw-on cap, 7-29-81, 8-oz., M . . . . . $75.00 D

Florida Forest Festival, 1995, NM . . . . $45.00 D

Florida Marlins, 1994, NM. . . . . $5.00 D

Gator Bowl, NM. . . . . $5.00 D

George C. Snyder D•A•Y commemorative, issued only to plant stockholders to honor founder of bottling plant in Charlotte, N.C., 1-30-96, 8-oz., M. . . . . $395.00 C

Georgia Tech 75th Anniversary, 1984, NM. $12.00 C

Glass jug with diamond paper label, 1910, one-gal., clear, EX . . . . $250.00 C

Glass jug with hoops at neck and embossed lettering, "Coca-Cola" in script, fairly rare, 1900s, one-gal., clear, EX. . . . . $1,200.00 C

Glass jug with paper label, 1960s, one-gal., clear, EX. . . . . $15.00 D

Glass jug with round paper label, 1910s, one-gal., clear, EX . . . . $300.00 B

Glass syrup jug with applied label, 1950, one-gal., clear, VG. . . . . $25.00 D

Gold bottle of Bellingrath Gardens & Homes, Mobile, Ala., limited edition, NM . . . . $35.00 D

Gold commemorative, 3-bottle set, from Atlanta, Ga., in display case, 1996, M . . . . $129.00 D

Gold dipped, "Bottled from the one millionth gallon December 22, 1959 by the Coca-Cola Bottling Co., Memphis, Tennessee," 1959, NM. . . . . . . $30.00 D

Guam Liberation Day. . . . . $10.00 D

Happy Holidays, 1994, NM . . . . $5.00 D

Hardee's LE commemorative celebrating opening of the 3000th restaurant, 1988, NM . . . . $50.00 D

Hardee's 3 great years LE commemorative, 1982–85, 1985, NM. . . . . $25.00 D

Hardee's 35th anniversary LE commemorative, NM. . . . . $75.00 D

Hawaii Mickey Mouse Toontown limited edition, 1994, NM. . . . . $20.00 D

Head Yai, Thailand, new bottling plant, rare, 1993, 10-oz., NM . . . . $100.00 D

Hutchinson style, "Birmingham Coca-Cola Bottling Co.," "DOC 13" on back, 1894, 7"h, NM . $1,000.00 B

Independent Grocers Alliance, 70th anniversary commemorative, only 960 produced, 1996, M . $110.00 C

Jacksonville Jaguars limited edition commemorative No. 1, M. . . . . $3.00 D

Jacksonville Jaguars limited edition commemorative No. 2, M. . . . . $3.00 D

Jacksonville Jaguars limited edition commemorative No. 3, M. . . . . $3.00 D

Jeff Gordon Winston Cup Champion, 1995, NM. . . . . $5.00 D

Kennesaw College National Softball Champs, 50 cases produced, M . . . . $14.00 D

Lamp with embossed "Coca-Cola" base, 1970s, 20", EX . . . . $6,000.00 B

Lamp with embossed "Coca-Cola" base, 1970s, 20", EX . . . . $6,000.00 C

Leaded glass display bottle, 1920s, 36" tall, EX .... $9,500.00 C

Long John Silver's LE commemorative, 8-oz., NM .... $95.00 C

Los Angeles Olympics set in boxes with tags, 1984, EX .... $100.00 D

Mardi Gras, 1996, NM .... $5.00 D

McDonald's 40th partners, M .... $120.00 C

McDonald's Hawaii I, M .... $50.00 D

McDonald's Hawaii II, M .... $50.00 C

Mexican Christmas commemorative, 1993, M .... $26.00 D

Mexican Christmas commemorative, 1994, EX .... $21.00 D

Mexican Christmas bottle, 1996, M ...... $22.00 D

Mexico, Christmas with Santa and girl, NM. $6.00 D

Mickey Mouse Hawaii Toontown limited edition commemorative, given away with $200 grocery purchase in Hawaii between May and July 1994, M .... $10.00 C

Miniature six-pack of gold-plated metal bottles, 1970, EX .... $15.00 D

Monsanto experimental with screw-on lid in various colors, 1960, EX .... $40.00 C

Nahunta Fire Dept. LE commemorative, M $80.00 C

North Dakota, embossed Coke with bottle in diamond, 10-oz., NM .... $20.00 D

Original paper label with script "Coca-Cola Beverage," reproduction labels are available, 1900–10, aqua, F $100.00

Orlando World Cup, NM .... $5.00 D

Pete Rose, NM .... $95.00 C

Pharmor, NM .... $275.00 D

Phoenix Coyotes hockey LE commemorative bottle with picture of moon, new, M .... $3.00 D

"Property of Coca-Cola Bottling Co., La Grange, Texas," in block print on body with embossed ribbon on shoulder, 6-oz., aqua, G .... $20.00 D

Republican National Convention LE commemorative, 1996, M .... $30.00 C

Ron Carew LE commemorative, NM ..... $25.00 C

Ronald McDonald House charity commemorative, 1996, M .... $105.00 C

Root Commemorative in box with gold clasp, 1965, aqua, EX .... $450.00 D

Root Commemorative in box with silver clasp, 1971, aqua, EX .... $350.00 D

San Diego Padres, 1993, NM .... $5.00 D

San Diego Padres, 1993, EX .... $3.00 C

San Francisco 49ers, NM .... $5.00 D

Santa Claus Christmas bottle carrier sleeve, Santa Claus & Christmas Greetings, 1930s, M ...... $1,900.00 B

Script "Coca-Cola" in shoulder from Verner Springs Water Co., Greenville, S.C., 9", aqua, EX . $55.00 C

Script "Coca-Cola" inside arrow circle, Louisville, Ky., 1910s, 6-oz., amber, EX .... $75.00 D

Script "Coca-Cola" on shoulder and Biedenharm in script on base, all lettering is embossed, 1900s, aqua, F .... $135.00 C

Seltzer, clear, from Coca-Cola Bottling Co., Cairo, Illinois, with applied color labeling featuring Ritz boy with tray, EX $100.00

Seltzer, from Bradford Pennsylvania Bottling Company, blue, VG .... $125.00 D

Seltzer, green fluted for Rock Springs Coca-Cola Bottling Company, Rock Springs Wyoming, green, VG .... $240.00 D

Seltzer, top marked "Coca-Cola B. Co. R.t. Ill.," 1930s, amber, NM. . . . . $200.00 D

Seltzer, with etched lettering, dark blue, EX. . . . . $175.00 D

Six miniature perfume bottles in miniature '50s style case, 1950s, EX . . . . $160.00 C

Small tray bottle for toy cooler, 1951, 3½" tall, EX. . . . . $15.00 C

Small tray bottle for toy cooler, 1951, 3½" tall, EX. . . . . $15.00 D

Southwest Airlines commemorative featuring artwork of wings on bottle, 8-oz., M . . . . $125.00 C

St. Louis Rams, NM. . . . . $5.00 D

Standard top, with "Coca-Cola" in block print from Mt. Vernon, IL, embossed at base, 6-oz., aqua, EX. . . . . $15.00 D

Straight-sided amber marked "Made at Williamstown, New Jersey," "Made by Williamstown Glass Company," made by mold, very rare, 1905–10, 3¼" tall, EX . . . . $3,200.00 B

Styrofoam display, 1961, 42" tall, VG . . . . $225.00 C

Super Bowl 28, NM . . . . $5.00 D

Syrup bottle with wreath logo, with original jigger cap, nice heavy transfer onto bottle, 1910, NM . . $700.00

Syrup can with paper label, 1930s, one-gal., red, EX. . . . . $200.00 D

Syrup can with paper label featuring Coca-Cola glass, 1940, EX. . . . . $325.00 D

Syrup can with paper label red on white, 1950s, one-gal., VG. . . . . $175.00 D

Syrup, applied label and original cap, EX. . $1,000.00 C

Syrup, with "Drink Coca-Cola" inside etched ribbon with bow at bottom, metal lid, 1910, clear, EX. . . . . $800.00 C

Syrup, with fired-on foil label, red lettering on white label, 1920s, NM. . . . . $775.00 C

Syrup, with foil label red script lettering on white background with gold outline, with original metal lid, 1920, blue, EX. . . . . $850.00 C

Syrup, with paper label "Coca-Cola" in block lettering, metal lid, 1900, clear, EX . . . . $700.00 C

"Tell City, IND," green, 28-oz., 1937, 12"h, NM . . . . $40.00 C

Test for 16 oz., "QC" on bottom for quality control, original sticker, scarce due to unusual size, 1940–60s, 16-oz., NM . . . . $90.00 C

Ty Cobb commemorative, birthplace Banks County, 8-oz., NM. . . . . $75.00 D

Ty Cobb LE commemorative five-piece: The Georgia Peach; Royston Lodge Remembers; First in the Hall of Fame; The Boy, the Man, the Legend; Birthplace, Banks County, NM. . . . . $1,375.00 C

Tyber Island Centennial limited edition commemorative, 10-oz., M. . . . . $8.00 C

Wal-Mart Christmas, 1994, NM. . . . . $5.00 C

White Castle 75th anniversary LE commemorative bottle, NM . . . . $85.00 C

World of Coca-Cola 5th anniversary limited edition commemorative, 8-oz., M. . . . . $6.00 D

Wooden keg with paper label, 1920–30, 10-gallon, VG. . . . . $225.00 B

Wooden keg with paper label on end, 1920–30s, 5-gallon, VG . . . . $200.00 B

York Rite Masonry, NM . . . . $20.00 D

Young Presidents commemorative, M. . . . . $55.00 D

Glasses

Anniversary glass given to John W. Boucher, 1936, NM, $375.00 B.
Muddy River Trading Co./Gary Metz.

50th Anniversary, gold-dipped with plastic stand, 1950s, EX, $250.00 B.
Muddy River Trading Co./Gary Metz.

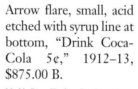

Arrow flare, small, acid etched with syrup line at bottom, "Drink Coca-Cola 5¢," 1912–13, $875.00 B.

Muddy River Trading Co./Gary Metz.

Bell, "Drink Coca-Cola," 1940 – 60s, $10.00 C. Mitchell Collection.

Bell, with "Enjoy," set of four different sizes, EX, $20.00 D.

Flare, modified, "Coca-Cola," 1926, EX, $175.00 C; Bell with trademark in tail of C, 1930–40s, $55.00 C; Flare with syrup line, "Drink Coca-Cola," 1910s, EX, $400.00 C. Mitchell Collection.

Glass holder, "Coca-Cola," new, EX, $25.00 C. Mitchell Collection.

Glass holder, silver, 1900, VG, $2,100.00 B. Beware: reproductions exist. Muddy River Trading Co./Gary Metz.

Pewter, bell-shaped, scarce, 1930s, EX, $300.00 B.
Muddy River Trading Co./Gary Metz.

Bell, "Enjoy Coca-Cola," 1970s. . . . . $5.00 C

Flare, "Bottle Coca-Cola," 1916, EX. $550.00

Flare with syrup line, 1900s, EX . . . . $450.00 C

Information paper showing all the strong points of the glass, VG. . . . . $15.00 C

Pewter, "Coca-Cola," with original leather pouch, 1930s, EX. . . . . $750.00 B

"Drink Coca-Cola Good with food,"
Wellsville China Co., 1940–50s, 7½", VG,
$750.00 B. Muddy River Trading Co./Gary Metz.

Sandwich plate, "Drink Coca-Cola Refresh Yourself," Knowles China Co., 1931, NM, $775.00 B.
Muddy River Trading Co./Gary Metz.

Sandwich plate, "Drink Coca-Cola Refresh
yourself," 1930s, 8¼", NM, $1,200.00 B.
Muddy River Trading Co./Gary Metz.

Sugar bowl complete with lid, "Drink Coca-Cola,"
1930, M, $350.00 C; Creamer, "Drink Coca-Cola,"
1930s, VG, $300.00 C. Mitchell Collection.

Dish, round, world, 1967, 7", EX . . . . $100.00 C

Dish, square, "Coca-Cola" world, 1960s, 11½"x11½",
EX. . . . . $125.00 C

Display bottle with original tin lid, 1923 bottle,
20" . . . . $260.00 D

Pitcher, red lettered "Coca-Cola" on glass,
M . . . . $55.00 C

Plate, Swedish, 1969, 8¼"x6¼", EX . . . . . $100.00 C

Dark headed woman facing forward with her head slightly to the left and looking upward, 10", EX, $375.00 D.

Western Coca-Cola™ Bottling Co., featuring brunette with red hair scarf holding a pink rose, 1908–12, EX, $375.00 C.

Western Coca-Cola™ Bottling Co., featuring dark haired woman turned at an angle to the plate, 1908, 10" dia., EX, $375.00 D.

Western Coca-Cola™ Bottling Co., featuring dark haired woman with low drape across shoulders, 1908, 10" dia., EX, $400.00 C.

Western Coca-Cola™ Bottling Co., featuring dark haired woman with yellow head piece, 1908–12, 10" dia., EX, $375.00 C.

Western Coca-Cola™ Bottling Co., featuring long haired woman body forward with head and eyes to the left wearing a white drape covering off the shoulders, 1908–12, EX, $450.00 C.

Western Coca-Cola™ Bottling Co., featuring woman with auburn colored hair with a red adornment on the right side of her head, 1908, 10" dia., EX, $375.00 C.

Western Coca-Cola™ Bottling Co., featuring woman with long red hair and off the shoulder apparel, 1908–12, 10" dia., EX, $325.00 C.

Western Coca-Cola™ Bottling Co., if any art plate is in its original shadow box frame value can be doubled, 1908–12, EX, $750.00 C. Mitchell Collection.

Western Coca-Cola™ Bottling Co., profile of dark haired woman with red head piece and yellow blouse, 1908–12, 10", EX, $375.00 C.

Celluloid and metal pocket mirror with the Hamilton King Coca-Cola girl on the front, 1911, 1¾" x 2¾", F, $150.00 B. Muddy River Trading Co./Gary Metz.

Celluloid and metal pocket mirror featuring Elaine, 1916, 1¾" x 2¾", G, $190.00 B. Muddy River Trading Co./Gary Metz.

Glass, Silhouette Girl, with thermometer, 1939, 10"x14¼", VG, $850.00 B. Muddy River Trading Co./Gary Metz.

"Drink Coca-Cola in Bottles," Coca-Cola Bottling Co, Madisonville, Ky., 1920–30s, 8"x17½", $500.00 C. Mitchell Collection.

Pocket mirror featuring the Coca-Cola girl, 1910, 1¾" x 2¾", EX, $250.00 B. Muddy River Trading Co./Gary Metz.

Pocket mirror, "Wherever you go you will find Coca-Cola at all fountains 5¢," 1900s, G, $900.00 C. Mitchell Collection.

Pocket mirror, folding cardboard cat's head, "Drink Coca-Cola in bottles" on inside cover, 1920, EX, $750.00 C.

Mitchell Collection.

Celluloid and metal, "Drink Coca-Cola," 1908, 1¾"x2¾", EX. Beware: reproductions exist.........$1,100.00 C

Celluloid and metal, "Drink Coca-Cola," Elaine, 1916, 1¾"x2¾", NM.................$600.00 C

Celluloid and metal, "Drink Coca-Cola 5¢," 1914, 1¾"x2¾", EX......................$625.00 C

Celluloid and metal, "Drink Coca-Cola," Golden Girl, 1920, 1¾"x2¾", EX. Beware: Reproductions exist.............................$700.00 C

Celluloid and metal, "Drink Delicious Coca-Cola" with the Coca-Cola girl, 1911, 1¾"x2¾", Hamilton King. Beware: Reproductions exist. NM..$550.00 C

Celluloid and metal, girl on beach beside parasol, much sought after piece, 1922, 1¾"x2¾", EX...$1,750.00 D

Celluloid and metal, Juanita, 1906, 1¾"x2¾", EX. Beware: Reproductions exist..........$600.00 C

Celluloid and metal, "Relieves Fatigue," 1907, 1¾"x1¾", EX......................$600.00 D

Celluloid and metal, St. Louis Fair, 1909, 1¾"x2¾", EX. Beware: Reproductions exist.......$600.00 D

Celluloid and metal, the Coca-Cola Girl, 1910, 1¾"x2¾", Hamilton King, NM........$550.00 C

Commemorative wall mirror featuring Hilda Clark produced for the 75th anniversary of the Chicago Coca-Cola Bottling Co., 1976, 28½" x 41", NM...........................$425.00 C

In frame under glass "Drink Coca-Cola in Bottles Delicious Refreshing," 1930s, 8"x12", EX...........................$150.00 D

Pemberton and Chandler with ceramic dispenser in center, 1977, M.....................$35.00 D

Pocket, "Coca-Cola Memos, 50th Anniversary, 1886–1936," 1936, EX..............$200.00 D

Pocket, "Coca-Cola Memos, Delicious and Refreshing," 1936, EX......................$225.00 C

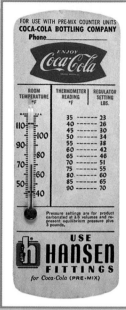

Cardboard pre-mix counter unit thermometer with mercury scale on left then comparison chart of thermometer reading to regulator setting right, 1960s, VG, $55.00 C.

Mitchell Collection.

"Drink Coca-Cola, Delicious and Refreshing," Silhouette Girl, 1930s, 6½"x16", EX, $425.00 C. Mitchell Collection.

Embossed die cut with 1923 Christmas bottle, 1931, VG, $200.00 B.

Muddy River Trading Co./Gary Metz.

Leather desk thermometer, 1930s, EX, $1,200.00 B. Muddy River Trading Co./Gary Metz.

Metal and plastic, "Drink Coca-Cola, Sign of Good Taste," Robertson, 1950s, 12" dia., EX, $130.00 C. Mitchell Collection.

Masonite, "Thirst knows no season," 1940s, 6¾"x17", EX, $425.00 C. Mitchell Collection.

Metal and plastic 12" Pam style with bottle outline in center on red background, outside circle is in green with black numbers, 1950s, $425.00 B. Muddy River Trading co./Gary Metz.

Metal, die cut bottle thermometer, 1956, 5" x 17", NM, $160.00 B. Muddy River Trading Co./Gary Metz.

Metal, "Drink Coca-Cola in Bottles, Quality Refreshment," features button at top, 1950s, EX, $150.00 C. Mitchell Collection.

Metal, embossed Spanish bottle thermometer, 1950s, 6" x 18", EX, $150.00 B. Muddy River Trading Co./Gary Metz.

Metal, gold version double bottle, "Drink Coca-Cola," metal composition, 1942, 7"x16", EX, $425.00 C. Mitchell Collection.

Metal French Canadian bottlers' thermometer, logo at top left with scale on left next to bottle, "Leo Aboussafy," 6" x 16", NM, $350.00 B. Muddy River Trading Co./Gary Metz.

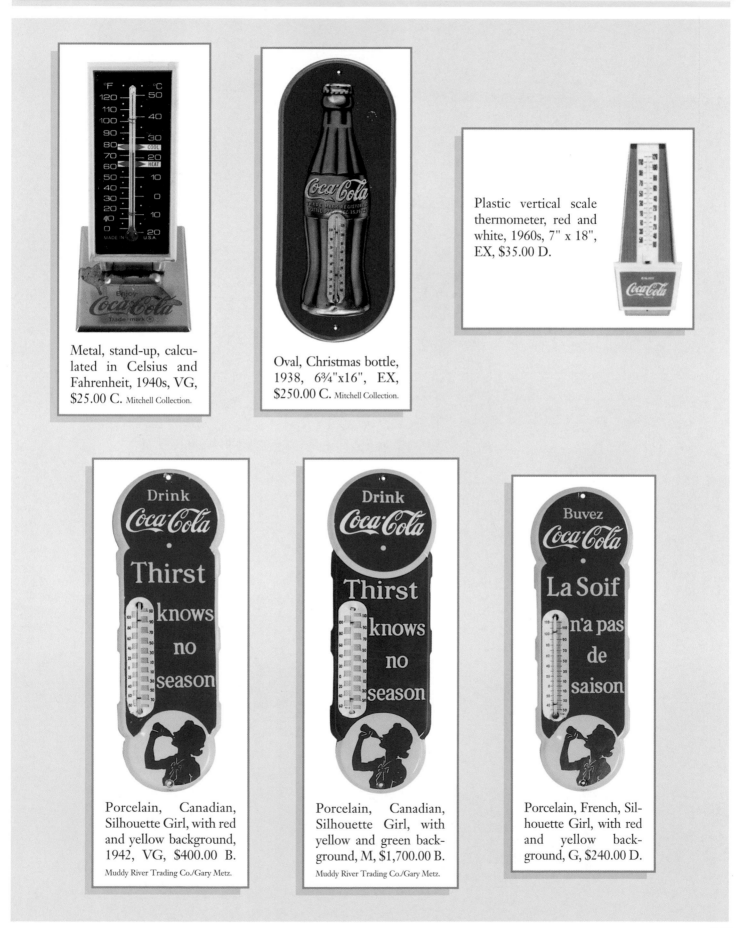

Metal, stand-up, calculated in Celsius and Fahrenheit, 1940s, VG, $25.00 C. Mitchell Collection.

Oval, Christmas bottle, 1938, 6¾"x16", EX, $250.00 C. Mitchell Collection.

Plastic vertical scale thermometer, red and white, 1960s, 7" x 18", EX, $35.00 D.

Porcelain, Canadian, Silhouette Girl, with red and yellow background, 1942, VG, $400.00 B.

Muddy River Trading Co./Gary Metz.

Porcelain, Canadian, Silhouette Girl, with yellow and green background, M, $1,700.00 B.

Muddy River Trading Co./Gary Metz.

Porcelain, French, Silhouette Girl, with red and yellow background, G, $240.00 D.

Round glass front, "Enjoy Coca-Cola" dial type thermometer, white lettering on red background, 1960s, 12" round, EX, $165.00 B.

Muddy River Trading Co./Gary Metz.

Tin, "Drink Coca-Cola in Bottles" Phone 612, Dyersburg, Tenn., with minder notations for oil, grease, and battery, 1940s, VG, $35.00 C.

Mitchell Collection.

Tin, bottle embossed die cut, 1933, G, $110.00 B.

Muddy River Trading Co./Gary Metz.

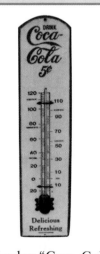

Wooden, "Coca-Cola 5¢" good graphics, red on white, 1905, 5" x 21", G, $400.00 B.

Muddy River Trading Co./Gary Metz.

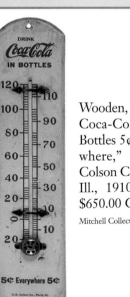

Wooden, "Drink Coca-Cola in Bottles 5¢ Everywhere," V. O. Colson Co., Paris Ill., 1910s, VG, $650.00 C.

Mitchell Collection.

Desk free-standing in leather case with a round dial, hard to find, 1930s, 3¼"x3¼", EX . . . . . $1,500.00 C

Dial, with gold bottle outline on red center button, black numbers on face, 1908, 12" dia., NM$375.00 C

Leather front, self-standing desk, 1930s, 3¼"x3¼", EX . . . . $1,600.00 C

Liquid crystal readout design showing temp in both Celsius and Fahrenheit, scarce, 1970s, 10¼" sq., NM. . . . . $165.00 C

Metal and plastic, Pam, "Drink Coca-Cola Be Really Refreshed," with fishtail, 1960s, 12" dia. . . $500.00 C

Metal "cigar" thermometer, red & white, 1950s, 30" tall, F. . . . . $130.00 C

Metal framed mirror with thermometer on left side and Silhouette Girl across bottom, 1930s, EX . . . $450.00 C

Metal, round, "Enjoy Coca-Cola," white on red, EX. . . . . $95.00 C

Metal, round, "Things Go Better With Coke," red on white, 1960s, EX. . . . . $160.00 C

Metal, "Things go better with Coke," 1960, 12", M . . . . $110.00 D

Plastic and metal, round, "Drink Coca-Cola," fishtail with green on white, 1960s, NM. . . . . $375.00 C

Plastic and metal, round, "Drink Coca-Cola in Bottles," white on red, VG . . . . $110.00 C

Porcelain, all red, French version of the Silhouette Girl, 1939, 5½"x18", M. . . . . $525.00 C

Porcelain, French, Silhouette Girl, with green and yellow background, VG . . . . $240.00 B

Porcelain, Silhouette Girl, red and green version, 1939, 5½"x18", EX . . . . $625.00 C

Porcelain, "Thirst Knows No Season," green background with red dot at top and Silhouette Girl at bottom, 1939, 18", EX. . . . . $600.00 D

Round, "Drink Coca-Cola," "Be Really Refreshed!," with fishtail logo, 1960s, 12" dia., NM . . . $475.00 C

Round, "Drink Coca-Cola In bottles," white on red with glass face, 1950s, 12", NM . . . . $225.00 C

Round, "Drink Coca-Cola, Sign of Good Taste," 1957, 12" dia., NM . . . . $155.00 D

Tin, "Coke Refreshes," white on red, 1950, 8"x36", NM . . . . $2,600.00 C

Tin, double bottle, 1941, VG . . . . $325.00 D

Tin, embossed bottle, 1936, G . . . . $160.00 D

Wooden, "Coca-Cola 5¢," 1905, F . . . . . . $275.00 C

Carriers

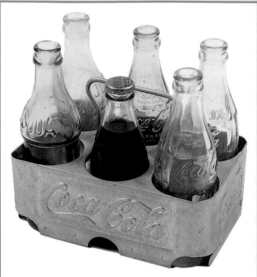

Aluminum six-pack carrier with separated bottle compartments, "Coca-Cola" is embossed on side, 1940–50s, EX, $85.00 C. Mitchell Collection.

Aluminum six-pack carrier with wood and wire handle, red lettered "Drink Coca-Cola," 1950s, EX, $85.00 C. Mitchell Collection.

Aluminum six-pack king size carrier with wire handle, red lettered "Drink Coca-Cola" and "King Size," 1950, EX, $95.00 C. Mitchell Collection.

Aluminum six-pack with wire handle, separated bottle compartments, "Delicious Refreshing Coca-Cola" in white on red center panel, 1950s, EX, $50.00 C. Mitchell Collection.

Bent wood with rounded corners and flat wood handle, 1940s, VG, $125.00 C. Mitchell Collection.

Cardboard carton display, "Take enough home today," 1950s, 14" x 20" x 38", EX, $210.00 B.

Muddy River Trading Co./Gary Metz.

Cardboard case, holds four 6-packs, EX, $75.00 D.

Wildflower Antique Mall.

Cardboard display rack, "Drink Coca-Cola Take Home a Carton," 1930s, VG, $725.00 B.

Muddy River Trading Co./Gary Metz.

Cardboard, showing "Season's Greetings" and holly leaves, 1930s, VG, $35.00 C. Mitchell Collection.

Cardboard six pack carrier, 6 for 25¢, red and white, 1939, EX, $45.00 B. Muddy River Trading Co./Gary Metz.

Cardboard six-pack, red background, 1930s, EX, $110.00 C. Mitchell Collection.

Cardboard six-pack, "Serve Ice Cold," 1930s, EX, $100.00 C. Mitchell Collection.

Cardboard with metal handles, "Drink Coca-Cola" on front, "Have a Coke" "Picnic Cooler" on sides, red with white lettering, 1956, EX, $130.00 C. Mitchell Collection.

Metal grocery cart two bottle holder with sign on front "Enjoy Coca-Cola while you shop, Place Bottles Here," 1950s, EX, $45.00 C. Mitchell Collection.

Metal stadium carrier with opener, white lettering on red, 1950s, EX, $275.00 D. Rare Bird Antique Mall/ Jon & Joan Wright.

Metal three case bottle rack with "Place Empties Here, Thank You" sign at top, red, G, $275.00 C. Mike and Debbie Summers.

Metal twelve-pack, red lettering on yellow body, 1920–30s, G, $325.00 C. Mitchell Collection.

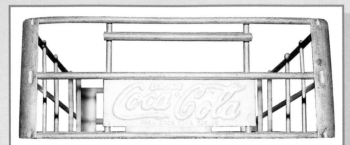

Wire carrier, case size with embossed aluminum "Drink Coca-Cola," 1940s, 24 bottle, EX, $45.00 D. Chief Paduke Antique Mall.

Wire case holder, sign on top, "Drink Coca-Cola Take enough home," EX, $165.00 D. Patrick's Collectibles.

Wire case rack with "Take some Coca-Cola home today" sign at top of rack, metal wheels on bottom, EX, $250.00 D.

Affordable Antiques/Oliver Johnson.

Wooden six-pack carrier with bottle separators, "Pause… Go Refreshed" white on red, 1930s, EX, $450.00 B.

Muddy River Trading Co./Gary Metz.

Wooden six-pack with wood and wire handle, wings on side of carrier, 1930–40s, yellow, EX, $95.00 C. Mitchell Collection.

Wooden six-pack with wooden handle featuring a cut out hand hold, 1940s, EX, $150.00 C. Mitchell Collection.

Wooden with dovetail corner joints, "Refresh yourself Drink Coca-Cola in Bottles," black lettering, 1920s, VG, $250.00 C. Mitchell Collection.

12 bottle aluminum carrier with red panel on side, 1950s, EX . . . . $85.00 C

24 bottle display case, 1950s, VG . . . . $170.00 C

48 bottle wooden shipping crate, 1910s, 9"x18"x25", VG . . . . $375.00 C

Cardboard, car window holder, 1950s, red and white, EX. . . . . $30.00 D

Cardboard, six bottle, bracket on end, 1924, red and green in white, EX . . . . $250.00 D

Cardboard, six bottle carrier for King Size, red, white, and light green, NOS, 1960s, NM . . . . $15.00 C

Cardboard, six-pack, "Serve Ice Cold," 1930s, EX. . . . . $85.00 C

Cardboard, red and white, will hold four Family Size bottles, NOS, 1958, NM. . . . . $15.00 D

Cardboard, six-pack "Money back bottles return for deposit," dynamic wave logo, red and white, NOS, 1970s, EX . . . . $10.00 D

Cardboard, triangle-shaped, NOS, 1950s, M$60.00 D

Cardboard, twelve bottle, white lettering on red background, 1950s, EX . . . . $20.00 D

Cardboard, twelve bottles, "Coca-Cola" in script, white on red, NOS, 1951, EX. . . . . $20.00 D

Cardboard, twelve regular size bottles, yellow on red, 1950s, EX . . . . $15.00 D

Cardboard, 24 bottle case, 1950s, EX . . . . $45.00 D

Cardboard, waxed "In 6 Bottle cartons" with "Coca-Cola" button at left, will hold four 6-pack cartons, NOS, 1940s, M . . . . $45.00 C

Cardboard, white lettering on red, "Chill...Serve..." banner at top by cut out carry handle, twelve bottles, NOS, 1950s, EX . . . . $20.00 C

Cardboard, white top with red lettering, red button, twelve bottles, NOS, 1960s, NM. . . . . $10.00 C

Cardboard with metal handles, "Drink Coca-Cola" on front, "Have a Coke," "Picnic Cooler" on sides, red with white lettering, 1956, EX. . . . . $130.00 C

Cardboard with top carrying handle, will hold six bottles, "Drink Coca-Cola Delicious and Refreshing," "Serve Ice Cold," 1929, EX. . . . . $75.00 D

Cardboard with wire handle, white lettering on red, six bottle, NOS, 1950s, NM. . . . . $45.00 D

Display case for giant 20" bottles, 1950s, VG . . . . $180.00 C

Masonite six-pack carrier, 1940s, EX . . . . . $75.00 D

Metal and wire Canadian carrier and vendor for 18 bottles "Drink Coca-Cola Iced" on side panels, 1930s, 18 bottle, G. . . . . $275.00 C

Metal and wire 18 bottle, Canadian, 1930–1940, red, VG . . . . $275.00 D

Metal for car window, 1940s, white and red, EX . . . . $75.00 D

Metal vendor's carrier, red with white lettering; embossed on ends, metal loop handle with on front, 1950s, red, VG . . . . $200.00 C

Miniature six pack, plastic bottles in red and white carton, 1970s, EX . . . . $15.00 D

Plastic miniature six-pack carrying case, red lettering on white, 1970s, EX . . . . $10.00 D

Plastic six-pack carrier, King Size, white lettering, 1950s, red, EX. . . . . $12.00 D

Plastic six-pack carrier, regular size, white lettering, 1950s, red, EX. . . . . $12.00 D

Salesman's sample for bulk case storage, 1960s, 6"x12"x13", EX . . . . $4,500.00 C

Six-pack cardboard, French, 1934, G . . . . . $85.00 C

Six-pack carton wrapper, July 4th, 1930s, red, white, and blue, EX . . . . $350.00 C

Vinyl 12 bottle, white lettering on red, 1950s, EX . . . . $35.00 D

Wooden, "Drink Coca-Cola in Bottles," with cut out carrying handle, wings at end, 1940s, yellow, EX. . . . . $95.00 C

Wooden six-pack, "Six bottles for 25¢ plus deposit," 1940s, red, EX. $150.00 C

Wooden six-pack, with end wings and bottle separators, white logo on red background, 1930–1940s, EX. . . . . $450.00 C

Wooden six-pack, with hand in bottle and wings logo on both ends, G. . . . . $100.00 C

Cooler, lift-top fiberglass, new, built to resemble a Vendo V-81 vending machine, new, EX, $325.00 C.

Floor cooler, with base, in form of picnic cooler, 1950s, 17"x12"x39", EX, $3,100.00 B. Muddy River Trading Co./Gary Metz.

Glascock junior size cooler complete with cap catcher, 1929, EX, $1,400.00 C. Mitchell Collection.

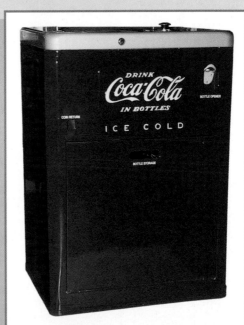

Glascock salesman's sample, complete with under cooler case storage metal, NM, $1,200.00 C. Mitchell Collection.

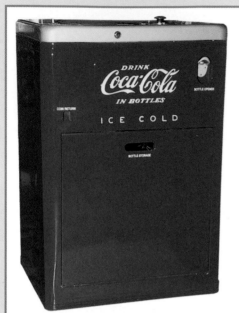

Vendo model #23, also known to collectors as the spin top machine, comes in standard and deluxe model, which has the silver top, vends 23 bottles and precools 7, with drop door in front for storage, 40-50s, 24"w x 36"h x 21"D, EX, $1,295.00 D.

Affordable Antiques/Oliver Johnson.

Vendo model 44, restored, red & white, 1950s, 16"w x 57½"h x 15½"D, NM, $2,400.00 B. Collectors Auction Services.

Vendo V-39, a fairly common machine, dispenses 39 bottles and precools 20 bottles, 1940 – 1950s, 27"w x 58"h x 16"D, NM, $2,995.00 D. Patrick's Collectibles.

Vendolator 72, dual chute machine with very large embossed Coca-Cola logo, dispenses 72 and precools 6, 1950s, 25"w x 58"h x 15"D, G, $1,500.00 D. Patrick's Collectibles.

Vendolator model Dual 27, successor to the table top version of this machine, dispenses 27 bottles while precooling 27, 1950s, 25½"w x 52"hx 17½"D, NM, $2,195.00 D, Patrick's Collectibles.

Westinghouse ten case master, electric "dry" box, lid hinges in middle and opens side to side instead of front to back, cools 240 bottles, stacked, 1950s, 30½"w x 36"h x 45. $172.00 D, NM, $1,850.00 D. Patrick's Collectibles.

Vendo coin changer with keys, reproduction sign, EX, $625.00 B. Muddy River Trading Co./Gary Metz.

Vendo V-81, much sought after for home use due to its compact design and ability to dispense different size bottles, 1950s, 27" x 58" x 16", white on red, VG, $795.00 C.

Mike and Debbie Summers.

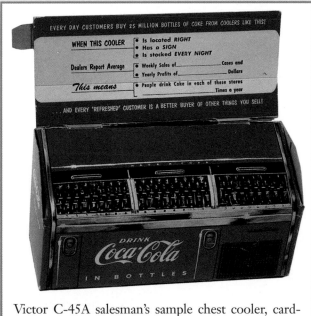

Victor C-45A salesman's sample chest cooler, cardboard, 1940–50s, G, $100.00 C. Mitchell Collection.

Westinghouse salesman's sample metal two-door lift-up cooler, EX, $2,600.00 B. Mitchell Collection.

Westinghouse salesman's sample, standard box, metal, EX, $1,800.00 C. Mitchell Collection.

Westinghouse WE-6, salesman's sample, 1940–50s, 4⅜" x 4" x 3", G, $275.00 C. Mitchell Collection.

Zinc lined wet box for cooling and dispensing, "Help Yourself Drink Coca-Cola Deposit in Box 5¢," wood exterior, 1920s, $310.00 B. Muddy River Trading Co./Gary Metz.

Bottle cooler, wet box, wood by Mengel, "Drink Coca-Cola Delicious Refreshing," 1920s, 32"x38", yellow and red, EX .... $1,700.00 B

Cavalier Coca-Cola vending machine, model 96, vends 96 bottles and precools 17 bottles, 1950s, EX .... $850.00 C

Cavalier 10 case giant chest electric cooler, dispenses 240 bottles, 1940–50, red and stainless steel, EX .... $425.00 D

Cavalier 10 case giant ice chest type cooler, dispenses 256 bottles, 1940–50, red, EX......... $450.00 D

Cavalier C-27, chest type machine that looks more like an upright, dispenses 27 bottles, uncommon and can be difficult to locate but most collectors could find one with a few contacts, 1940–50s, 18"x41"x22", red, EX.. $1,000.00 C

Cavalier C-51, upright that will dispense 51 bottles with a pre-cooling shelf under the dispensing unit, 1950s, red, EX .... $425.00 C

Cavalier CS72, upright that dispenses 72 bottles, will dispense many brands and sizes of bottles, still fairly easy to find, 1950s, red and white, EX ... $625.00 C

Glascock table top cooler chest type wet box, very sought after, 1930s, red and white, G, $350.00 C; Restored........................ $1,250.00 C

Jacobs vending machine model #26, upright shaped like a mailbox, very sought after but also the most common of Jacobs machines, 1940–50s, red, EX .... $1,350.00 C

Vendo coin changer with keys and "Have a Coke" sign under glass, 12"x15", F............... $325.00 D

Vendo model 39, a top entry drum type box with the coin mechanism on top, vends 39 bottles and precools 42 bottles, not highly sought after in the past, but a nice machine whose value will increase, white lettering on red, 1940s, 34½"w x 34"h x 27½"d, EX .... $800.00 C

Vendo model 56, similar to the model 81, but without fluorescent tube in door, and the door on most versions has to be opened to observe selection, red & white, 1950s, 25"w x 52"h x 18¾"d, F ... $500.00 D

Vendo model 56, similar to the model 81, but without fluorescent tube indoor, and the door on most versions has to be opened to observe selection, red & white, 1950s, 25"w x 52"h x 18¾"d, F........ $500.00 D

Vendo model 83 vending machine, not in heavy demand due in large part to the fact they are so heavy, red & white, 1940s, 32½"w x 63"h x 18" d, F . . . . . $225.00 D

Vendo V-23, box cooler that will vend 23 bottles, made in a standard and deluxe version, fairly easy to find, 1940–50s, red and silver, EX . . . . $600.00 C

Vendo 39 vending machine, chest type with top drum and coin entry box, 1940s, 34½"wx34"hx27¼"d, F. $250.00 D

Vendo V-23, box cooler that will vend 23 bottles, made in both a standard and deluxe version, fairly easy to find, 1940 – 50s, red and silver, NM . . . $1,250.00 D

Vendo V-44, an upright box that is highly sought after by collectors, will dispense 44 bottles, 1950s, red and white, EX . . . . $1,800.00 C

Vendo V-56, upright, will dispense 56 bottles, 1950s, red and white, EX . . . . $1,500.00 D

Vendo V-56, upright, will dispense 56 bottles, 1950s, red and white, EX . . . . $1,400.00 C

Vendo V-59 top chest cooler electric, dispense 59 bottles, not very sought after by collectors, 1940s, red, EX . . $575.00 C

Vendo V-80, upright, will dispense 80 bottles, not aggressively sought after so still relatively easy to find and easy to buy, 1950s, red and white, EX . $450.00 D

Vendo 81 Coca-Cola vending machine, one of the most sought after machines due in part to its compact design, original unrestored, red & white, 1950s, 27"w x 58"h x 16"d, NM . . . . $1,950.00 C

Vendo V-81, dispenses 81 bottles, upright, this machine is also sought after by collectors but is still fairly easy to find, 1950s, red and white, G . . . . $750.00 C

Vendo V-81, dispenses 81 bottles, upright, this machine also sought after by collectors but is still fairly easy to find, 1950s, red and white, NM . . . . $2,000.00 C

Vendo V-83, dispenses 83 bottles, very common, 1940–50, red, EX . . . . $550.00 C

Vendolator 27, known as the table top, this machine would sit on a desk or special stand, dispenses 27 bottles, still fairly easy to find, 1940s, 24"x27"x19", red, F . . . . $750.00 C

Vendolator 27, known as the table top, this machine would sit on a desk or special stand, dispenses 27 bottles, still fairly easy to find, 1940s, 24"x27"x19", red, NM . . . $1,750.00 C

Vendolator 33, upright that dispenses 33 bottles, relatively common, 1950s, red, EX . . . . $500.00 D

Vendolator 44, upright that dispenses 44 bottles, not hard to find, 1950s, red and white, EX . . $1,200.00 B

Vendolator 72, upright will dispense 72 bottles, will serve only 6½-oz. bottles, 1950s, red, EX . $695.00 B

Vendor V-39, box type cooler that will vend 39 bottles and will pre-cool slightly more than this number, 1940s, red, EX . . . . $625.00 C

Westinghouse 3 Case Junior electric chest box, dispenses 75 bottles, 1940–50s, red, EX . . . . $795.00 D

Westinghouse 3 Case Junior, water cooled chest box, 1940–50s, red, G . . . . $375.00 C

Westinghouse 6 Case Master dispenses 140 bottles, chest box electric, 1940s, red and stainless steel, G . $425.00 D

Westinghouse 6 Case Master wet chest type box dispenses 144 bottles, 1940s, red, EX . . . . . . $425.00 D

Westinghouse Master electric chest cooler, dispenses 144 bottles fairly common, 1930–40, red, EX . . . . $495.00 D

Westinghouse Master electric chest cooler, dispenses 144 bottles, fairly common, 1930–40, red, NM . . . $795.00 C

Westinghouse model 42, embossed "Here's A Coke For You" on sides, early models were solid red, red & white, 1950s, 25"wx53½"hx20"d, NM . . . . $1,200.00 D

Westinghouse model 96, vends 96 bottles and will dispense both regular and King Size bottles, 1950s, 25"w x 75"h x 19½"d, NM . . . . $975.00 C

Westinghouse salesman's sample, featuring open front, white on red, F . . . . $900.00 D

Westinghouse Standard ice chest, dispenses 102 bottles, 1930s, red, EX . . . . $425.00 C

Westinghouse 3 Case Junior, water cooled chest box, 1940–50s, red, NM . . . . $1,150.00 C

Airline Coca-Cola cooler with stainless steel cooler, white lettering on red, 1950s, G, $300.00 B. Muddy River Trading Co./Gary Metz.

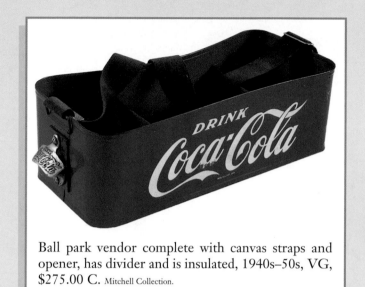

Ball park vendor complete with canvas straps and opener, has divider and is insulated, 1940s–50s, VG, $275.00 C. Mitchell Collection.

Coolers, metal cooler with dynamic wave, "It's the real thing," 18"x13"x16½", G, $150.00 D.

Patrick's Collectibles.

Coolers, wood and metal cooler with tin sides," Serve yourself... Please pay the clerk," 32"x29"x21¼", F, $1,700.00 B.

Collectors Auction Services.

Junior stainless steel cooler, 1950s, 12" x 9" x 14", EX, $650.00 B.

Muddy River Trading Co./Gary Metz.

Picnic cooler with original hand in bottle decals on each side, with bail handle, red, 1940s, 8" x 12" x 13", EX, $100.00 B.

Muddy River Trading Co./Gary Metz.

Floor chest, embossed lettering, yellow and white lettering on red background with bottle at left side, 29"x32½"hx22"d, VG, $950.00 B.

Muddy River Trading Co./Gary Metz.

Metal picnic, small, "Drink Coca-Cola in Bottles," 1950s, VG, $130.00 C. Mitchell Collection.

Salesman's sample counter dispenser with original carrying case and complete presentation unit, light inside lights up glasses, very rare, 1960s, 4½"wx6½"dx6¾"h, EX, $2,500.00 B. Muddy River Trading Co./Gary Metz.

Salesman's sample sale aid shaped like box cooler, EX, $125.00 C. Mitchell Collection.

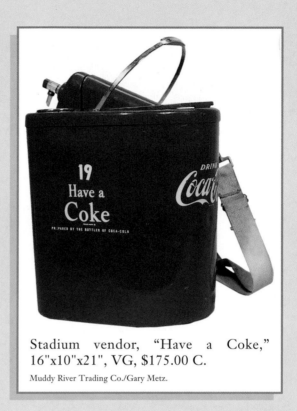

Stadium vendor, "Have a Coke," 16"x10"x21", VG, $175.00 C.
Muddy River Trading Co./Gary Metz.

Wooden cooler for iced bottles, with the original zinc lined tub, red on yellow, 1920s, 38" x 20" x 35", F, $950.00 B.
Muddy River Trading Co./Gary Metz.

Stainless steel picnic cooler "Drink Coca-Cola" on front in red, 1950s, 6-pack, EX, $425.00 B. Muddy River Trading Co./Gary Metz.

Airline style painted cooler with stainless liner, with opener on end, white lettering on red, 1950s, NM . . . . $375.00 C

Airline, with top handle, 1950s, red, NM . $450.00 C

Aluminum, 12 pack, 1950s, 12 pack, G . . . . $85.00 C

Aluminum, 12 pack, 1950s, 12 pack, EX . . $125.00 D

Floor chest, embossed lettering, yellow and white lettering on red background with bottle at left side, 29" x 32½"h x 22"d, VG . . . . $950.00 C

Dispenser, fountain, red with white lettering, 1940s, EX . . . . $425.00 D

Dispenser, refills from top, red metal with cream lettering, 1950s, VG . . . . $325.00 D

Dispenser, soda fountain, red and white, 1940–50s, EX . . . . $675.00 D

Dispenser, soda fountain, red sides with chrome lid, two tops, 1930s, EX. . . . . $675.00 D

Floor, large, resembling a large picnic cooler, 1950s, red, NM . . . . $3,000.00 C

Hemp Model 9022 picnic, white "Drink" on red, metal latch and handle, NOS, 1950s, M . . $500.00 D

Insulated stadium vendor, no strap or opener, red, 1930s, F . . . . $175.00 C

Metal picnic, small, "Drink Coca-Cola in Bottles," 1950s, VG . . . . $130.00 C

Metal picnic, with bottle in hand decal, 1940–50s, 13"x12"x8", EX . . . . $110.00 D

Metal picnic, with bottle in hand decal, 1940 – 50s, 13" x 12" x 8", F . . . . $55.00 C

Metal, Progress Refrigerator Company, Louisville, Ky., featuring "Things go better..." logo embossed on front. With lift top lid, metal handles with opener under handle, white lettering on red background, F . . . . $100.00 D

Plastic covered metal, by Royal Mieco Inc. Clinton, Okla., metal handles featuring "Drink" opener on side, white on red, P . . . . $75.00 C

Vinyl cooler bag featuring "drink" fishtail on front, red & white, 1960s, 1" x 10" x 6", G . . . . $85.00 D

Vinyl picnic with fishtail logo, shaped like a box with a fold-over top and strap "Refreshing New Feeling," NM . . . . $45.00 D

Bottle shaped, AM/FM, plastic, 1970s, EX, $35.00 C. Mitchell Collection.

Can with the dynamic wave, 1970s, EX, $45.00 C. Mitchell Collection.

Cooler design, upright, 1960s, G, $165.00 C. Mitchell Collection.

Cooler design, upright, 1980s, EX, $75.00 C. Mitchell Collection.

Cooler design, upright, J. Russell, 1970s, EX, $110.00 C. Mitchell Collection.

Cooler design, upright, with dynamic wave, 1970s, EX, $125.00 C. Mitchell Collection.

Cooler, prices on these vary greatly, some will go into the thousands, while others fall below the book price, remember condition, 1950s, red, VG, $625.00 B. Muddy River Trading Co./Gary Metz.

Cooler-shaped crystal with ear piece, if all parts including instructions present, increase price to $200.00, EX, $175.00 C. Mitchell Collection.

Cooler, upright, 1950s, F, $200.00 C. Mitchell Collection.

Extremely rare and hard to find, radio designed to resemble an airline cooler, top lifts to reveal controls, red & white, 1950s, G, $3,800.00 B.

Muddy River Trading Co./Gary Metz.

Bottle-shaped, 1933, VG . . . . $3,300.00 B

Cooler, lights up and plays, 1950s, EX . . . $900.00 C

Cooler, lights up and plays, 1950s, EX . . . $900.00 D

Anniversary style dome, 1950s, 3"x5", EX, $850.00 C. Mitchell Collection.

Boudoir, leather with gold logo at bottom, "Drink Coca-Cola So Easily Served," 1910, 3"x8", $1,500.00 B.

Muddy River Trading Co./Gary Metz.

Celluloid desk, Hilda Clark seated at table holding a glass in a holder, clock is in lower left portion of piece, working, rare and hard to find, 1901, 5½"x7¾", EX, $8,500.00 C.

Counter, "Drink Coca-Cola Please Pay When Served," yellow numbers on black background, 19¼"x9", VG, $525.00 D.

Desk, leather composition with "Drink Coca-Cola in Bottles 5¢" at top center over clock works and smaller bottles at hour right and left hand corners, 1910, 4⅓"x6", EX, $1,250.00 C.

"Drink Coca-Cola 5¢ Delicious, Refreshing 5¢," Baird Clock Co, 15 day movement, working, 1896–99, EX, $6,500.00 B.

"Drink Coca-Cola in Bottles," wooden frame, 1939–40, 16"x16", G, $175.00 B.

Muddy River Trading Co./Gary Metz.

"Drink Coca-Cola" red and white plastic, round, EX, $450.00 C. Mitchell Collection.

Gilbert case, "Drink Coca-Cola" in red lettering on clock face and decal of girl with a bottle on bottom glass door, 1910, 18"x40", EX, $4,500.00 B.

Gilbert key wound case, "Drink Coca-Cola" in red lettering on white clock face, "In Bottles 5¢" on pendulum door glass, 1916-20s, Beware: Reproductions exist. EX, $1,450.00 D.

Gilbert pendulum with original finish, 1930s, VG, $1,200.00 B.

Muddy River Trading Co./Gary Metz.

Gilbert regulator with Gibson girl decal on glass, 1910, EX, $6,000.00 B.

Muddy River Trading Co./Gary Metz.

Glass and metal light up clock, with red spot center, 14½" dia., EX, $550.00 B. Collectors Auction Services.

Ingraham with restored regulator on bottom glass, some fade in to clock face, 1905, VG, $950.00 B.

Muddy River Trading Co./Gary Metz.

Light-up clock made by Modern Clock Advertising Company in Brooklyn, N.Y., aluminum case with solid plastic face that lights up, 1950s, 24" dia., EX, $550.00 B. Muddy River Trading Co./Gary Metz.

Light-up counter top clock and sign, restored, 1950, $525.00 B. Muddy River Trading Co./Gary Metz.

Light-up glass front clock with "Drink Coca-Cola" in red fishtail in center, NOS, in original box, 1960s, M, $550.00 B.
Muddy River Trading Co./Gary Metz.

Light-up fishtail clock, NOS, 1960s, EX, $240.00 B. Muddy River Trading Co./Gary Metz.

Maroon, on wings, 1950s, 17½" dia., EX, $275.00C.

Neon clock with rainbow panel for 3 to 9 o'clock, "Drink Coca-Cola, Sign of good taste," red and white, 1950s, 36" across, NM, $1,550.00 B.
Muddy River Trading Co./Gary Metz.

Light-up neon counter, "Pause Drink Coca-Cola," showing bottle spotlighted, restored, rare, and hard to find piece, 1930s, EX, $5,000.00 C.
Mitchell Collection.

Neon clock with spot-lighted bottle at 6 o'clock, square, green wrinkle on outer case, 1930s, 16", EX, $825.00 B.
Muddy River Trading Co./Gary Metz.

Neon, octagonal, "Ice Cold Coca-Cola," Silhouette Girl, 1940s, 18", VG, $1,600.00 B.
Muddy River Trading Co./Gary Metz.

Plastic and metal, "Things go better with Coke," 16"x16", EX, $75.00 D.

Reverse glass metal frame clock "Drink Coca-Cola in bottles" in red center, original jumpstart motor, 1939–42, EX, $550.00 B.
Muddy River Trading Co./Gary Metz.

Rocking bottle clock made by Swihart Products, red and green on white background, 1930s, 20", G, $750.00 C. Mitchell Collection.

Round Silhouette Girl with metal frame, 1930 – 40s, 18" dia., VG, $750.00 C. Mitchell Collection.

Swihart electric Coke clock, unusual size, 1960s, 8"x6½", EX, $350.00 B. Muddy River Trading Co./Gary Metz.

Telechron, red dot in hour position with white background and white wings, 1948, 36" wing span, VG, $475.00 C. Mitchell Collection.

Travel, German-made with brass case, 1960s, 3"x3", $120.00 C. Mitchell Collection.

Wall, spring-driven pendulum, "Coca-Cola, The Ideal Brain Tonic," Baird Clock Co., 1891–95, 24" tall, EX, $5,000.00 B.

Wooden Welch Octagon School House, 1901, EX, $1,700.00 B. Gene Harris Antique Auction Center, Inc.

Dome, white lettering "Drink Coca-Cola" in red center, 1950s, 6"x9", EX . . . . $1,000.00 C

Electric, plastic white background, 1970s, EX . $85.00 C

Light-up advertising by Modern Clock Advertising Company in Brooklyn N.Y, aluminum case with plastic face, 1950s, 24" dia., red on white, VG. . . . . $350.00 D

Light-up counter top, "Serve Yourself," 1940–50s, EX. . . . . $750.00 B

Light-up, "Drink Coca-Cola in Bottles," button in center with white on red, numbers are black on white, by Swilhart, 1950s, 15" dia., EX . . . . $375.00 D

Light-up fishtail with green background, "Drink Coca-Cola" in white lettering on red fishtail background, 1960s, EX . . . . $175.00 C

Light-up fishtail with white background, 1960, EX. . . . . $175.00 C

Light-up glass front clock, white lettering in center on red button, 1950s, NM . . . . $600.00 C

Light-up round with "Drink Coca-Cola" in red on white background with bottle above number 6, 1950s, VG . . . . $400.00 D

Maroon, on wings with Sprite Boy on each end, it's hard to find these with wings still attached, even harder to find them with the Sprite Boy on the ends, 1950s, EX. . . . . $850.00 C

Metal and plastic construction dot logo at 4 and 5, "Things Go Better With Coke" where 10 and 11 should be, 16"x16", EX. . . . . $95.00 C

Metal framed electric with silhouette girl above number 6, 1930–40, 18" dia., EX. . . . . $800.00 C

Metal framed glass front by Lackner, has bottle in circle at top of number 6, 1940s, 16"x16", M . . . . $950.00 C

Neon, bottle on octagon with logo, metal case with yellow border, 1942, 16"x16", EX . . . . . . $900.00 B

Neon, octagonal, featuring Silhouette Girl logo on center disc, "Ice Cola Cola Coca-Cola," 1941, EX . . . . $1,450.00 B

Neon, octagonal, with Silhouette Girl above number, 1930s, EX. Beware: Reproductions exist $1,200.00 D

Neon surrounded by rainbow banner from 9 to 3, "Drink Coca-Cola-Sign of Good Taste" on rainbow panel, 1950s, 24" dia., NM. . . . . $2,700.00 C

Plastic body electric with fake pendulum and a light-up base with "Coca-Cola" in base, 1970s, G . . . . $45.00 D

Plastic body, white background with red lettering and "Coca-Cola" written in lower right hand corner, 1960s, 16"x16", EX. . . . . $125.00 D

Plastic pocket watch, 1970s, EX . . . . $35.00 C

Plastic pocket watch shape, "Drink Coca-Cola," 18" dia., EX. . . . . $45.00 D

Pocket watch, with second hand dial at bottom, VG. . . . . $85.00 C

Reproduction Betty, 1974, VG . . . . $50.00 D

Reproduction plastic regulator style, 1972, EX. $50.00 D

Round, pulsating Silhouette Girl, cut number 6 on dial, fairly rare, 1930s, 18" dia., EX . . . . $2,900.00 C

Wood framed with "Drink Coca-Cola in Bottles" in white on red background, 1930s, 16"x16", EX. . . . . $400.00 C

Wood framed with Silhouette Girl at bottom center, 1930s, 16"x16", EX . . . . $850.00 B

Wooden regulator, pendulum, oak case, key wound "Drink Coca-Cola In Bottles" in black on white face, 1980s, 23"h, M . . . . $225.00 C

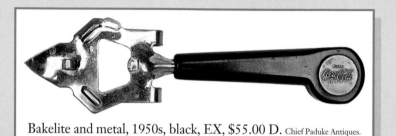

Bakelite and metal, 1950s, black, EX, $55.00 D. Chief Paduke Antiques.

Bottle shaped, EX, $50.00 C. Mitchell Collection.

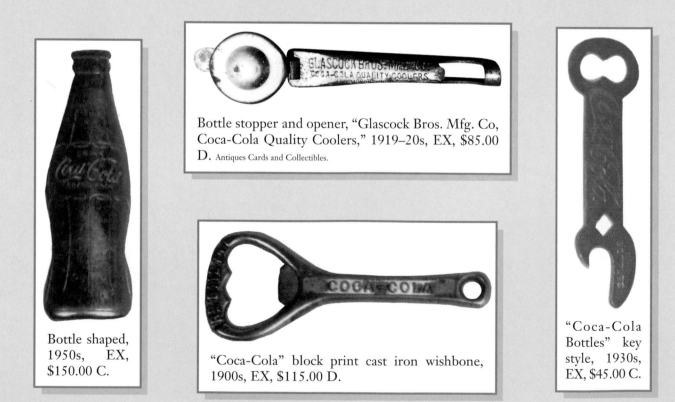

Bottle stopper and opener, "Glascock Bros. Mfg. Co, Coca-Cola Quality Coolers," 1919–20s, EX, $85.00 D. Antiques Cards and Collectibles.

Bottle shaped, 1950s, EX, $150.00 C.

"Coca-Cola" block print cast iron wishbone, 1900s, EX, $115.00 D.

"Coca-Cola Bottles" key style, 1930s, EX, $45.00 C.

Top, from left: Corkscrew, wall mounted, 1920s, EX, $85.00 C; Corkscrew, wall mounted, 1950s, EX, $35.00 C; Cast "Drink Coca-Cola" wall mount, 1930s, EX, $10.00 C. Center: Wall mounted metal "Drink Coca-Cola," also has been referred to as bent metal opener, 1950, EX, $20.00 C. Bottom: Opener, formed hand version, several versions exist, ca. 1930s, $25.00 C; Opener, over the top "Drink Coca-Cola," several version, ca. 1940s, $30.00 C. Mitchell Collection.

"Drink Bottled Coca-Cola" saber shaped opener, 1920s, EX, $200.00 C.

"Drink Coca-Cola™ in Bottles," 1920–40s, EX, $20.00 D.

"Drink Coca-Cola in Bottles" brass key, 1910s, EX, $100.00 C.

"Drink Coca-Cola™ in Sterilized Bottles" lollipop-shaped, 1930s, EX, $85.00 C.

"Drink Coca-Cola" key-shaped with bottle cap facsimile at top, 1920–50s, EX, $35.00 C.

"Drink Coca-Cola," plastic and metal, red and white, EX, $5.00 C. 75th Anniversary from Columbus Ohio, plastic and metal, 1970s, EX, $15.00 C.

"Drink Coca-Cola™," straight, 1910 – 50s, EX, $20.00 C.

Top row: Formed hand, many versions, ca. 1940s, $20.00 C; formed hand, many versions, ca. 1920s, $25.00 C; formed hand, P, ca. 1940s, $10.00 C. Second row: ca. 1940s, $25.00 C; formed hand version, ca. 1950s, $15.00 C; can piercer, metal, "…Coke," ca. 1970s, $10.00 C. Third row: combination can and bottle, 1980s, $8.00 C; plastic handle can piercer and cap opener, ca. 1950s–70s, $8.00 C. Fourth row: 50th Anniversary, 1950s, EX, $55.00 C; Spoon opener, 1920–30, 7½", EX, $75.00 C. Bottom: plastic handle with dynamic wave, 1960s, $8.00 C; metal, "Drink Coca-Cola," $5.00 C. Mitchell Collection.

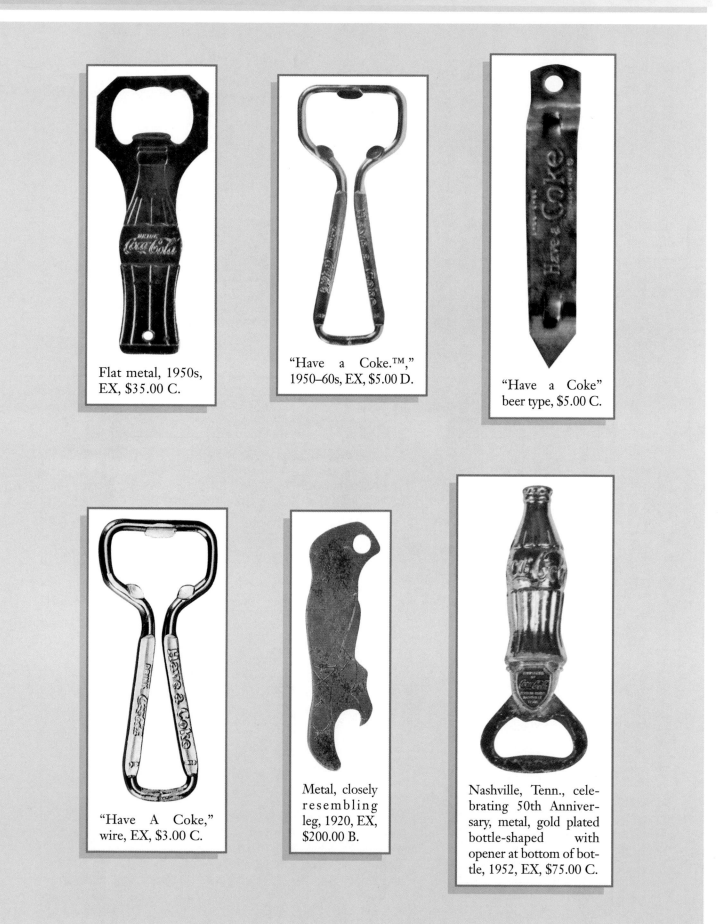

Flat metal, 1950s, EX, $35.00 C.

"Have a Coke.™," 1950–60s, EX, $5.00 D.

"Have a Coke" beer type, $5.00 C.

"Have A Coke," wire, EX, $3.00 C.

Metal, closely resembling leg, 1920, EX, $200.00 B.

Nashville, Tenn., celebrating 50th Anniversary, metal, gold plated bottle-shaped with opener at bottom of bottle, 1952, EX, $75.00 C.

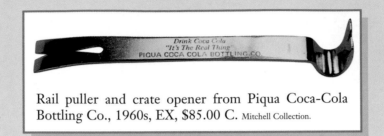

Rail puller and crate opener from Piqua Coca-Cola Bottling Co., 1960s, EX, $85.00 C. Mitchell Collection.

Starr "X" wall mount in original box, 1940–1980, EX, $15.00 D.

Card suit, stainless steel set in marked carrier sleeves, 1970s, EX.............................$45.00 C

Cigar box cutter, "Delicious & Refreshing," 1905 – 15, EX ....$85.00 C

Fishtail spinner, 1910–30, EX.........$150.00 C

Hand spinner, "You Pay," 1910–20, EX .. $120.00 C

Metal, eagle head, "Drink Coca-Cola," engraved, 1919–20s, EX......................$165.00 C

Metal lion head, 1910–30s, EX.........$160.00 C

Metal, logo at end with "Drink Bottled Coca-Cola," hard-to-find, 1908, EX...............$160.00 C

Metal with a solid handle, "Shirts For the Coke Set," EX ....$20.00 C

Opener and spoon combination, 1930s, EX ....$125.00 D

Steel, black with red background, outing style, 1910–20s, EX......................$100.00 D

Turtle style with four devices, "Drink Coca-Cola in Bottles," 1970s, EX..................$12.00 C

Top: One blade and one opener, "Coca-Cola Bottling Company," 1910s, EX, $275.00 C. Bottom: "The Coca-Cola Bottling Co." blade has to be marked Kaster & Co. Coca-Cola Bottling Co., Germany, 1905–15, brass. Beware: Reproductions exist. EX, $425.00 C. Mitchell Collection.

Pearl handle with corkscrew blade and opener, 1930s, EX, $115.00 C. Mitchell Collection

Two blade, "Drink Coca-Cola," G, $40.00 D.

Two blade pen knife, "Enjoy Coca-Cola," all metal, EX, $15.00 D.

Stainless steel with one blade and nail file, 1950–60s, EX, $30.00 C. Mitchell Collection.

Small metal utility with a cutting blade, an opener, and a nail file with key chain, "Enjoy Coca-Cola," EX, $12.00 C.

Bone handle combination knife and opener, red lettering, "Drink Coca-Cola in Bottles," 1915–25, EX. $125.00 C

Bone handle, two blade, "Delicious and Refreshing," 1920, VG. . . . . $100.00 C

Combination Henry Sears & Son, Solingen, one blade with case shaped like boot as opener, "Coca-Cola," 1920s, white, EX. . . . . $400.00 D

"Compliments – The Coca-Cola™ Co," 1930s, EX . . . . $75.00 D

"Drink Coca-Cola™ in Bottles," 1940s, EX. . . $75.00 D

Pearl handle, "Serve Coca-Cola™," 1940s, EX. . . . . $175.00 D

Switchblade, Remington, "Drink Coca-Cola in Bottles," 1930s, EX. . . . . $225.00 D

"The Coca-Cola™ Bottling Co." embossed on side, 1940s, EX . . . . $45.00 D

Truck shaped from seminar, 1972, EX . . . . $20.00 D

"When Thirsty Try A Bottle" embossed on side with bottle, 1910, EX . . . . $350.00 D

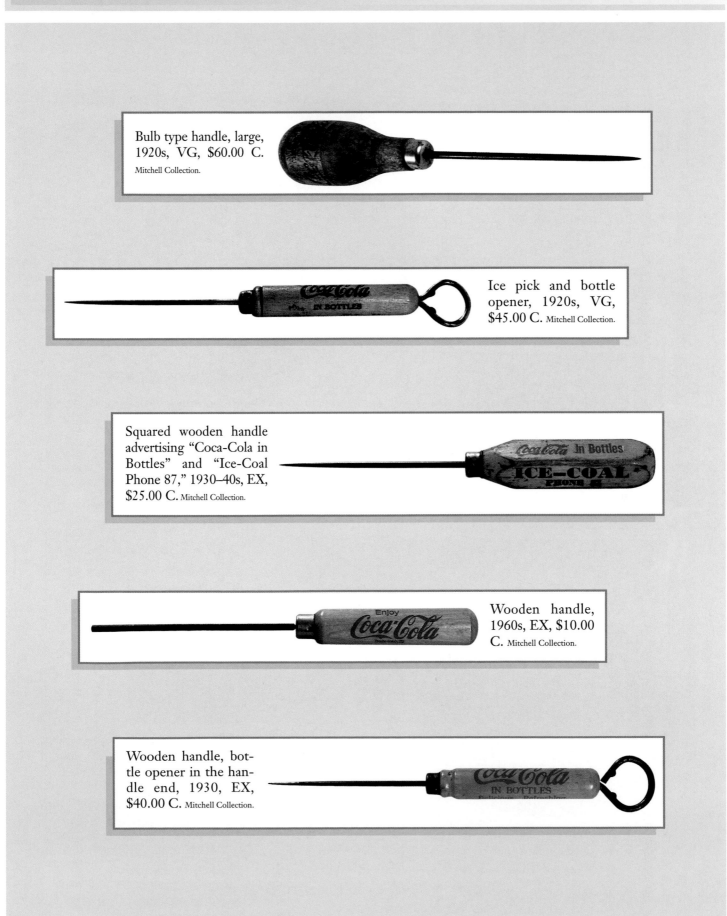

Bulb type handle, large, 1920s, VG, $60.00 C. Mitchell Collection.

Ice pick and bottle opener, 1920s, VG, $45.00 C. Mitchell Collection.

Squared wooden handle advertising "Coca-Cola in Bottles" and "Ice-Coal Phone 87," 1930–40s, EX, $25.00 C. Mitchell Collection.

Wooden handle, 1960s, EX, $10.00 C. Mitchell Collection.

Wooden handle, bottle opener in the handle end, 1930, EX, $40.00 C. Mitchell Collection.

Ashtrays

Ashtray with bottle lighter featuring "Drink" logo from Canadian bottler red & white, 1950s, NM, $250.00 B.

Muddy River Trading Co./Gary Metz.

Bronze colored, depicting 50th Anniversary in center, 1950s, EX, $55.00 C. Mitchell Collection.

From Mexico, Wave logo, 1970s, EX, $3.00 D.

"High in energy, Low in calories," tin, 1950s, EX, $20.00 C. Mitchell Collection.

Glass from Dickson, Tennessee, EX, $15.00 C. Mitchell Collection.

Metal with molded cigarette holder, EX, $20.00 D. Mitchell Collection.

Left: Top match pull Bakelite, rare, 1940s, EX, $1,000.00-C. Right: Bottle lighter, 1950s, EX, $125.00 C. Mitchell Collection.

Set of four, ruby red, price should be doubled if set is in original box, 1950s, EX, $375.00 C. Mitchell Collection.

Bottle, 1950s, EX . . . . $100.00 D

"Drink Coca-Cola™," round, 1960, EX . . . . $5.00 D

"Drink Coca-Cola™," round with scalloped edge, 1950s, EX . . . . $8.00 C

"Support Your Fireman, Compliments of Coca-Cola," tin rectangular, EX . . . . $225.00 C

"The pause that refreshes & J.J. Flynn Co.," square glass, red round center, 1950s, EX . . . . $70.00 D

"Things go Better with Coke™," square metal, 1960s, red, EX . . . . $8.00 D

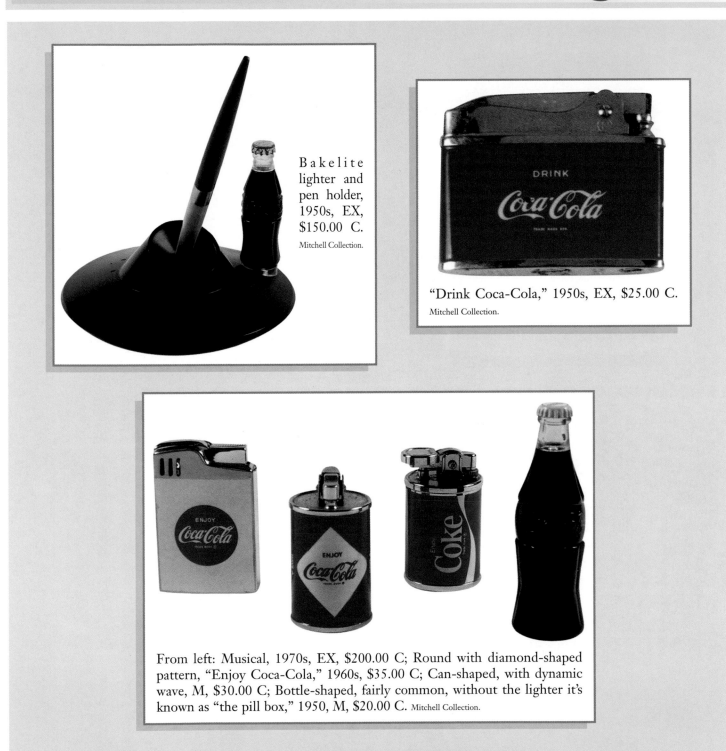

Bakelite lighter and pen holder, 1950s, EX, $150.00 C.
Mitchell Collection.

"Drink Coca-Cola," 1950s, EX, $25.00 C.
Mitchell Collection.

From left: Musical, 1970s, EX, $200.00 C; Round with diamond-shaped pattern, "Enjoy Coca-Cola," 1960s, $35.00 C; Can-shaped, with dynamic wave, M, $30.00 C; Bottle-shaped, fairly common, without the lighter it's known as "the pill box," 1950, M, $20.00 C. Mitchell Collection.

Dispose-a-lite in original box, 1970s, EX . . $15.00 D

"Enjoy Coca-Cola" on bottom, flip top, gold plate, NM . . . . $85.00 D

Executive award, 1984, NM . . . . $25.00 D

Gold Sygnus standup, 1962, EX . . . . $140.00 D

Musical, red "Drink" on white dot, EX. . . $155.00 D

Red lettering on the diagonal with gold-tone background, 1962, EX . . . . $135.00 D

Silver with embossed bottle, flip top, M . . . $35.00 D

Matches

Book, 50th Anniversary, 1936, EX, $8.00 C. Mitchell Collection.

Book, "A Distinctive Drink in a Distinctive Bottle," 1922, EX, $125.00 C. Mitchell Collection.

Left: Book for Westinghouse coolers for the Bottlers of Coca-Cola, G, $3.00 C. Right: Book from the Coca-Cola Bottling Co. at Fulton, Ky., Telephone 447, EX, $3.00 C. Mitchell Collection.

Top: Book from 1982 World's Fair at Knoxville, Tenn., 1982, EX, $1.00 D. Bottom: Book from New York World's Fair, 1964, $8.00 C. Mitchell Collection.

Book, "Have a Coke," 1950s, VG, $5.00 C. Mitchell Collection.

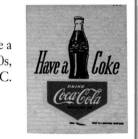

Book, "Have a Coke," bottle in hand, 1940–50s, VG, $5.00 C. Mitchell Collection.

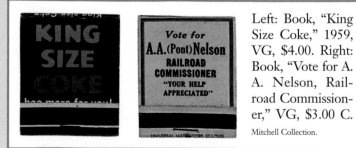

Left: Book, "King Size Coke," 1959, VG, $4.00. Right: Book, "Vote for A. A. Nelson, Railroad Commissioner," VG, $3.00 C. Mitchell Collection.

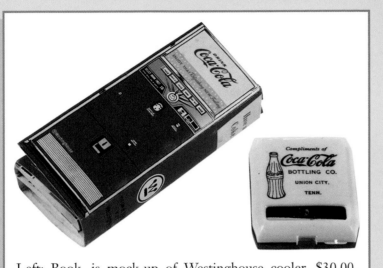

Left: Book, is mock-up of Westinghouse cooler, $30.00.
Right: Safe & strikes, 1930s, EX, $250.00 C. Mitchell Collection.

Holder, tin, "Drink Coca-Cola in Bottles," 1940s, F, $350.00 C. Mitchell Collection.

Matchbook holder with matches, metal, 1959, EX, $125.00 C. Mitchell Collection.

Porcelain match striker, "Drink Coca-Cola, Strike matches here," 1939, NM, $400.00 B. Muddy River Trading Co./Gary Metz.

Book with bottle on cover, 1910–20s, VG. $750.00 D

Book with woman on front, 1910s, VG. . . $950.00 C

Matchbook holder, celluloid, 1910, EX. . . $300.00 C

Matchbook holder, "Compliments of The Coca-Cola Co. Coca-Cola Relieves Fatigue," 1907, EX . . . . . $350.00 C

Matchbook holder, "Drink Coca-Cola at Soda Fountains 5¢," 1907, EX . . . . $350.00 C

Match strikes, porcelain, French, NM. . . . $250.00 C

Safe, "Drink Coca-Cola in Bottles," 1908, EX. . . . . $700.00 C

Striker, "Drink Coca-Cola, Strike Matches Here" beginning to be a scarce item, 1939, red, white, yellow, VG . . . . $400.00 D

Striker, porcelain, "Drink Coca-Cola Strike Matches here," English, yellow and white lettering with red background and black match strike field, NM . . . $500.00 C

Clockwise from top: Foil showing lady with a bottle, square, M, $5.00 C; Foil showing a street car scene, M, $5.00 C; Foil showing party tray and cooler, square, M, $5.00 C; Foil showing hand in bottle with world globe behind square, M, $5.00 C. Mitchell Collection.

Paper program for the 37th National Convention in Miami, Fla., Oct. 10, 11, 12, 13 (55), American Legion, Drink Coca-Cola, 1955, VG, $35.00 C.

Top: "Please put empties in the rack," green and white, $10.00 D; "Things go better with Coke," red letter-ing on white background, round, $5.00 D. Bottom: "Have a Coke" with Sprite Boy in bottle cap hat, M, $10.00 D; "Things go better with Coke," red and white, square with scalloped edges, M, $5.00 D. Mitchell Collection.

Aluminum, 1960s, green, EX $4.00

Cardboard, "Go with Coke," 1960s, red and white, EX. . . . . $5.00 D

"Drink Coca-Cola ice cold," with Silhouette Girl, 1940s, M . . . . $15.00 C

"Have a Coke" with Sprite Boy, 1940s, M. . $12.00 C

Metal, "Drink Coca-Cola," EX. . . . . $5.00 D

Metal, Hilda Clark artwork, EX . . . . $5.00 D

Metal with Juanita, 1984, EX . . . . $5.00 D

Metal with Santa Claus, white. . . . . $5.00 D

Plastic with dynamic wave, "Enjoy Coca-Cola," red, EX . . . . 1970s, $5.00 D

No Drip Protectors

Left: Bottle bag, the distinctive Coca-Cola glass, EX, $7.00 C. Right: Bottle bag, used in the days of "wet" coolers to keep the customer dry, 1931, EX, $8.00 C. Mitchell Collection.

Bottle protector, 1932, VG, $8.00 C. Mitchell Collection.

Dispenser for no drip protectors, unmarked, red, 1930s, 4½" x 8" x 2¾", EX, $75.00 C. Bill Mitchell.

"A Great Drink...With Good Things To Eat," 1938, NM . . . . $5.00 C

Bottle protector, 1934, EX . . . . $6.00 C

Bottle protector, 1944, EX . . . . $5.00 C

Bottle protector, 1948, EX . . . . $5.00 C

Featuring a couple dancing, 1946, NM . . . . . $5.00 C

"In Bottles" protector, 1930, NM . . . . $5.00 C

Paper bottle protector, 1946, EX . . . . $5.00 C

Rear view of man drinking from a bottle, 1936, NM . . . . $5.00 C

"The Pause That Refreshes," featuring three bottles, 1936, NM . . . . $5.00 C

Cardboard menu board, "Sign of Good Taste," with bottle on each side of board, difficult to locate in cardboard, 1959, 19" x 28" NM, $180.00 B. Muddy River Trading Co./Gary Metz.

Cardboard and wood in tin frame menu board for pricing 6.5 and 12 oz. Coke, this piece isn't found very often, red on black, 1950s, 25" x 15", G, $145.00 B. Muddy River Trading Co./Gary Metz.

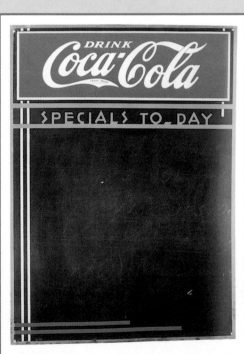

"Drink Coca-Cola Specials Today," 1930s, G, $175.00 B.
Muddy River Trading Co./Gary Metz.

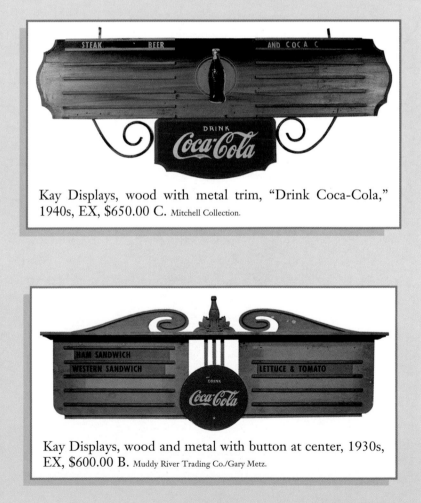

Kay Displays, wood with metal trim, "Drink Coca-Cola," 1940s, EX, $650.00 C. Mitchell Collection.

Kay Displays, wood and metal with button at center, 1930s, EX, $600.00 B. Muddy River Trading Co./Gary Metz.

Metal and wood, "Drink Coca-Cola" in white lettering inside red fishtail on green background, metal menu strips, 1950s, VG, $135.00 C. Mitchell Collection.

Metal Canadian, "Drink Coca-Cola Specials to-day," embossed, scarce and difficult to locate, 1938, 17" x 24", NM, $650.00 B.

Muddy River Trading Co./Gary Metz.

Plywood Kay Displays menu board with "Drink" logo at top, 1930–40s, 20" x 37", G, $325.00 B.

Muddy River Trading Co./Gary Metz.

Tin, arched top embossed with fishtail design at top, NM, $375.00 B. Muddy River Trading Co./Gary Metz.

Tin, die cut, "Drink Coca-Cola Be Refreshed," Canadian, 1950, EX, $300.00 B. Muddy River Trading Co./Gary Metz.

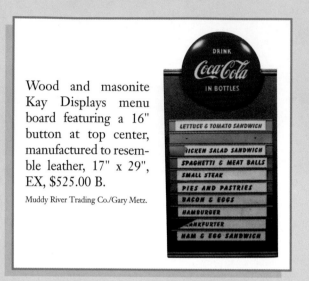

Wood and masonite Kay Displays menu board featuring a 16" button at top center, manufactured to resemble leather, 17" x 29", EX, $525.00 B.
Muddy River Trading Co./Gary Metz.

Wood and metal Kay Displays menu board, rare and hard to find, 1940s, F, $500.00 B.
Muddy River Trading Co./Gary Metz.

Cardboard stand-up, "Refreshing You Best," 1950s, EX. . . . . $150.00 C

Kay Displays, 1940–50s, 3'x1', NM. . . . . $2,400.00 B

Kay Displays, "Drink" on spotlight with full glass and gold tone slots on both sides, 1940–50s, 36"x12", EX . . . . $475.00 C

Light-up design with clock, 1960s, EX . . . $125.00 C

Metal, "Drink Coca-Cola Delicious and Refreshing," Silhouette Girl in lower right corner, 1930s, VG. $250.00 C

Metal French Canadian board, embossed, 1938, 17" x 24", F . . . . $45.00 D

"Refresh Yourself" with bottle and cap lower right hand corner, 1930, 20"x28", VG . . . . $450.00 D

Tin, "Drink Coca-Cola" at extreme top with "Specials Today" under that and on top of blackboard section, 1934, 20"x28", VG . . . . $350.00 C

Tin, "Specials Today, Coca-Cola" oval at top and bottle in lower right hand side, blackboard for easy menu changes, 1929, 20"x28", F . . . . $150.00 C

Wave logo at top, 1970s, 20"x28", M . . . . . $30.00 D

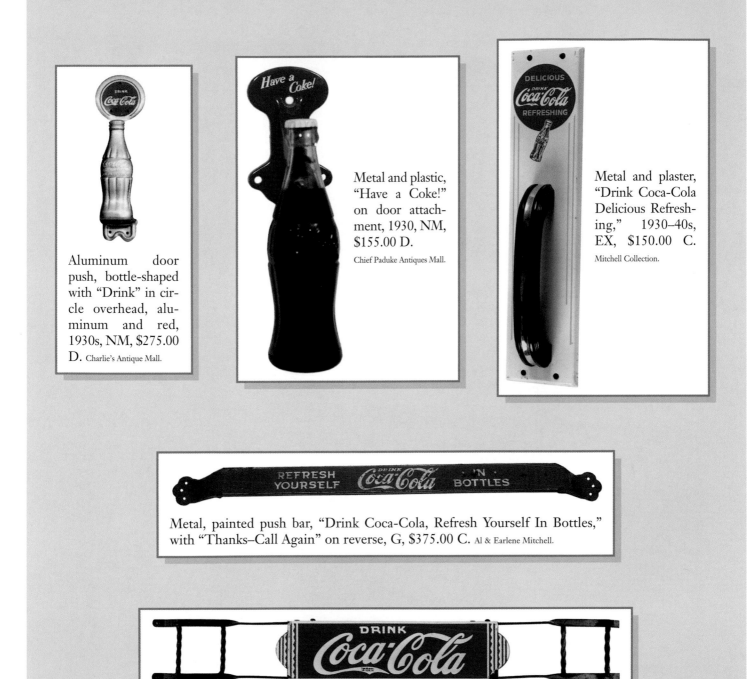

Aluminum door push, bottle-shaped with "Drink" in circle overhead, aluminum and red, 1930s, NM, $275.00 D. Charlie's Antique Mall.

Metal and plastic, "Have a Coke!" on door attachment, 1930, NM, $155.00 D.

Chief Paduke Antiques Mall.

Metal and plaster, "Drink Coca-Cola Delicious Refreshing," 1930–40s, EX, $150.00 C.

Mitchell Collection.

Metal, painted push bar, "Drink Coca-Cola, Refresh Yourself In Bottles," with "Thanks–Call Again" on reverse, G, $375.00 C. Al & Earlene Mitchell.

Porcelain and wrought iron, "Drink Coca-Cola," 1930s, EX, $425.00 C. Mitchell Collection.

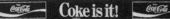

Porcelain "Coke is it" with two wave logo boxes, white on red, 1970s, NM, $65.00 B.
Muddy River Trading Co./Gary Metz.

Porcelain "Ice Cold Coca-Cola In Bottles," 1930s, 30" x 2½", NM, $300.00 B.
Muddy River Trading Co./Gary Metz.

Porcelain, "Ice Cold Coca-Cola In Bottles" on front with "Thank You, Call Again" on reverse side, white lettering on red background, 1930s, 25" x 3¼", NM, $475.00 B.
Muddy River Trading Co./Gary Metz.

Porcelain, "Thanks Call Again for a Coke," very heavy piece, Canadian, yellow and white on red, 3½" x 13½", NM, $300.00 B.
Muddy River Trading Co./Gary Metz.

Porcelain "Take some Coca-Cola Home Today," white lettering on red, 1950s, 34" long, NM, $525.00 B. Muddy River Trading Co./Gary Metz.

"Refreshing Coca-Cola New Feeling," 1950–60s, EX, $150.00 C. Mitchell Collection.

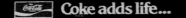

Steel with heavy paint featuring wave logo, white on black with red & white logo, 1970 – 80s, NM, $55.00 B. Muddy River Trading Co./Gary Metz.

Tin push plate with Silhouette Girl in yellow spotlight, "Drink Coca-Cola delicious refreshing," red with white & yellow lettering, 1939, 28" x 3½", NM, $500.00 B.
Muddy River Trading Co./Gary Metz.

Aluminum bottle, 1930–40, NM . . . . $275.00 D

"Drink Coca-Cola/Ice Cold/In Bottles," porcelain, red and white lettering on red and white background, 35" long, NM . . . . $255.00 C

Porcelain and wrought iron, adjustable, "Drink Coca-Cola" in center, 1930s, G . . . . $260.00 C

Porcelain, "Come In! Have a Coca-Cola," yellow and white lettering on red background, 3½"x11½", NM . . . . $290.00 C

Porcelain, horizontal, "Have a Coca-Cola," yellow and white lettering on red background trimmed in yellow, 6½"x3½", VG . . . . $260.00 C

Porcelain, "Ice Cold in Bottles," red on white, 1960s, 30", EX . . . . $300.00 C

Porcelain, "Iced Coca-Cola here," yellow and white on red, Canadian, 1950s, 30", NM . . . . $200.00 D

Porcelain, "Iced Coca-Cola Here," yellow and white lettering on red background, 1950s, 31", EX . . . . $175.00 C

Porcelain, oversized, outdoor style, with original box, 1942, 18"x54", NM . . . . $1,700.00 B

Porcelain, "Thanks Call Again For A Coca-Cola," yellow and white lettering red background, 4"x11½", VG . . . . $250.00 C

Porcelain, "Thanks Call again for a Coca-Cola," yellow and white lettering on red, Canadian, 1930s, EX . . . . $225.00 C

Porcelain, vertical, "Thanks Call Again for a Coca-Cola," yellow and white lettering on red background, 3½"x13½", NM $350.00-C

Tin, arched top embossed with fishtail design at top, NM . . . . $375.00 B

Tin, die cut, "Drink Coca-Cola Be Refreshed," Canadian, 1950, EX. $300.00

Tin, "Refresh Yourself," 1940–50, 3"x6", G . . $275.00 C

Tin, "Refresh Yourself," 1940–50, 3"x6", NM . $350.00 D

Tin, silhouette, 1939–41, 33"x3½", EX . . . $375.00 D

"Big Wheel," "Drink Coca-Cola," add $30.00 if MIB, 1970, EX, $65.00. Mitchell Collection.

Buddy L #5646 GMC with all original accessories in box, 1957, yellow, EX, $650.00 B.

Muddy River Trading Co./Gary Metz.

Buddy L #5546 International in original box with all accessories, 1956, NM, $725.00 B.

Muddy River Trading Co./Gary Metz.

Buddy L, "Enjoy Coca-Cola," complete with hand truck that mounts in side compartment, add $20.00 if MIB, 1970, EX, $65.00 C. Mitchell Collection.

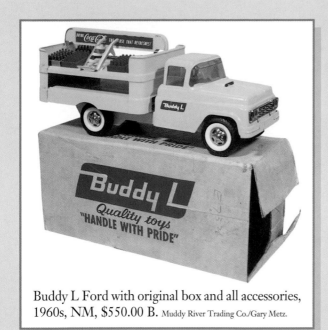

Buddy L Ford with original box and all accessories, 1960s, NM, $550.00 B. Muddy River Trading Co./Gary Metz.

Buddy L with cases and bottles, 1960s, EX, $300.00 C. Mitchell Collection.

Cargo style with working headlights and taillights, 1950, VG, $275.00 B. Muddy River Trading Co./Gary Metz.

Gas, made in Germany, model #426-20, a rare and desirable tin wind-up litho with great detailing with a full load of tin and plastic cases, 1949, yellow, EX, $2,600.00 B. Muddy River Trading Co./Gary Metz.

Marx #991 with gray cab and frame in original box, 1953, yellow and gray, NM, $900.00 B. Muddy River Trading Co./Gary Metz.

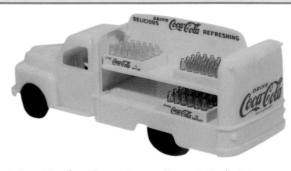

Marx Ford style, 1950s, yellow, EX, $375.00 B. Muddy River Trading Co./Gary Metz.

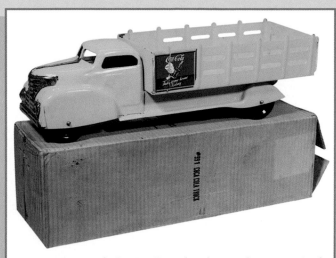

Marx #991 with Sprite Boy decal on side, in original box, 1951, yellow, NM, $625.00 B.
Muddy River Trading Co./Gary Metz.

Marx, if in MIB condition with original box this value would nearly double, 1950, G, $225.00 C. Mitchell Collection.

Marx, metal, 1950s, yellow, VG, $450.00 C.
Mitchell Collection.

Marx plastic with original six Coca-Cola cases, Canadian, 1950s, red, EX, $525.00 B. Muddy River Trading Co./Gary Metz.

Marx, stake, yellow bed with red cab and frame with Sprite Boy decal on side of bed, 1950, G, $295.00 B. Muddy River Trading Co./Gary Metz.

Maxitoys made in Holland, hard to find since only 500 were made, 1980s, 11" long, NM, $300.00 B.

Metalcraft with rubber tires, if this item were MIB price could go up by as much as $400.00, 1930s, G, $750.00 C. Mitchell Collection.

Plastic Marx Canadian truck with 6 plastic cases, wooden wheels, in original box, hard to find, red, 1950s, 11", G, $1,300.00 B.

Sanyo truck made in Japan, distributed by Allen Haddock Company in Atlanta, Ga., with original box, battery operated, 1960s, 12½" long, EX, $275.00 B.

Muddy River Trading Co./Gary Metz.

Smith Miller, metal, GMC #2 of 50 stamped on bottom, with six original cases of 24 green bottles in original box, #1 is in the Smith Miller Museum, rare, 1979, red, EX, $1,700.00 B.

Muddy River Trading Co./Gary Metz.

VW van with friction motor by Taiyo, 1950s, 7½" long, VG, $225.00 C. Mitchell Collection.

Vending machine style ⅟₂₅-scale model kit, 1970, MIB, $75.00 C.

Bank, wooden van with stamped logo, driver, and cases, 1980s, 7", EX . . . . $25.00 C

Barclay open bed, even load, 1950, 2", yellow, EX . . . . $175.00 C

Bedford, Oinky, even load, open body, 1950s, 4½", red and white, NM . . . . $325.00 C

Berlist Stradair of France, 1960s, 4¼", EX . $300.00 C

Buddy L #420C, 1978, G . . . . $45.00 C

Buddy L #591-1350, steel, Japan, 1980s, 11", EX . . . . $75.00 C

Buddy L #666 set, 15 pieces, 1980s, M . . . . $45.00 D

Buddy L #4969, scarce tractor-trailer rig, 1970s, NM . . . . $125.00 C

Buddy L #4973 set, 7 pieces, 1970s, NM . . $75.00 C

Buddy L #5215, 1970s, NM . . . . $45.00 C

Buddy L #5215 H, big tires, pressed steel, 1980s, red and white, M . . . . $35.00 C

Buddy L #5216 plastic A-frame, will hold eight cases, in original box, 1962, yellow, EX . . . . $375.00 C

Buddy L #5426, pressed steel, 1960, 15", NMIB . . . . $500.00 B

Buddy L #5426 truck, steel, Ford style with chrome grille, 1960s, yellow, NM . . . . $125.00 C

Buddy L #5646, GMC loader with case loading line, 1950s, yellow . . . . $450.00 C

Buddy L, 5-piece set, 1981, NM . . . . $95.00 C

Budgie even load, 1950, 5", yellow, EX . . . $450.00 D

Chevy delivery, tin, Smokeyfest Estb. 1930, 1995, MIB . . . . $225.00 C

Corgi, Jr. double decker bus, 1974, 3", EX . . . $15.00 D

Corgi, Jr. featuring contour logo, 1982, NM . $20.00 D

Durham Industries van in original packaging, 1970–80s, NM . . . . $25.00 D

El Camino given away at convention in Ohio, plastic, 1995, red and white, MIB . . . . $15.00 C

Goodies van, Canadian, contour logo, 1970s, 12", M . . . . $110.00 C

Lemerzarugyar plastic van, friction, 7", silver, MIB . . . . $105.00 C

Lemezarugyar van, Hungary, plastic friction, 1970s, red, MIB . . . . $215.00 D

London, "Drink Coca-Cola" decal on side, 1960s, EX . . . . $265.00 C

Marx #21 open side, 1950s, yellow, EX . . . $450.00 D

Marx #21, open divided double decker bed, 1954, 12½", yellow and red, NM . . . . $275.00 D

Marx #991, pressed steel, Sprite Boy decal, 1950s, gray, MIB . . . . $1,000.00 D

Marx #991, pressed steel, Sprite Boy decal, 1950s, red and yellow, G . . . . $150.00 D

Marx #1090, tin, open bed, 1956, 17", yellow and red, EX . . . . $450.00 B

Marx, stake, Sprite Boy, 1940s, yellow, EX . . $650.00 B

Matchbox, tractor-trailer, Super King, 1978, NMIB . . . . $45.00 D

Matchbox with even load bed, "Drink Coca-Cola," 1960s, 2", yellow, EX . . . . $65.00 D

Matchbox with staggered load bed, "Drink Coca-Cola," 1960s, yellow, EX . . . . $125.00 D

Maxitoys/Holland metal van with open sided driver's seat, 1980s, 11", yellow and black, EX . . . . $275.00 D

Maxwell Co., plastic delivery van, India, 1970s, EX . . . . $45.00 D

Metalcraft #171 A-frame, 1932, red and yellow, EX . . . . $900.00 D

Metalcraft #171 pressed steel, rubber wheels, A frame, 1932, red and yellow, NMIB . . . . $2,500.00 B

Model T, cast iron, 1980s, M. Warning: Fantasy item . . . . $10.00 C

Model T, scale kit in original box, 1970s, MIB . $55.00 C

Osahi, Japan, van, tin and plastic, friction, 1970s, EX . . . . $75.00 C

Panel type, AMBO with smooth tires tin litho, 1960s, EX . . . . $550.00 D

Plastic Fun Mates from Straco, wind-up, 1970s, EX . . . . $30.00 D

Plastic, smooth tire, 1940–50s, yellow, EX . $95.00 D

Renault, solid metal, 1970s, red, NM . . . . . $55.00 D

Renault, solid metal, 1970s, yellow, NM . . . $55.00 D

Rico Sanson-Junior with contour logo, 1970s, 13½", red, EX . . . . $45.00 D

Rosko friction motor, beverage delivery, 1950, 8", EX . . . . $475.00 C

Sanyo/A. Haddock Co route, battery operated, in original box, 1960s, yellow, white, red, EX . . . . . . $275.00 D

Siki Eurobuilt, Mack tractor trailer, die cast, 1980s, 12½", MIB . . . . $45.00 D

Siku-Oldtimes, metal, 1980s, 5¼", EX . . . . $40.00 D

Smith-Miller A-frame, wood and aluminum, rubber tires, 1944, 14", red, EX . . . . $1,600.00 D

Smith-Miller, wood and metal with bottle logos on bed, 1947–53, 14", red, EX . . . . $695.00 D

Smokeyfest Estb. 1930, 1995, MIB . . . . $25.00 C

Straco, plastic Wee People, Hong Kong, 5½", EX . . . . $40.00 D

Supervan, plastic, 1970s, 18"x11", NM . . . $110.00 D

Tin van, "Drink Coca-Cola, Delicious, Refreshing," Japanese, 1950, 4", yellow . . . . $150.00 D

Tin, even load, Japanese, 1950s, 4", yellow, EX . . . . $150.00 D

Tin Lincman, friction power, 1950s, VG . $200.00 D

Tootsie Toy van copy, die cast metal, white lettering, 1986, M . . . . $15.00 D

Uni Plast, Mexican #302, van with contour logo, plastic, 1978–79, red, NM . . . . $25.00 D

Van, cardboard, Max Headroom, 1980s, 6", NM . . . . $15.00 D

Winrose, Atlanta Convention, 1994, MIB . $165.00 D

Clockwise, from top: Bang gun with Santa in sleigh, 1950s, M, $20.00 C; Bang gun with clown, yellow, red, and white, 1950s, $20.00 C; Bang gun, "It's the real thing," M, $20.00 C. Mitchell Collection.

Bank, dispenser shaped, plastic, if this is in original box double the price, 1960s, VG, $75.00 C. Mitchell Collection.

Bank, dispenser shaped with glasses, add $200.00 if in original box, metal, 1950s, VG, $375.00 C. Mitchell Collection.

Bank, plastic cooler shaped, there is a reproduction of this that has two sets of five horizontal lines on the face, plus bottles on both sides of the bottom slot, 1950s, EX, $100.00 C. Mitchell Collection.

Bank, plastic vending machine-shaped, if found in original box value will climb to $200.00 C, 1950s, EX, $100.00 C. Mitchell Collection.

Bank, metal, vending shaped with coin slot on top, 1940s, 2¼"x3", EX, $135.00 C. Mitchell Collection.

Baseball Hall of Fame information featuring both National and American League from 1901 to 1960, baseball-shaped, 1960, G, $80.00 B.

Muddy River Trading Co./Gary Metz.

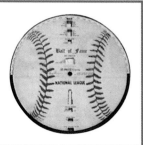

Buddy Lee doll in homemade uniform with original patches worn by "Aunt" Earlene Mitchell's father when he worked for Coca-Cola in Paducah, Ky., 1950s, EX, $500.00 C. Mitchell Collection.

Buddy Lee composition doll with original uniform bearing the original Lee tag, 1950s, 12" tall, EX, $875.00 B.

Muddy River Trading Co./Gary Metz.

Dispenser with original glasses, "Drink Coca-Cola," 1950s, EX, $125.00 C.

Mitchell Collection.

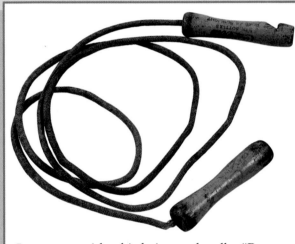

Jump rope with whistle in one handle, "Pure as Sunlight" on other handle, 1920s, G, $350.00 C.

Mitchell Collection.

Kit Carson stage coach, EX, $125.00 C.

Al and Earlene Mitchell.

Lionel train complete with original box and transformer, 1970s, EX, $425.00 C. Mitchell Collection.

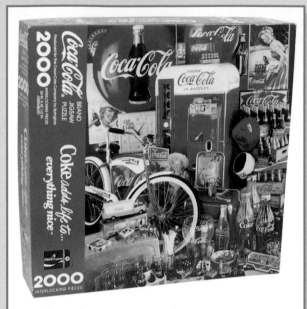

Puzzle with 2,000 pieces featuring a potpourri of Coke-Cola items, EX, $55.00 C. Mitchell Collection.

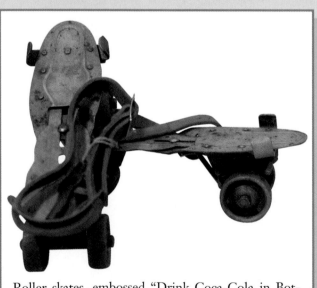

Roller skates, embossed "Drink Coca-Cola in Bottles" on the face with "Pat. Aug 16, 1914" under first line, probably from the St. Louis Bottling Company, 1914, VG, $900.00 B. Muddy River Trading Co./Gary Metz.

Shopping basket, child's size with grocery graphics printed on both sides of basket liner, complete with contents, 1950s, EX, $400.00 C. Mitchell Collection.

American Flyer kite, bottle at tail end of kite, 1930s, EX . . . . $400.00 C

American Flyer train car, "Pure As Sunlight," a complete train set with track and original box would push this price to around $4,500.00, 1930s, red and green, EX. . . . . $1,200.00 C

Bank, bottle cap with slot in top, plastic, 1950s, M. . . . . $30.00 C

Bean bag, "Enjoy Coca-Cola," with dynamic wave, 1970s, red, VG. $25.00 C

Bicycle, EX . . . . $700.00 D

Boomerang, 1950s, EX . . . . $35.00 C

Buddy L can car, 1970s, EX. . . . . $60.00 D

Bus, cardboard double decker with dynamic contour logo, Sweetcentre, 1980s, red, M. . . . . $45.00 C

Caboose with wave logo, 1970s, 6½" long, EX. . . . . $45.00 D

Car kit, Bill Elliott's thunderboat with logo, plastic, 1:24 scale . . . . $15.00 C

Car, tin Taiyo Ford taxi, friction power, "Refresh With Zest," 1960s, 9", white and red, NM . . . . . $225.00 D

Corvette, die cast, convention banquet gift, 1993, MRFB . . . . $30.00 C

Dart board with "Drink Coca-Cola" in center, 1950s, EX. . . . . $75.00 D

Dispenser, "Drink" on panel sides, image of two glasses over the spigot, 1960s, red and white, EX. . . . . $45.00 D

Dispenser, plastic "Drink Coca-Cola" with dynamic wave logo on tank, 1970s, red and white, EX. . . . . $35.00 D

"Express Cafe Snackbar," plastic and tin, "Drink Coca-Cola" button on front and advertisement on back, 1950–60s, NM . . . . $175.00 C

Fanny pac, Jeff Gordon, shaped like pace car, logo, M . . . . $15.00 D

Friction car by Taiyo, 1960s, red and white, EX . . . . $250.00 B

Marbles in bag that were given away with every carton, 1950, EX . . . . $50.00 C

Model airplane with Coca-Cola circle for wings, 1960s, red and white, EX. . . . . $45.00 D

Pedal car, metal and rubber, 1940–50s, 19"x36", M . . . . $1,350.00 B

Pedal car, white lettering, 1940–1950, 19"x36", red, EX. . . . . $1,300.00 B

Picnic cooler, plastic, 6", EX . . . . $95.00 C

Play town hamburger stand made of wood, metal, and plaster in original box, very desirable piece, 1950s, EX . . . . $375.00 C

Puzzle, jigsaw in original can, 1960, EX . . . $65.00 D

Puzzle, wire, with "Drink Coca-Cola in Bottles" on flat portion of puzzle, 1960s, EX . . . . $35.00 D

Stove, "Drink Coca-Cola with Your Meals," 1930s, green, EX . . . . $2,200.00 C

Train tank car HO gauge, "Enjoy Coca-Cola," 1980s, EX. . . . . $45.00 C

Tic-Tac-Toe with bottle pawns, 1950s, EX $125.00 C

Top, plastic, "Coke Adds Life To...Fun Times," 1970s, VG. . . . . $10.00 C

Whistle, plastic, "Merry Christmas Coca-Cola Bottling, Memphis Tenn., 1950, EX . . . . $20.00 C

Whistle, thimble-shaped, 1940s, EX . . . . . $60.00 C

Whistle, tin, "Drink Coca-Cola," 1930, red and yellow, VG. . . . . $125.00 D

Whistle, wood, "Drink Coca-Cola," 1940s, EX. . . . . $30.00 D

Yo-yo, Russell Championship, "Drink Coca-Cola" on side, 1960, EX . . . . $25.00 D

Yo-yo, wooden, VG . . . . $100.00 C

Games

Baseball glove, left-handed, MacGregor, 1970, EX, $175.00 C. Mitchell Collection.

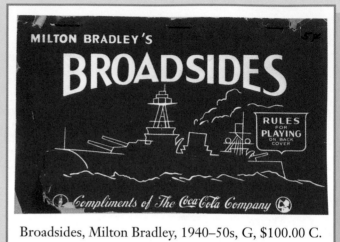

Broadsides, Milton Bradley, 1940–50s, G, $100.00 C. Mitchell Collection.

Checkers, modern, 1970s, EX, $65.00 C. Mitchell Collection.

Flip game, early, showing boy drinking from a bottle with a straw, 1910–20s, VG, $875.00 C. Mitchell Collection.

Checkers, wooden, Coca-Cola name in script on top, 1940–50s, EX, $45.00 C. Mitchell Collection.

Game box, contains two decks of 1943 cards unopened, plus marbles, dominos, chess, and checkers, 1940s, NM, $450.00 B.

Muddy River Trading Co./Gary Metz.

Game in original cardboard box, contains table tennis, bingo, dominos, two decks of cards, chess, checkers, 1940s, EX, $1,100.00 D. Antiques Cards and Collectibles/Ray Pelly.

Game of Steps To Health, Based on the Malden Health Series, cardboard tri-fold board game, Prepared and Distributed by The Coca-Cola Company Of Canada, Limited, 1940-50s, EX, $125.00 C.

Al and Earlene Mitchell.

Playing cards, top row: Coca-Cola and Don Nelson of the Milwaukee Bucks, 1970s, M, $95.00 C; Mexico, 1971, M, $65.00 C; "Coca-Cola adds life to everything nice," 1976, M, $30.00 C; Betty, 1977, M, $30.00 C. Bottom: Gold box, 1974, M, $15.00 C; Dynamic wave trademark, 1985, M, $15.00 D; Girl sitting in field, 1974, M, $20.00 D; Bottle and food, 1974, M, $25.00 C. Mitchell Collection.

Playing cards, complete with Joker and Bridge scoring cards, featuring girl with bottle, 1928, NM, $2,500.00 B. Muddy River Trading Co./Gary Metz.

Playing cards, double deck in container similar to six pack holder, 1970s, EX, $65.00 C.
Mitchell Collection .

Playing cards, friends and family, 1980, M, $55.00 C.

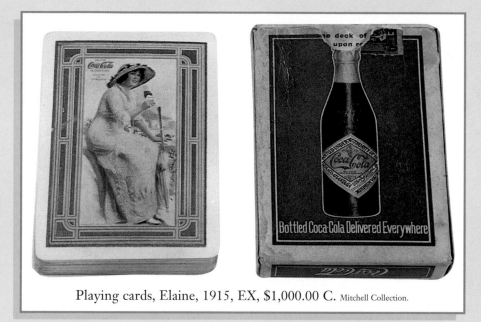

Playing cards, Elaine, 1915, EX, $1,000.00 C. Mitchell Collection.

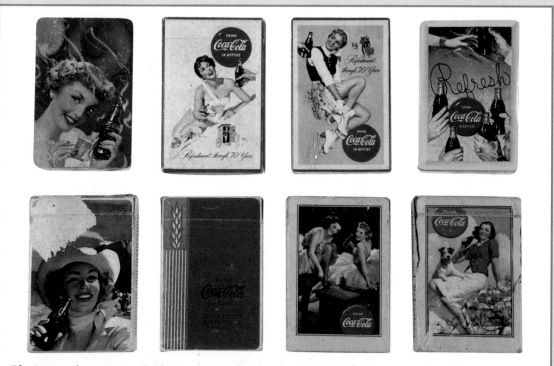

Playing cards, top row: Lady at party with a bottle, 1951, M, $80.00 C; Girl at beach, 1956, M, $80.00 C; Girl putting on ice skates, 1956, M, $80.00 C; "Refresh," 1958, M, $85.00 C. Bottom: Cowgirl in hat with a bottle, 1951, M, $80.00 C; "Drink Coca-Cola In Bottles," 1938, M, $135.00 C; 1943, EX, $200.00 C; Lady with dog and bottle, 1943, EX, $225.00 C. Mitchell Collection.

Playing cards, top row: Santa Claus, 1979, M, $25.00 C; Sprite Boy and bottle, 1979, M, $35.00 C; "Coke Is It," 1985, M, $25.00 C; Red and white, 1986, M, $25.00 C. Bottom: Hamilton King Coca-Cola girl on the cover, 1977, M, $25.00 C; "Have a Coke and a Smile," double check, 1979, $35.00 C; Kansas City Spring Fling '82, M, $55.00 C. Mitchell Collection.

Playing cards, top row: Spotter lady, 1943, M, $100.00 C; Blue wheat, 1938, M, $155.00 C; Great Bend, Kansas, EX, $175.00 C; Military nurse in uniform, 1943, EX, $135.00 C. Bottom: 1943, M, $100.00 C; "Drink Coca-Cola in Bottles," 1938, red wheat, M, $155.00 C; "Drink Coca-Cola in Bottles," 1938, green wheat, $150..00 C; Woman in uniform with wings below photo, 1943, EX, $125.00 C.

Mitchell Collection.

Playing cards from Campbellsville, Ky., Bottling Co., M, $65.00 C. <small>Mitchell Collection.</small>

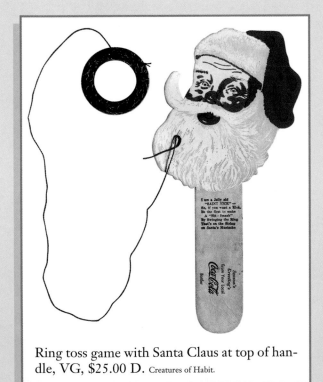

Ring toss game with Santa Claus at top of handle, VG, $25.00 D. <small>Creatures of Habit.</small>

Score keeper, cardboard, keeps score of runs, hits, and errors by both teams, by score wheels, 1900s, VG, $135.00 C. <small>Mitchell Collection.</small>

Sprite Boy ball game with glass cover and metal back, VG, $100.00 C. Mitchell Collection.

Sprite Boy Double Six Domino set in original vinyl case, 1970s, EX, $25.00 C. Mitchell Collection.

Arkansas Chapter "Holiday Happening" in plastic, 1995, EX............................$30.00 D

Ball and cap game, wooden, 1960s, EX....$35.00 C

Baseball bat, 1950s, EX...............$175.00 C

Baseball bat, wooden, featuring Coca-Cola at end, 1968, EX............................$55.00 D

Baseball glove, left-handed, 1920s, EX...$350.00 C

Bingo card, "Drink Coca-Cola" in center spot, 1950s, EX...................................$10.00 D

Bingo card with slide covers, "Play Refreshed Drink Coca-Cola From Sterilized Bottles," 1930s, EX..............................$45.00 D

Canned Wizzer Coke game, EX..........$5.00 D

Checkers, dominos, cribbage board, two decks of cards, and a bridge score pad in a carrying box, 1940s, VG...............................$200.00 D

Chinese Checkers board with Silhouette Girl logo, 1930–40s, EX........................$75.00 D

Cribbage board, 1940s, EX............$40.00 D

Dominos, wooden in original box, 1940–50s, EX . $55.00

Football, miniature, 1960s, black and white, EX...................................$10.00 D

Frisbee, plastic with dynamic wave logo on top, "Coke adds life to having fun," 1960s, EX.......$12.00 C

Horse Race, in original box, EX........$350.00 C

Magic kit, 1965, EX ....$175.00 D

Playing cards, Arkansas Chapter "Holiday Happening" in plastic, 1995, EX................$30.00

Playing cards, Atlanta Christmas, 1992, EX $45.00 D

Playing cards, Atlanta Christmas, 1993, EX $40.00 D

Playing cards, Atlanta, Ga. convention cards, 1990s, NRFB............................$15.00 D

Playing cards, Beach scene, 1960, M......$85.00 D

Playing cards, "Coca-Cola adds music to my life," 1988, EX............................$25.00 D

Playing cards, Bottle on ice man, 1958, M ....$75.00 C

Playing cards, "Coke Refreshes You Best," girl with bowling ball, 1961, M . . . . $70.00 C

Playing cards, "Coke Refreshes You Best," 1961, M . . . . $70.00 C

Playing cards, Couple at beach with surf board, 1963, M . . . . $95.00 C

Playing cards, Couple playing tennis, 1979, M . $35.00 D

Playing cards, Couple playing tennis, 1979, M . . . . $40.00 D

Playing cards, Couple sitting and resting under tree in planter, 1963, M, ... $100.00 C

Playing cards, Dearborn Convention, 1993, EX . $25.00 D

Playing cards, "Drink Coca-Cola," party scene, 1960, M . . . . $70.00 D

Playing cards featuring a Coca-Cola bottle, 1963, white and red, EX . . . . $35.00 D

Playing cards featuring the bobbed hair girl, "Refresh Yourself," in original box, 1928, EX . . . . . $575.00 C

Playing cards, Friends and family, 1980, M . . . $55.00 D

Playing cards from Campbellsville, Ky, Bottling Co, M . . . . $65.00 C

Playing cards from the California Chapter of the Cola Clan, 1986, EX . . . . $100.00 D

Playing cards, girl in circle surrounded by leaves, in original box, 1943, EX . . . . $105.00 D

Playing cards, Girl in pool, "Sign of Good Taste," 1959, EX . . . . $80.00 D

Playing cards, Kansas City Convention, 1995, NRFB . . . . $15.00 C

Playing cards, Kansas City Spring Fling, 1993, EX . . . . $60.00 D

Playing cards, Louisville Ky. convention, 1980s, NRFB . . . . $15.00 C

Playing cards, model that was used on 1923 calendar, 1977, M . . . . $45.00 D

Playing cards, "Refreshing New Feeling," featuring couple in front of fireplace, 1963, M . . . . . $75.00 C

Playing cards, Smokeyfest Chapter, 1994, EX . . $25.00 C

Playing cards, Smokeyfest Chapter, 1995, EX . . $20.00 C

Playing cards, Snowman in a bottle cap hat, 1959, M . . . . $75.00 D

Playing cards, woman with tray of bottles, 1963, M . . . . $55.00 C

Pool cue, dynamic wave logo, EX . . . . $55.00 C

Pool cue with dynamic contour logo, EX . . $35.00 D

Puzzle, bottles in tub, 1950s, 12"x18" . . . . . $85.00 D

Puzzle, jigsaw, "An Old Fashioned Girl," in original box, 1970–80s, NM . . . . $15.00 D

Puzzle, jigsaw, Coca-Cola Pop Art, in sealed can, 1960, NM . . . . $15.00 C

Puzzle, jigsaw, Hawaiian beach, rare, in original box, NM . . . . $165.00 C

Puzzle, jigsaw, in original box, "Crossing The Equator," NM . . . . $135.00 D

Puzzle, jigsaw, Teen Age Party, NM . . . . . . $75.00 D

Puzzle, miniature, in box, 1983, NM . . . . . $15.00 D

Puzzle, wooden blocks that spell "Ice Cold Coca-Cola," 15", NM . . . . $275.00 D

Record chart, baseball-shaped, National League Hall of Fame, 1960, EX . . . . $55.00 D

Shanghai, MIR . . . . $15.00 D

Steps to Health with original playing pieces and envelope, 1938, 11"x26", NM . . . . $130.00 D

Tower of Hanoi, EX . . . . $225.00 D

Left: Case, snap lid with raised bottle in center, all metal, EX, $75.00 C. Right: Money clip, compliments Coca-Cola Bottling Works, Nashville, Tenn., EX, $45.00 C. Mitchell Collection.

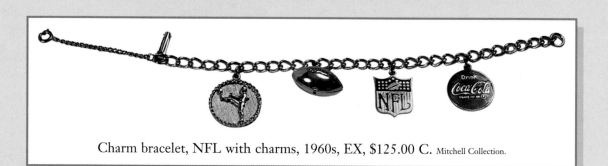

Charm bracelet, NFL with charms, 1960s, EX, $125.00 C. Mitchell Collection.

Charm bracelet with bottle and glass charms, EX, $125.00 C. Mitchell Collection.

Cuff links, gold finish, "Enjoy Coca-Cola," glass-shaped, 1970s, EX, $35.00 C. Mitchell Collection.

Key chain, 1900s, EX, $135.00 C. Mitchell Collection.

Key chain, compliments of Coca-Cola Bottling Works, Nashville, Tenn., in original box with Merry Christmas card inside, VG, $75.00 C. Mitchell Collection.

Money clips, top row: bottle in horseshoe, EX, $30.00 C; 50th year, from the Coca-Cola Bottling Co, Piqua, OH, EX, $45.00 C. Key chain, bottom: 50th Anniversary, G, $20.00 C. Mitchell Collection.

Match safes, top: for wood matches, "Drink Coca-Cola in Bottles" on side in cameo, EX, $350.00 C. Bottom: "Drink Coca-Cola," F, $175.00 C. Mitchell Collection.

Money clips, top row: gold plate with "Drink Coca-Cola" button in center, F, $35.00 C; "Coca-Cola" in white lettering on gold plate, EX, $30.00 C. Bottom: Silver plate, "Enjoy Coca-Cola," dynamic wave with knife, $30.00 C; "Enjoy Coca-Cola" with dynamic wave on silver plate, VG, $30.00 D. Mitchell Collection.

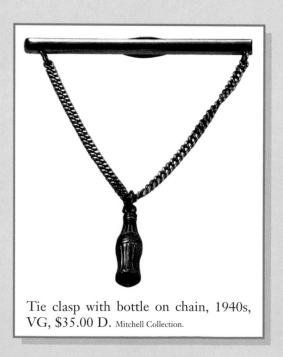

Tie clasp with bottle on chain, 1940s, VG, $35.00 D. Mitchell Collection.

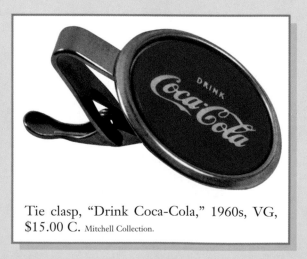

Tie clasp, "Drink Coca-Cola," 1960s, VG, $15.00 C. Mitchell Collection.

Watch fob with likeness of Duster Girl, Coca-Cola logo on reverse side, 1911, E, $800.00 B.

Muddy River Trading Co./Gary Metz.

Belt and buckle, "All Star Dealer Campaign Award," 1950–60s, M . . . . $25.00 D

Brooch, "Drink Coca-Cola," EX, $40.00-D; Necklace with bottle, EX . . . . $85.00 C

Button, pin lock, bottle is hand club pen, VG. $15.00 C

Coca-Cola Bottlers convention pin, shield-shaped, 1912, EX. . . . . $500.00 D

Coca-Cola Bottling Company annual convention pin, 1915, red, white, blue, EX. . . . . $600.00 D

Coca-Cola Bottling company annual convention pin, 1916, EX. . . . . $600.00 D

Coca-Cola 100th anniversary wrist watch, featuring a diamond chip at 12 o'clock, NM . . . . $120.00 B

Compact with 50th Anniversary spot on front center, 1950s, red, M . . . . $55.00 D

Hat pin from driver's uniform, "Drink Coca-Cola," 1930, EX. . . . . $175.00 D

Money clip, "All Star Dealer Campaign Award," 1950–60s, NM . . . . $25.00 D

Pledge pin, bottle-shaped, EX. . . . . $25.00 D

Service pin, 5 year, EX . . . . $70.00 C

Service pin, 10 year, EX . . . . $75.00 C

Service pin, 15 year, EX . . . . $75.00 C

Service pin, 20 year, EX . . . . $75.00 C

Service pin, 30 year, EX . . . . $125.00 D

Service pin, 50 year, as you might expect this pin is hard to find and is extremely rare, EX. . . . $375.00 C

Watch fob, 50th Anniversary, EX . . . . $75.00 C

Watch fob, brass, "Drink Delicious Coca-Cola in Bottles," girl drinking from bottle with straw, 1912, EX. $175.00 C

Watch fob, brass swastika (this was a good luck symbol until the 1930s when the Nazi connection made it an ugly form), 1920s, EX . . . . $150.00 C

Watch fob, brass with gold wash, "Relieves Fatigue" on front, "Drink Coca-Cola Sold Everywhere 5¢" on back, 1907, EX . . . . $150.00 C

Watch fob, brass with red enamel lettering, 1900s, EX. . . . . $135.00 C

Watch fob, brass with red enamel lettering, "Drink Coca-Cola," 1920s, EX. . . . . $150.00 C

Watch fob, bulldog, 1920s, EX . . . . $110.00 C

Watch fob, "Coca-Cola 5¢," applied paper label bottle . . . . $50.00 C

Watch fob, "Drink Delicious Coca-Cola in Bottles," brass with black enamel, EX . . . . $175.00 C

Watch fob, Duster Girl, 1911, EX . . . . . . $700.00 D

Watch fob, Hilda Clark in center, EX. . . . $125.00 C

Watch fob, horseshoe-shaped with paper label bottle in center, 1905, EX. . . . . $950.00 D

Watch fob, oval, girl drinking from a bottle with a straw, 1910, 1¼"x1¾", EX . . . . $800.00 D

Watch fob, round celluloid girl in bonnet with red ribbon, 1912, EX . . . . $1,800.00 D

Watch fob, with swastika, 1915 . . . . $150.00 C

Wrist watch, in original metal tin, NM. . . . $35.00 D

Apron, cloth, "Be Really Refreshed" with button on chest portion, 1950s, white, VG, $30.00 C. Mitchell Collection.

Bandanna, Kit Carson, 1950s, 20"x22", red, EX, $65.00 C. Mitchell Collection.

Cap, felt beanie, 1930 – 40s, 8" dia., VG, $45.00 C. Mitchell Collection.

Bowler's shirt, "Things go better with Coke," 1960s, EX, $30.00 C. Mitchell Collection.

Driver's cap with hard bill, red, white, and yellow, 1930s, EX, $75.00 C. Mitchell Collection.

Driver's shirt, short sleeve, white with green stripes and large back patch with white background, VG, $35.00 C. Mitchell Collection.

Driver's shirt, short sleeve, 1960s, VG, $50.00 C. Mitchell Collection.

Driver's folding cap, 1950s, VG, $65.00 C. Mitchell Collection.

Hat, soda person, cloth, 1940, EX, $25.00 C. Mitchell Collection.

Hat, soda person, note the term Soda Jerk wasn't coined until the 1940s, EX, $20.00 C. Mitchell Collection.

Hat, soda person paper fold-up, featuring Sprite Boy, 1950s, VG, $25.00 C. Mitchell Collection.

Kerchief, "The Cola Clan," with Silhouette Girl from Coca-Cola Collectors' banquet, 1970s, white and red, EX, $20.00 C. Mitchell Collection.

Patch, "Coca-Cola," red outline and lettering on white background, VG, $8.00 C. Mitchell Collection.

Patch, "Drink Coca-Cola in Bottles" with yellow and white lettering, 1960s, red, EX, $8.00 C. Mitchell Collection.

Patch, large, back, "Enjoy Coca-Cola," with yellow and white lettering, 1950–60s, red, EX, $15.00 C. Mitchell Collection.

Apron, "Enjoy Ice Cold Coke" on bib, 1941, EX . . . . $55.00 C

Apron, salesman's sample, "Drink...In Bottles," EX . . . . $50.00 C

Apron with red change pockets, "Drink Coca-Cola," 1950–60s, VG . . . . $25.00 C

Bandanna, Kit Carson, new, white, EX . . . . $15.00 C

Belt, vinyl, with "Drink Coca-Cola" blocks, 1960, white $15.00

Bow tie, white "Coca-Cola" on red, NM . . $35.00 C

Cowboy hat, convention, 1937, EX . . . . . $200.00 C

Patch, small shirt, "Drink Coca-Cola," with red and black lettering, 1960s, EX . . . . $5.00 C

Painter's hat, 1950s, F . . . . $10.00 C

Coin purse with gold lettering engraved in leather "When thirsty try a bottle," "Coca-Cola Bottling Company" with a paper label bottle to the left of lettering, 1907, maroon, EX, $100.00 C. Mitchell Collection.

Left: Leather, black, 1920s, EX, $85.00 C. Right: Leather, "Drink Coca-Cola, Delicious, Refreshing," 1920s, EX, $45.00 C. Mitchell Collection.

Left: Coin purse with snap closures, leather, arrow, "Whenever you see an arrow think of Coca-Cola," 1909, VG, $175.00 C. Right: Coin purse with snap closure top, leather, compliments of Coca-Cola Bottling Co., Memphis, TN, 1910–1920s, VG, $185.00 C.

Mitchell Collection.

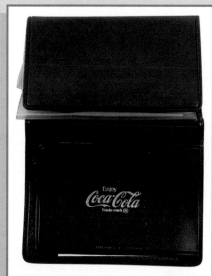

Plastic, "Enjoy Coca-Cola," 1960s, black, EX, $8.00. Mitchell Collection.

Coin purse, leather with gold embossed lettering, "Drink Coca-Cola in Bottles Delicious Refreshing" with gold colored rounded metal snap, 1910, black, EX. $150.00 C

Coin purse, leather with silver colored rounded metal snap top and silver embossed lettering, 1920s, black, EX..............................$150.00 C

Embossed wallet with bottle on front, 1920s, black, EX.................................$45.00 C

Leather with gold embossed lettering, 1907, black, EX.................................$90.00 C

Tri-fold with calendar and photo sleeves, leather, gold embossed lettering, 1920s, black, EX.....$75.00 C

Tri-fold with calendar, leather with gold embossed lettering, 1918, black, EX...............$85.00 C

Banner, horizontal paper, Santa Claus, "The gift for thirst," 1952, G, $45.00 C. Mitchell Collection.

Black Rushton doll holding a bottle, one of the harder dolls to find, 1970s, 16" tall, EX, $225.00 C. Mitchell Collection.

Cardboard cut out, "Free Decorations in cartons of Coke," Santa standing on ladder in front of Christmas tree with a small girl on stool at bottom of ladder, 1960s, EX, $25.00 C. Mitchell Collection.

Cardboard cut out, "Free new Holiday Ideas in cartons of Coke," Santa standing on ladder with small child playing with a jack-in-the-box on floor, 1960s, 36", EX, $25.00 C. Mitchell Collection.

Cardboard cut out, Santa Claus, "Greetings from Coca-Cola," 1946, 6"x12", EX, $225.00 C. Mitchell Collection.

Cardboard cut out, Santa Claus in front of an open refrigerator door holding a bottle, this folds in the middle, easelback, 1948, 5' tall, F, $225.00 C. Mitchell Collection .

Cardboard cut out, Santa Claus, "Greetings," ribbon on bottom, G, $350.00 C. Mitchell Collection.

Cardboard cut out, Santa Claus, "The gift for thirst," 1953, 9"x18", EX, $200.00 C.
Mitchell Collection.

Cardboard cut out, Santa Claus trying to quiet small dog in front of Christmas tree, while holding a bottle, 1960s, EX, $75.00 C. Mitchell Collection.

Cardboard cut out sign featuring Sprite Boy and Santa Claus with reindeer, has original easel back attachment, 1940s, 26" x 52", EX, $525.00 B.

Muddy River Trading Co./Gary Metz.

Cardboard cut out, "Free new Holiday Ideas in cartons of Coke," Santa standing on ladder with small child playing with a jack-in-the-box on floor, 1960s, 36", EX, $20.00 C.

Mitchell Collection.

Cardboard cut out showing small boy peering around a door facing at Santa who's opening a bottle, easelback, 3-dimensional, 1950s, VG, $225.00 C. Mitchell Collection.

Cardboard die cut hanging sign "Christmas Greetings," 1932, NM, $4,200.00 B.
Muddy River Trading Co./Gary Metz.

Cardboard stand up Santa Claus holding three bottles in each hand with a button behind Santa, 1950s, VG, $175.00 C. Mitchell Collection.

Cardboard poster, artwork of Santa with bottle, "Sign of Good Taste… anytime!" EX, $85.00 C. Al and Earlene Mitchell.

Cardboard Santa hanger, "Add Zest to the Season," Canadian, 1949, 10½" x 18½", EX, $900.00 B.
Muddy River Trading Co./Gary Metz.

Cardboard truck sign featuring Santa with both hands full of Coke bottles "Santa's Helpers," 1960s, 66" x 32", G, $120.00 B.
Muddy River Trading Co./Gary Metz.

Cut out Santa Claus on stool holding wooden rabbit, EX, $100.00 C. Mitchell Collection.

In America, we, too, like to use words in our own way. No doubt the Dutch "Sant Nikolaas" was changed to the easier said "Santa Claus" by the little boys and girls of long ago who waited so eagerly for his yearly visit.

Many countries have contributed to the history of Santa Claus, to what he should wear, how he should travel, even to his personal appearance. His reindeer must have come from the icy areas of northern Scandinavia where reindeer and sleigh are used for travel. The chimney he descends on Christmas Eve with his sack and his short pipe are Dutch traditions. The fur-trimmed clothes could have been added by anxious folk of cold lands who were fearful lest Santa's comfort be disturbed in his long night's journey.

But his twinkling eyes, cherry nose and plump body are purely American. It was a scholarly New Yorker, Dr. Clement Moore, who saw the "jolly old elf" most clearly and recorded for the whole world, the classic picture of him in the poem which begins, "'Twas the night before Christmas."

Here Santa Claus comes to life, merry, affectionate, a friend of little children; one who finds a great joy in giving. Through him the spirit of mankind is lifted, soaring up the snow-blown path of the sleigh and eight tiny reindeer to a happy world where anything is possible.

Copyright 1950, The Coca-Cola Company

Christmas card with possible origin of Santa clothing on reverse side, VG, $45.00 C. Mitchell Collection.

Display topper, cardboard, "Stock up for the Holidays," Santa holding a bottle behind a six-pack, 1950s, EX, $135.00 C. Mitchell Collection.

Hanging display sign, cardboard, "Serve Coke and add Punch to your holidays," Santa at bottom of sign holding a glass, 1958, EX, $30.00 C. Mitchell Collection.

Light hanger, 1960, EX, $18.00 C. Mitchell Collection.

Porcelain, large animated, Santa holding a bottle and holds up a finger to quieten a small porcelain dog, new, EX, $115.00 C. Mitchell Collection.

Porcelain, large animated, Santa holding a book that has good boys and girls list, new, EX, $120.00 C. Mitchell Collection.

Porcelain, large, Santa holding a bottle and a string of lights standing beside a small wooden stool with a striped package sitting on the top step, new, EX, $135.00 C. Mitchell Collection.

Poster, cardboard, "A Merry Christmas calls for Coke," Santa seated in green easy chair while elves bring him food, 1960s, 16"x24", VG, $45.00 C. Mitchell Collection.

Poster, cardboard, "Bring Home The Coke," Santa at his work bench, 1956, 14"x28", EX, $200.00 C. Mitchell Collection.

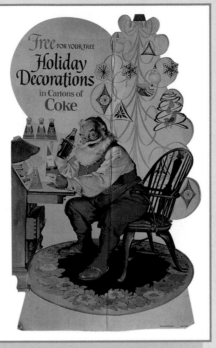

Poster, cardboard cut out, "Free for your tree Holiday Decorations in Cartons of Coke," Santa seated at desk with a bottle, 1960s, VG, $35.00 **C.** Mitchell Collection.

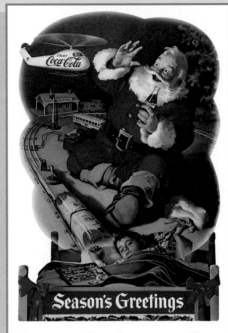

Poster, cardboard, cut out, "Season's Greetings," Santa sitting in the middle of a train set with a white helicopter flying around his head, 1962, 32"x47", EX, $375.00 **C.** Mitchell Collection.

Poster, cardboard, vertical, "The gift for thirst, Stock up for the Holidays," children with presents and a hatless Santa with a bottle, EX, $50.00 **C.** Mitchell Collection.

Poster, large, cardboard, "Holiday Refreshment Starts Here Enjoy Coca-Cola," Santa pointing to the lettering with one hand and holding a bottle with the other, EX, $45.00 **C.** Mitchell Collection.

Royal Orleans porcelain figurine featuring Santa holding a bottle and looking at a globe, one part of a six series set, 1980, EX, $175.00 C. Mitchell Collection.

Royal Orleans porcelain figurine featuring Santa hushing a small dog and holding a bottle, one in a limited six part series, 1980, EX, $135.00 C. Mitchell Collection.

Royal Orleans porcelain figurine featuring Santa seated holding a child and a bottle while a small boy kneels at a dog sitting up, one in a limited set of six, 1980s, $125.00 C. Mitchell Collection.

Royal Orleans porcelain fig-urine featuring Santa standing beside a sack of toys and drink-ing from a glass, part of a six-piece limited edition set, 1980, EX, $150.00 C. Mitchell Collection.

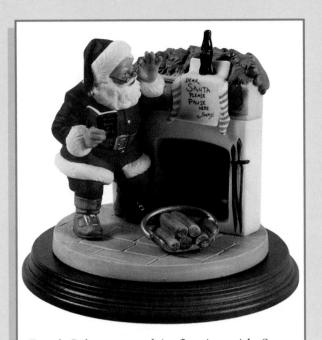

Royal Orleans porcelain figurine with Santa holding a book in front of a fireplace that has a bottle on the mantel, part of a limited six-part series, all six pieces together MIB $1,200.00, 1980s, EX, $125.00 C. Mitchell Collection.

Sign, cardboard, double sided hanging, "Things go better with Coke," Santa and a couple kissing, 1960, 13½"x16", EX, $45.00 C. Mitchell Collection.

Sign, cardboard rocket, "Drink Coca-Cola Fes-tive Holidays," die cut dimen-sional Santa, 1950s, 33" tall, VG, $325.00 C.

Mitchell Collection.

Sign, cardboard, "Santa's Helpers," Santa holding six bottles, 1950s, VG, $85.00 D. Mitchell Collection.

Wreath, cardboard, Santa holding six bottles, 1958, EX, $25.00 C. Mitchell Collection.

Cardboard cut out, "It's the real thing. Coke Stock up for the Holidays," featuring Santa standing in back of elves decorating a Christmas tree, 1970s, VG . . . . . $35.00 C

Cardboard cut out, "Things go better with Coke," scenes of people over Santa's head, 1960s, 36", EX . . . $45.00 C

Cardboard cut out, "Things go better with Coke," Santa and little boy with dog, 1960s, 36", EX. . . . . . $30.00 C

Cardboard stand up, Santa Claus resting one arm on a post while holding a bottle with the other, a holly Christmas wreath is shown in the rear, 1960s, EX . . . . . . $85.00 C

Carton stuffer Santa Claus, "Good taste for all," EX . . . . $45.00 D

Doll, Rushton, holding a bottle, 1960s, 16" high, EX . . . . $135.00 C

Paper hanger, Season's Greeting's with Santa and helicopter, 1962, 16"x24", NM . . . . $425.00 B

Poster, cardboard, "Coke adds life to Holiday Fun," lettering on sign in front of Santa, 1960s, EX. . . . $25.00 C

Poster, cardboard, "Extra Bright Refreshment" Santa beside a Christmas tree with a six-pack in front, 1955, 16"x27", VG . . . . $65.00 C

Poster, cardboard, "Get your Santa Collector's Cup," Santa holding a glass, EX . . . . $15.00 C

Poster, cardboard, "Real holidays call for the real thing," Santa holding a Christmas wreath, 1970s, 36" tall, EX . . . . $20.00 C

Poster, paper, "Coke adds life to Holiday Fun," Santa beside fireplace holding a bottle, EX. . . . . . $30.00 C

Poster, paper, "The pause that refreshes," Santa in his workshop, EX . . . . $25.00 C

Royal Orleans Santa plate, first plate, 1983, MIB . . . . $75.00 C

Santa doll in black boots, original, 1950s, 16", EX . . . . $175.00 C

Sign, cardboard rocket, "Drink Coca-Cola Festive Holidays," die cut dimensional Santa, 1950s, 33" tall, VG . . . . $375.00 D

Sign, cardboard, "The More the Merrier," Santa sitting in front of Christmas tree with sacks of toys and Coca-Cola and Sprite in front of him, 1970s, EX . . . . $35.00 D

Astro-Float mounts on top of bottle, designed to put ice cream in for a Coke float or ice to help cool down your drink, 1960s, VG, $20.00 C.

Mitchell Collection.

Axe, "For Sportsmen" "Drink Coca-Cola," 1930, EX, $950.00 C. Mitchell Collection.

Bank, cooler style, "Have a Coke" embossed in top, 1940s, 5"x5"x3½", EX, $1,000.00 B.

Muddy River Trading Co./Gary Metz.

Bookmark, celluloid, "Drink Coca-Cola at Soda Fountains 5¢," 1898, F, $550.00 C.

Bookmark, paper, "Drink Coca-Cola Delicious and Refreshing" featuring Lillian Nordica at stand table with a glass, 1900s, 2¼"x5¼", NM, $1,500.00 B. Muddy River Trading Co./Gary Metz.

Bookmark, celluloid oval, "What Shall We Drink? Drink Coca-Cola 5¢," 1906, 2"x2¼", EX, $750.00 C. Mitchell Collection.

Bookmark, celluloid, "Refreshing Drink Coca-Cola Delicious 5¢," 1900s, 2"x2¼", F, $500.00 C. Mitchell Collection.

Bookmark, Lillian Nordica, 1904, 2"x6", EX, $300.00 C. Mitchell Collection.

Bookmark with white cat, Tell City Coca-Cola Bottling Co., Inc., EX, $75.00 D.
Antiques, Cards, Collectibles.

Bottle lamp, with cap and original marked brass base, very rare and highly desirable, 1920s, 20", NM, $7,200.00 B.
Muddy River Trading Co./Gary Metz.

Bowl, green, scalloped edge Vernonware, "Drink Coca-Cola Ice Cold," 1930s, green, EX, $450.00 C. Muddy River Trading Co./Gary Metz.

Brass book ends in shape of bottle, 1960s, EX, $200.00 B.
Gene Harris Antique Auction Center, Inc.

Cardboard display of Coca-Cola bottling plant in San Diego, note the streamline architecture; this has been designated a historic cultural monument, 14"x4½"x6½", EX, $50.00 B.
Muddy River Trading Co./Gary Metz.

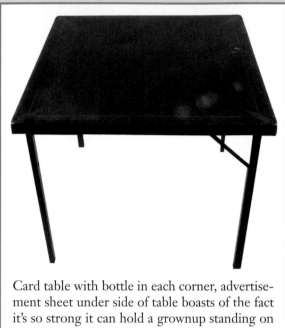

Card table with bottle in each corner, advertisement sheet under side of table boasts of the fact it's so strong it can hold a grownup standing on it, 1930, VG, $250.00 C. Mitchell Collection.

Cash register topper, "Please Pay When Served," light-up, 1950s, EX, $950.00 B.
Muddy River Trading Co./Gary Metz.

Chewing gum display box, held twenty 5¢ packages cardboard, rare, 1920s, VG, $1,500.00 B.

Cigarette box, 50th Anniversary frosted glass, 1936, EX, $700.00 C. Mitchell Collection.

Coke pepsin gum jar with embossed lid, 1905 – 11, NM, $900.00 B.

Muddy River Trading Co./Gary Metz.

Desk pen holder with music box attached, 1950s, EX, $275.00 C. Mitchell Collection.

Counter dispenser, bolt-on, 1940–50s, VG, $725.00 D. Patrick's Collectibles.

Dispenser with porcelain base, frosted glass body and lid, white lettering on red base, 1920s, 17" tall, NM, $6,200.00 B.

Muddy River Trading Co./Gary Metz.

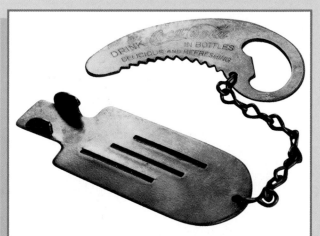

Door lock, metal, "Drink Coca-Cola in Bottles, Delicious and Refreshing," 1930s, EX, $55.00 C.

Mitchell Collection.

Educational poster, chart four in the electricity series, distributed to schools for teaching aids, great graphics, but low in demand, 1940s, EX, $15.00 D. Creatures of Habit.

Fact wheel, United States at a glance, EX, $85.00 C. Mitchell Collection.

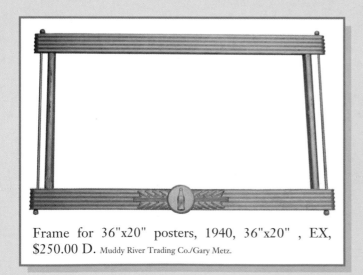

Frame for 36"x20" posters, 1940, 36"x20", EX, $250.00 D. Muddy River Trading Co./Gary Metz.

Globe, leaded glass, round, "Coca-Cola," rare, 1920s, EX, $10,000.00 D.

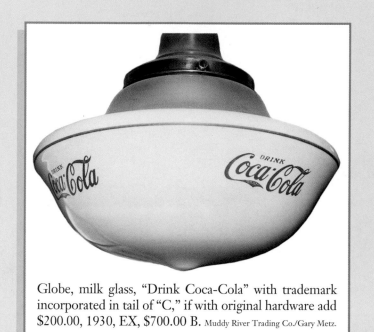

Globe, milk glass, "Drink Coca-Cola" with trademark incorporated in tail of "C," if with original hardware add $200.00, 1930, EX, $700.00 B. Muddy River Trading Co./Gary Metz.

Globe, milk glass, from ceiling fixture, "Drink Coca-Cola," 1930–40s, EX, $450.00 C. Mitchell Collection.

Key tag, Coca-Cola Bottling Co., Indianapolis, showing 2 cents postage guaranteed, VG, $35.00 C. Mitchell Collection.

Light fixture, rectangular colored leaded glass, with bottom beaded fringe, "Coca-Cola 5¢," "Pittsburgh Mosaic Glass Co, Inc, Pittsburgh, Pa," 1910, 11"wx22"x7½"h, EX, $12,000.00 C.

Metal string holder with six pack in spotlight, "Take Home In Cartons," red, 1930s, 14" x 16", EX, $1,000.00 B. Muddy River Trading Co./Gary Metz.

Mileage meter, "Travel refreshed," originating from Asheville, N.C., white on red, 1950s, EX, $1,550.00 B. Muddy River Trading Co./Gary Metz.

Our America, Iron and Steel, poster number three in a series of four posters, great graphics but demand for educational material has remained low, 1946, EX, $15.00 C. Mitchell Collection.

Pencil sharpener, cast metal in shape of bottle, 1930s, VG, $40.00 C. Mitchell Collection.

Pepsin gum jar with thumbnail type lid, 1910, EX, $1,600.00 **B.** Muddy River Trading Co./Gary Metz.

Popcorn box, "Drink Coca-Cola," 1950s, EX, $35.00 C. Mitchell Collection.

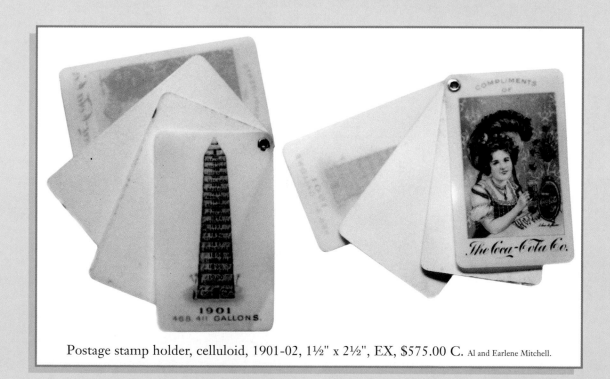

Postage stamp holder, celluloid, 1901-02, 1½" x 2½", EX, $575.00 C. Al and Earlene Mitchell.

Refrigerator water bottle, green glass "Compliments Coca-Cola Bottling Co.," embossed, EX, $135.00 C.

Mitchell Collection.

Ricky Nelson set, consisting of poster and a 45LP, personally autographed, framed, difficult to find these, 1960s, 18"x14½", G, $575.00 B.

Muddy River Trading Co./Gary Metz.

Ruler, 12", wooden, "A Good Rule," very common item, 1920–1960, EX, $2.00 C.

Screwdriver, pocket clip set, one straight and one Phillips blade, EX, $8.00 C.

Mitchell Collection.

Sewing needle case with packaging featuring the same model that appeared on the 1924 calendar, 1920s, EX, $75.00 C.

Mitchell Collection.

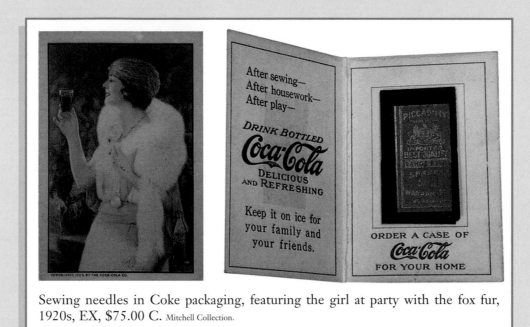

Sewing needles in Coke packaging, featuring the girl at party with the fox fur, 1920s, EX, $75.00 C. Mitchell Collection.

Shade, ceiling, milk glass with original hardware, 1930s, 10", EX, $1,500.00 D.

Shade, colored leaded glass, with the chain edge that originally had a border of hanging beaded fringe, "Property of the Coca-Cola Co. to be returned on demand" must be on top band, 1920s, 18" dia., EX, $5,000.00 C.

Statue holding bottles of Coca-Cola, "Tell me your profit story, please" on base, 1930–40s, EX, $125.00 C. Mitchell Collection.

Street marker, brass, "Drink Coca-Cola, Safety First," fairly rare piece, 1920, VG, $175.00 C. Mitchell Collection.

Syrup dispenser, ceramic, complete, marked "The Wheeling Pottery Co.," 1896, VG, $5,500.00 B.

Muddy River Trading Co./Gary Metz.

Syrup dispenser, reproduction made of hard rubber, 1950s, EX, $325.00 B. Muddy River Trading Co./Gary Metz.

Thimbles, left: red band, 1920s, EX, $65.00
C. Right: blue band, 1920s, EX, $95.00 C.
Mitchell Collection.

Tumbler, showing "Drink
Coca-Cola," 1950–70s,
EX, $10.00 C. Mitchell Collection.

Umbrella, "Drink Coca-Cola... Be Really
Refreshed," F, $575.00 C. Mitchell Collection.

Wall pocket, 3-dimensional press
fiber board, 9"x13", EX, $650.00 C.
Mitchell Collection.

Water cup with handle, tin, "This cup for water but Drink Coca-Cola in Bottles, Coca-Cola Bottling Co. Greencastle, Ind." is printed in black in bottom of cup, rare piece, 1930s, EX, $125.00 C. Mitchell Collection.

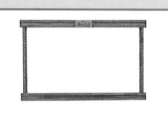

Wooden Kay Displays frame with unusual crest at top, will accommodate 40" x 24" poster, 1930s, F, $160.00 B. Muddy River Trading Co./Gary Metz.

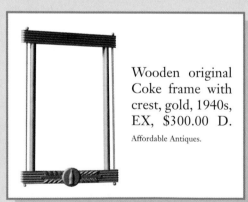

Wooden original Coke frame with crest, gold, 1940s, EX, $300.00 D.

Affordable Antiques.

Wooden transistor radio with battery compartment behind back door, Philippines, 1940s, 7"w x 4"d x 5"t, EX, $400.00 C. Mitchell Collection.

45 RPM record, Trini Lopez, with dust cover advertising Fresca, 1967, EX . . . . $15.00 D

Badge holder, Bottler's Conference, metal and celluloid, 1943, EX . . . . $55.00 C

Bell, stamped metal, "Refresh Yourself Drink Coca-Cola In Bottles" on both sides, 1930s, 3¼" tall, NM . . . . $500.00 B

Bolo tie, Kit Carson, neckerchief in original mailer envelope, 1950s, EX . . . . $75.00 C

Bookmark, plastic with wave logo, 1970, white and red, EX, $5.00 C. Shoe spoon with wave logo, plastic, 1970s, white and red, EX. . . . . $8.00 C

Chewing gum jar with thumb nail type lid, 1930s, M . . . . $500.00 D

Cigar band, 1930, EX . . . . $150.00 D

Comb, plastic, 1970s, red, EX . . . . $3.00 D

Cup, paper, red lettering "Things Go Better With Coke" on white square, 1960s, NM. . . . . . $5.00 D

Dialing finger, "It's the real thing," 1970s, EX . . . . $15.00 D

Display bottle, hard rubber, 1948, 4' tall, EX . $975.00 D

Display bottle, plastic, with embossed logos, 1953, 20" tall, VG. . . . . $210.00 D

Dust cover, Lone Ranger, 1971, EX . . . . $35.00 D

Dust cover, Superman, 1971, EX. . . . . . $35.00 D

Fence post topper made from heavy cast iron, used to decorate fence pillars outside bottling plants, has a threaded base, 20" tall, EX . . . . $500.00 D

Flashlight in original box, 1980, EX . . . . $35.00 D

Fly swatters, "Drink Coca-Cola In Bottles," EX . . . . $90.00 D

"Drink Coca-Cola" with net end, EX . . . $15.00 C

Glass negative for the 1940s poster featuring the tennis girl, very unusual and rare, 20"x24", G . . . . $100.00 D

Globe, leaded glass, round, "Coca-Cola," rare, 1920s, EX. $10,000.00 D

Golf divot remover, metal, EX . . . . $5.00 D

Ice bucket, "Drink Coca-Cola In Bottles," 1960s, EX . . . . $15.00 D

Ice tong with metal handle, 1940s, EX . $250.00 D

Ice tong with wood handle, "Drink Coca-Cola, Greencastle, Ind.," 1920s, EX . . . . $300.00 D

Ice tongs from Coca-Cola Bottling Co., Green Castle, Ind, has a 3-digit phone number, 1920s, EX . . . . $500.00 D

"Jim Dandy" combination tool that has a screwdriver, button hook, cigar cutter, and bottle opener, rare, 1920, EX. . . . . $300.00 D

Jug with paper label in original box, 1960s, one gallon, EX . . . . $30.00 D

Letter opener, metal and plastic with bottle on handle, 1950, red and white, EX. . . . . $30.00 D

Letter opener, plastic from Coca-Cola Bottling Co. Dyersburg, Tenn., clear, EX . . . . $15.00 C

Letter opener, plastic, white and red, EX . $5.00 C

Light, hanging adjustable, with popcorn insert on one of four sides, with red and white Coca-Cola advertising on the other panels, 1960s, 18"x18", M . . . . $525.00 D

Light, octagonal hanging Art Deco motif, believed to have been made for the San Francisco World's Fair Exhibition in 1939, 1930s, 20"w x 24"t, EX . . . . $1,800.00 D

Light shade for ceiling fixture, milk glass, "Drink Coca-Cola" with red lettering, 1930s, 14" dia., G. . . . . $600.00 D

Magic lantern slide, hand colored glass, "A Home Run" from Advertising Slide Co., St. Louis, 1970s, EX . . . . $125.00 D

Magic lantern slide, hand colored slide, "Daddy-here it is," 1920s, EX . . . . $150.00 D

Magic lantern slide, hand colored glass, "Good Company!" features a couple toasting with Coke bottles, 1920s, EX . . . . $135.00 D

Magic lantern slide, hand colored glass, "People say they like it because...," 1920s, EX . . . . . $100.00 D

Magic lantern slide, hand colored glass "Stop at the Red Sign" Coca-Cola Bottling Co, Festus, MO, 1920s, EX . . . . $130.00 D

Magic lantern slide, hand colored slide, "Unanimous good taste!," Festus, Mo, 1920s, EX . . . . . $135.00 D

Message pad shaped like a case of Coke, 1980s, EX . . . . $10.00 D

Mileage meter with home location of Crescent Beach, South Carolina, also has bottom stamp Marion Coca-Cola Bottling Company, 1950s, VG . . . . $1,000.00 D

Money bag, vinyl zippered, "Enjoy Coca-Cola," 1960s, VG . . . . $10.00 C

Music box, cooler shaped, in working order, 1950s, EX $130.00

Nail clippers, samples with advertising, EX . . . . $20.00 D

Nail file, "Coca-Cola In Bottles" embossed in early script, metal pocketknife style, EX . . . . . $10.00 D

Napkin holder with Sprite Boy panel on side, "Have a Coke 5¢," 1950, VG . . . . $700.00 B

NCAA final four commemorative 16 oz. can and pin set, 1994, EX . . . . 15.00 B

Night light, "It's the real thing" with the dynamic wave logo rectangular shaped, 1970s, EX. . . . . $25.00 C

Note pad holder for candlestick phone, price includes phone which also has a courtesy coin box, 1920s, EX . . . . $900.00 B

Olympic disc in original box, 1980, M . . . $10.00 D

Pen and pencil set by Cross with logo on pocket clips, in original case, M . . . . $65.00 D

Pen and pencil set in plastic case celebrating the 50th anniversary of Coca-Cola Bottling in Frankfort, IN, 1965, EX . . . . $45.00 D

Pen, baseball bat-shaped, 1940s, white and black, EX . . . . $50.00 D

Pen, "Drink" and bottle on pocket clip, with prices for specific quantities on barrel, NM . . . . $45.00 D

Pen, ink, red and white, 1950s, EX . . . . . $40.00 D

Pencil box, pencil-shaped, Sprite Boy, 1948, NM . . . . $145.00 D

Pencil holder, celluloid, 1910, EX . . . . . $135.00 D

Pencil holder, white with red button, 1950s, 5" tall . . . . $300.00 D

Pencil, mechanical, 1930s, EX . . . . $30.00 D

Pencil sharpener, rectangular, 1960s, EX. $10.00 D

Pencil sharpener, round, plastic, "Drink Coca-Cola," 1960s, white and red, EX . . . . $10.00 D

Penlight, push button with wave logo, 1970s, white and red, EX . . . . $10.00 D

Pin set, 100th Anniversary, limited edition, framed under glass, 1986, EX . . . . $275.00 D

Plaque for dispenser steel, stepped corners, 1950s, 7"x3", EX . . . . $75.00 D

Play dollar bill, "Refresh Yourself At The Bar," NM . . . . $90.00 D

Pocket protector, "Coke adds life to everything nice," 1960s, white and red . . . . $8.00 C

Pocket protector, vinyl, Union City, TN, 1950s, red and black, G . . . . $15.00 C

Polaroid camera, "Coke adds life to Happy Times," EX. . . . . $95.00 C

Popcorn bag, Jungleland, 5"x14", NM . . $12.00 D

Popcorn bucket, "Drink Coca-Cola in Bottles" spot in center, waxed cardboard, 1950s, M . . . $10.00 D

Postage stamp carrier, celluloid, 1902, EX. . . . . $500.00 C

Pot holder, "Drink Coca-Cola every bottle sterilized," red lettering on yellow, 1910–1912, G. . . . . $275.00 C

Printer's block with Sprite Boy, 1940s, M $35.00 C

Record album, "The Shadow," 1970, EX. $30.00 C

Record carrier for 45 rpms, plastic and vinyl, 1960s, 9"x8", red and white . . . . $40.00 C

Record dust cover featuring Dick Tracy scenes and the dynamic wave, 1971, EX . . . . $35.00 D

Record dust cover, Sgt. Preston, 1971, EX$35.00 D

Record dust cover, W. C. Field, 1971, EX$25.00 D

Refrigerator bottle, "Compliments of Coca-Cola Bottling Company" on one side with two horses and riders on the other side, 1940–1950s, 9" tall, EX. . . . . $125.00 C

Ruler, 12", plastic with wave logo, 1970, white and red, EX. . . . . $4.00 D

Ruler, 12", wooden, "Coca-Cola refresca en grande," 1950–60s, VG. . . . . $5.00 D

Salt and pepper shaker, thimble-shaped, 1920s, EX . . . . $350.00 D

Sandwich toaster, "Coke," used at soda fountains to toast sandwiches and would imprint the bread, hard to find, 1930s, EX. . . . . $700.00 D

School set, "Drink Coca-Cola Delicious Refreshing," complete with pencils, rulers, erasers in box, 1930s, red, EX . . . . $75.00 D

Shade, window, "Drink Coca-Cola, The Pause that Refreshes in Bottles," very rare, 4'x7', VG . $3,500.00 C

Shotgun, model 1500XLT, Coca-Cola Centennial, embossed Coca-Cola on receiver and barrel never fired, 1986, MIB. . . . . $1,100.00 C

String dispenser, tin, red with carton in yellow circle, 12"x16", EX . . . . $450.00 C

String holder, curved panels, "Take Home 25¢" six-pack in spotlight, 1930s, NM . . . . $1,000.00 C

Syrup dispenser, reproduction, made of hard rubber, unusual piece, 1950s, EX. . . . . $700.00 C

Tape for reel-to-reel for radio play, contains 16 advertising spots prepared by McCann & Erickson, Inc. New York, New York, 1970s. . . . . . . $25.00 C

Tap knob, doubled sided, "Coke," 1960–70, NM. . . . . $25.00 D

Tap knob, enameled double sided, "Drink Coke or Coca-Cola, Ask for it Either Way," 1940–50s, EX. . . . . $85.00 C

Tap knob, one side, "Coca-Cola," 1970 . . $20.00 C

Tape measure, horseshoe-shaped, Coke advertising on side, NM . . . . $8.00 C

Telephone, bottle-shaped, new, MIB . . . . $15.00 D

Telephone, can-shaped, new, MIB. . . . . . $20.00 D

Telephone in the shape of a 10 oz. bottle, EX . . . . $50.00 D

Thimble, aluminum, 1920s, EX . . . . . . $30.00 D

Thimble, "Coca-Cola," red lettering, M . $25.00 D

Training kit for sales complete with record, film strips, and charts, 1940s, EX . . . . $100.00 D

Tumbler, tulip shaped with syrup lines, EX . . . . $35.00 D

Umbrella, orange, black, and white, "Drink Coca-Cola," 1930s, EX. . . . . $800.00 C

Winchester model #94, Coca-Cola Centennial, only 2,500 produced, never fired, 1986, MIB . . . . $1,200.00 C

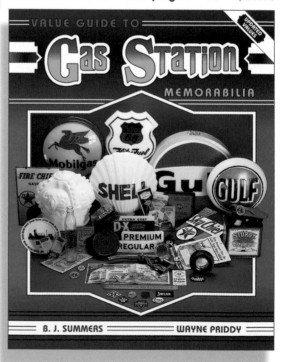

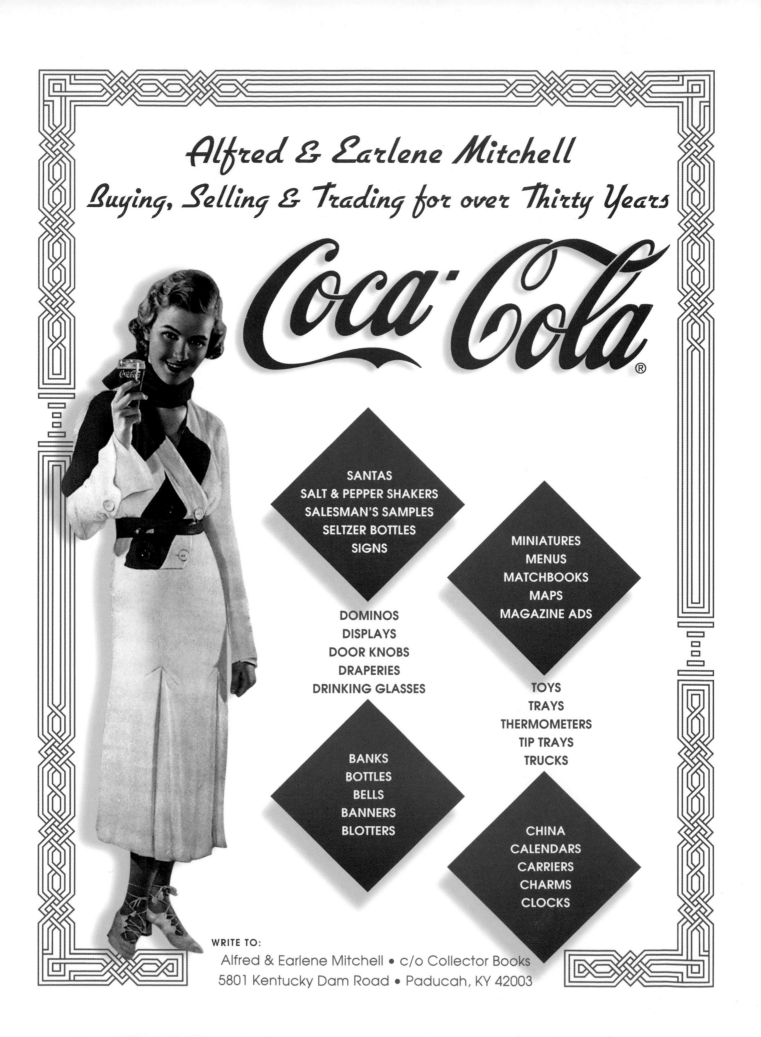

BUFFALO BAY AUCTION CO.

SPECIALISTS IN COLOR CATALOGUE MAIL & TELEPHONE AUCTIONS

THE ITEMS PICTURED ABOVE ARE JUST A SMALL SAMPLING FROM OUR MAY & JULY 1998 ADVERTISING AND COUNTRY STORE AUCTIONS. OVER 2,800 QUALITY AND INVESTMENT GRADE ITEMS ARE OFFERED ANNUALLY IN FULL COLOR WITH COMPLETE DESCRIPTIONS, GRADE, PRE-AUCTION ESTIMATES & PRICES REALIZED. IF YOU ARE INTERESTED IN CONSIGNING ITEMS FOR UPCOMING AUCTIONS, OR WOULD LIKE TO BE ON OUR MAILING LIST FOR FUTURE CATALOGUES, PLEASE CALL OR WRITE:

BUFFALO BAY AUCTION CO. • 5244 QUAM CIRCLE • ROGERS, MN 55374

E-Mail buffalobay@aol.com

Phone (612) 428-8480   Fax (612) 428-8879